TOUGH
COP

ALL THE BEST

Mike Cilum

— from me, as well!
Jeff

TOUGH
COP

MIKE
CHITWOOD
VS. THE "SCUMBAGS"

HAROLD I. GULLAN

Camino Books, Inc.

Philadelphia

Manufactured in the United States of America
1   2   3   4   16   15   14   13

Library of Congress Cataloging-in-Publication Data

Gullan, Harold I., 1931-
  Tough cop: Mike Chitwood vs. the scumbags / Harold I. Gullan.
     pages cm
   ISBN 978-1-933822-77-8 (alk. paper)
  1. Chitwood, Mike, 1944- 2. Police chiefs—United States—Biography. 3. Police—United States. 4. Crime—United States. I. Title.

  HV7911.C475G85 2013
  363.2092—dc23
  [B]   2013028548

ISBN 978–1–933822–77–8
ISBN 978–1–933822–76–1 (ebook)

Cover and interior design: Jerilyn Bockorick

This book is available at a special discount on bulk purchases for promotional, business, and educational use.

Publisher
Camino Books, Inc
P.O. Box 59026
Philadelphia, PA 19102
www.caminobooks.com

TO THE FUTURE:

Lindsay, Meggie, Kerrianne, Kayley, Kyle,
Christopher, Gracie and Winston

CRIME SCENE //// CRIME SCENE //// CRIME SCENE

Homicide detective Chitwood urges a
barricaded killer to surrender.

Philadelphia Inquirer, November 8, 1980.
Used with permission of *The Philadelphia Inquirer*,
copyright © 2013. All rights reserved.

CONTENTS

BY WAY OF INTRODUCTION

In a manner of speaking, this book actually began with a wedding—that of Becky Lakin to our son, Bill. Seven years later, Dr. Becky Gullan, now assistant professor of psychology at Gwynedd-Mercy College, and Bill Gullan, today president of Finch Brands marketing group, have given us not only two adorable grandchildren, but the idea that evolved into what you now hold in your hands (or in your hand-held device).

Having completed my prior work, an account of a memorable senate race, I had decided that my next book should chronicle someone's compelling career. Bill came up with a list of possible candidates, really interesting people who for one reason or another had not yet been the subject of a book. One of them was Michael Chitwood, virtually a living legend in law enforcement, currently police superintendent of the bustling community of Upper Darby, Pennsylvania.

The more I read about him, the more intriguing the prospect became. Here, in a career spanning nearly half a century, was the most decorated cop in Philadelphia history—who went on to head police departments in three disparate localities, becoming a national celebrity. Perhaps the reason there had been no previous biography of Mike Chitwood was the inability of anyone simply to keep up with him. It's funny. The few other Chitwoods I'd heard of, none related, were all inclined to activity: the noted race car driver Joie Chitwood; the fictional name for the hero of *Hoosiers*, Jimmy Chitwood; and the fabled Robertson Chitwood, a Canadian mountie who always got his man.

Becky's colleague, Walt Zdunowski, director of Gwynedd-Mercy's criminal justice program, a man whose own remarkable career is worthy of a book, had invited Chitwood to speak to his students. And so I got to meet him. Chitwood has an uncommon ability to talk conversationally to an audience of any size, relaxed and with a good deal of humor. Yet there is an evident intensity just under the surface.

As we got to talk further, often at the renowned Llanerch Diner (no, we didn't make it into *Silver Linings Playbook*), our potential book took shape. Fortunately, Mike Chitwood's career has been so thoroughly publicized, almost from its inception, that I had no lack of sources. And so, in a way, this book also represents a welcome re-acquaintance with writers and reporters I'd long admired—many, alas, now gone.

One recent columnist actually spent an entire day making the rounds with the indefatigable Chitwood, something I lack the energy even to contemplate. But over a year, I got to share his insights and supplement them with those of a great many others, past and present.

This is not intended to be a customary biography, but rather the account of an ongoing career. Still it has benefited immeasurably from the reflections of Mike's wife, Liz; his daughter, Beth Ann; and his police chief son, Mike Jr. I'm indebted to them all. Since *Tough Cop* is roughly half immersed in action and half in administration, reflecting Chitwood's own career path, it may also represent a relevant case study for criminal justice courses throughout the nation.

In its preparation, I am also indebted to Edward Jutkowitz, innovative publisher of Camino Books; Brad Fisher, my wise and perceptive editor; Elsa Efran, my overqualified and insightful literary associate; and my remarkably patient wife, Betsy, who has contributed immeasurably to all eight of my books. Among many others, I'd like to thank all those who helped uncover photographs from many sources, particularly Jessica Stremmel and Susan Drinan; our talented designer Jerilyn Bockorick; Scott Richards, Finch Brand's outstanding artist, for his creative input; and Patty Cook, whose technical skills kept us on track.

In referring to the parallels even in Mike's presentations, informal yet intense, it may seem as if there are dual Chitwoods. But the parallels are all of a piece. The career crime-fighter, tough as necessity demands, with a vocabulary to match, and the personal Chitwood, invariably considerate, almost courtly in demeanor, as observed in Chapter 1. Mike's wife, Liz, already saw that side of him, distinctive from other boys in the neighborhood, when they met in middle school. My own wife commented on it when she met Mike only a year ago.

It is, of course, imprudent to try to anticipate the reaction to any creative work. But I suspect some critics may find these observations of an extraordinary career excessively positive. If so, my plea is guilty. I can only write what I see, in hopefully well-considered conclusions. In the passages of everyone's life, there is tragedy even in triumph. It may seem tragic that Mike Chitwood, unlike a Bill Bratton or a John Timoney, never headed a police department in one of our greatest cities, as he had seemed destined to. If so, that is our loss. That he keeps on going so strong, as enthusiastic today as on his first day pounding a beat, remains Mike Chitwood's transcendent triumph—and ours.

TOUGH COP

Launched Into
the Limelight

"Hold on to the baby! Don't drop her!" With smoke pouring out of her third-floor window, young mother Virginia Brigden dangled from a rope between floors, desperately clutching five-month-old Lydia, the youngest of her five children. The exhortations were coming from a roving patrolman named Mike Chitwood. You never know where you'll be when an emergency propels you into action.

This predawn drama in a North Philadelphia row house during a frigid February started when neighbors saw and smelled the smoke, now coming from all three floors of the Brigden home. Could the fire department possibly get there in time? All that smoke, whatever had caused it, wakened Virginia's husband, Sam, who grabbed two of their children and instinctively found his way to the street. By luck he ran into patrolman Anthony Cacciatore and shouted that his wife and their three other kids were still inside the burning building. The patrolman rushed in, found the two eldest on the second floor, and got them out with no more serious result than mild smoke inhalation.

By now Chitwood and his partner, Michael Muto, had arrived on the scene. Fighting their way through the thick miasma up to the second floor, Chitwood yelled encouragement to the dangling young woman, while Muto held him out of a window by clutching Chitwood's belt and one of his legs. Minutes after Chitwood had managed to take little Lydia out of her mother's arms, all the while holding on to Virginia and tightening her tenuous grasp on the rope, the firemen arrived and rescued her via a ladder.

All the police officers were subsequently commended. Chitwood was cited for heroism. It was not the first citation for a man destined to become the most decorated police officer in Philadelphia history. Nor was it his first exposure to the glare of the media. In the years to come his image would be of "Dirty Harry" and yet sometimes more like Mother Teresa. But he would always seem to be making news.

*   *   *

You get a lot of on-the-job training at the police academy, not all of it in the classroom. Only 20 in 1964, Chitwood was assigned with his fellow trainees to "riot duty." Riots and the threat of riots were as big in the '60s as drug busts would be in the '70s. On patrol in Philadelphia, Chitwood and his partner were nearly hit by a reckless driver hurtling down Broad Street. Jumping into their car, they finally cornered him after a 15-block chase. Of course, it turned out that this particular driver was wanted for a series of holdups. More commendations, more publicity. It also didn't hurt his upright image when Chitwood was involved in a celebrated flag desecration case, pitting civil libertarians against the symbolic emphasis of those in authority who revere the American flag.

*   *   *

"Stop or I'll shoot!" Fresh out of the academy and assigned to a North Philadelphia district, Chitwood and his partner spotted three young toughs mugging and robbing an older man in the street. When the rookies leapt out of their patrol car, firing a warning shot into the air, all three thugs ran. In the frantic chase that followed, two got away, but one was shot in the back and killed. Chitwood's partner, John Dillon, fired the bullet, but both young patrolmen were commended for their quick action. The deceased, his mother insisted, was only 17, although police records indicated him to be two years older. It was the first of many instances in which Chitwood would be involved in accusations of using excessive force, including what is today termed "enhanced" interrogation techniques. He went quite literally by the book, aggressive and assertive. In an emergency, hesitation can be fatal.

And somehow, whatever his methods, Chitwood always seemed to be right at the scene of action. He was already being featured in the media as the quintessential tough cop, a law-and-order stalwart in the image of future mayor Frank Rizzo, another son of South Philadelphia. Chitwood's rise was rapid, leading to the highway patrol and ultimately the elite special investigations squad headed by celebrated Captain Clarence Ferguson, whose flair for publicity rivaled Rizzo's.

Like virtually all of his future performance evaluations, Chitwood's report of June 1965 included only "outstanding performance" grades, the equivalent of all A-pluses. His supervisor glowed, "You have maintained the same commendable degree of effort at all times. Your high number of quality arrests . . . were a credit to this command. . . . I know I can rely on you at all times." He even noted the six-foot-one Chitwood's "neat appearance." Indeed, the rather burly, clean-shaven, curly-haired professional of the 1960s would always retain that careful look. Sideburns and a mustache would make a very visible change in his outward appearance in the 1970s, as he traded his uniform for a trim suit. However, the major transition was in his weight and fitness, from 190 or more to a trim, sinewy 165. At 69,

Chitwood starts his day at 4:00 a.m. at the gym, his schedule more controlled ever since a regular regimen of physical fitness could be sustained.

While still in the highway patrol, Chitwood, with his partner Anthony Kane, got a foretaste of the kind of confrontations he would face too often in the future. From *The Philadelphia Inquirer* of November 1965, "Two highway patrolmen disarmed and captured a pistol-wielding burglar in a North Philadelphia house Wednesday morning after they were alerted by neighbors who spotted the intruder climbing a seven-foot fence at the rear of the property." Chitwood and Kane found that the place had been ransacked and that there was a man hiding in an upstairs closet. When he emerged and pointed a loaded .38 revolver at them, Chitwood calmly knocked it out of his hand. Disarmed, the suspect had only $15 on him, a stolen diamond ring, and six marijuana cigarettes in his pocket. It would not always be so easy to pin down an armed adversary, but Chitwood's proclivity for swift action never waned.

*   *   *

What has broadened and deepened over the years, along with his responsibilities, is perspective. In his late sixties, his hair gray, his manner almost courtly, his gait as effortless as ever, his reflexes seemingly as swift, and his puckish humor very intact, Mike Chitwood reflects that for all the millions invested in crime prevention, he's till striving to hold that thin blue line of protection against the same sort of adversaries he faced nearly half a century ago. It transcends race or class. The bluntest vernacular comes readily enough to anyone engaged in police work, including Chitwood. But he is better known for a distinctive epithet. The perpetual enemy of civil society is simply the all-encompassing "scumbag," which the *American Heritage Dictionary* defines as "a person regarded as despicable." Indeed, Chitwood, today the popular police superintendent of urban, exceedingly diverse Upper Darby, Pennsylvania, raised the ire of his few remaining critics when he sponsored fund-raising T-shirts bearing the slogan, "Not in My Town, Scumbag." All this did was raise thousands for art and music scholarships in the hard-pressed local schools. Each year, it raises more. His son, Mike Jr., a police chief himself down in Daytona Beach, Florida, is using T-shirts with the same slogan, gaining the same positive results. Funny. He also seems to have a proclivity for publicity.

Since being launched into the only profession he ever sought, Chitwood has served three very different communities as their police chief, been involved in solving more murders than Agatha Christie, escaped from more close calls than the Clint Eastwood character, and been proposed as a potential nominee for Congress in Pennsylvania and a candidate for governor of . . . Maine. It might be worth considering just how such an extraordinary career got started.

2

"I Hope It Doesn't Say 'Mom'!"

T he vibrant community of South Philadelphia is today an amalgam of every conceivable ethnicity and income level. In memory, however, its melodies—from Lanza to Fabian—its flavors and its very essence still seem peculiarly Italian. Of all the waves of immigrants who sought work and opportunity in what was then the greatest industrial arsenal of America, it was most visibly those from places like Calabria and Sicily whose families formed the neighborhoods of endless row houses that became "South Philly"—an ever-expanding Roman Catholic enclave within a predominantly Protestant city. It was the Irish, however, whose own gradual ascent was from working class through politics, the priesthood, and the police force, who were first to wrest a share of power from the established elite. There was a Mayor Tate before a Mayor Rizzo.

Vivid memories remain of growing up in the distinctive South Philly of the 1950s and '60s by a couple whose own merger joined Irish and Italian-American antecedents. Even 50 years since they eloped as teenagers, Liz Chitwood still cherishes recollections of the warmth of her hospitable childhood home, and Mike Chitwood affirms the stricter standards of his own, only a few blocks away on Oregon Avenue. It may not take a village to raise a child, but having a close-knit neighborhood doesn't hurt. Elizabeth Pino grew up in the comforting midst of so many outgoing relatives and extended family, with her own home the hub of it all. "It was like a party every night," she recalls. "You never knew who was going to come through the front door . . . and my mom was always prepared!"

If it wasn't quite a party at the Chitwood home, both parents in their uncompromising fashion were highly supportive of all three of their sons. Walter Chitwood, a career chief petty officer in the navy's submarine service, raised Baptist in his native Tennessee, had met and married Marie Carroll, a devout Philadelphia Irish-American Catholic, while he was stationed at the bustling Philadelphia Naval Base. When he was away at sea, she was in charge not only of their home but of raising their sons. Which hardly changed the standards both parents expected, but at least elevated the domestic vocabulary.

*   *   *

Born at Saint Agnes Hospital on January 18, 1944, Michael Jude Chitwood, their first son, was naturally expected to set an example for the two who were to follow. As they grew, all three were encouraged to excel at school and beyond and to avoid the temptations of the streets. These seem positively placid compared with what was to come. However, even as teenagers, the Chitwood boys were not permitted to go out on weekday nights, and on weekends their curfew was 10 p.m. The neat row houses of Oregon Avenue and its environs were hardly the congested slums of New York's Lower East Side, but they were very small and confining for a family of five, modest by South Philly standards, including three healthy, growing boys. The constraints they faced were shared by few of those they hung out with. Mike, particularly, resented such limitations, although in later years he would credit his "strong, strict upbringing with my success in life." By then, with the drug culture escalating, many of his childhood friends were dead, and he'd been obliged to arrest too many others.

Growing up, there was no shortage of friends. Without being overly gregarious, Mike was a kid who just naturally seemed to fit in as one of the guys. Yet there was already something different about him, a kind of ambivalence. These were hardly the organized gangs that would cause such havoc in later years—simply informal groups of restless teenagers hanging around the South Philly street corners, as so many pop vocalists have portrayed them. They were game for almost anything, any challenge or dare, the excitement of breaking out to try something new, and the older kids had wheels. Initially, Mike, so confined at home, seemed up for it all. Certainly, he was as tough as any of his companions, having already shown prowess as an amateur boxer in Golden Gloves competition. Yet he retained a certain reticence, even a sense of propriety. Mike might blow off steam with the others, but he was uncommonly serious about his future. The spontaneous pranks that sometimes alarmed his parents and teachers were in the end rather harmless. In what mattered, he already had a kind of maturity.

Liz Pino had noticed it when at only 13 she met the 15-year-old Mike Chitwood in middle school. "He was different than most of the boys in the neighborhood," she recalls, "polite and respectful, and if you can imagine it, shy and quiet." He'd invariably open the door for a woman of any age and stand up when she entered a room. Perhaps his parents had stressed manners, but there was something more. Even in small ways it was important to protect others. Such discernment didn't translate to school. It was clear Mike could do better, but here the duality was simply between what he liked and didn't like. School was something he had to get through. That it was rigorous Catholic school simply made the process more challenging, not more stimulating. For whatever reasons, Mike had no ambition to go on to college. His two younger brothers, however, flourished, justifying the ambitions and the standards of Marie and Walter Chitwood. Today, Mark is a retired school principal in Florida and Walt a distinguished psychologist residing in Wisconsin.

*   *   *

In seventh grade, Mike had something akin to a revelation that put everything in focus. Despite middling grades, he'd managed to be named to the school safety patrol. Once he put on his white banner and started guiding other students across the street, that was it. His career would be in police work. Now, of course, lots of kids envision themselves a firefighter or police officer, but it tends to be only a stage they pass through. Mike was constituted differently. He already knew instinctively that this was intended to be his life's work. Even then it wasn't the lure of guns or the appeal of authority. As Mike recalls, "Every day I would talk to a police officer, and the majority of his conversations dealt with helping people in crisis and need. These interactions stayed with me" all the way to the police academy some 13 years later, and indeed to this day. Protecting others would be his profession

Now school seemed even more irrelevant, yet completing it successfully and on time mattered more than ever. Mike had to do just well enough, grade after grade, until high school graduation. It didn't help that most of his early teachers were nuns, if anything more tenacious than his ever-observant parents. In any school setting, underachieving students who are at least trying tend to receive a more sympathetic appraisal than those who could obviously excel but don't exert the effort. From Epiphany of Our Lord grade school through Stella Maris middle school to what was then all-boys Bishop Neumann High School, it never got much easier. One particular experience stands out, with which many similar students could identify. In a critical high school chemistry course, Mike found his average slipping below even his customary 70s or 80s. Indeed, threatened with failing, he prepared for the final exam with all the up-all-night thoroughness absent from his prior work, and aced it, scoring nearly 100. The only problem was that his teacher initially couldn't buy such suspiciously sudden aptitude and insisted that Mike must have cheated, which not only offended young Chitwood's sense of equity, but also soured any residual regard for academics. Somehow, the situation was resolved, and Mike passed and graduated, sparing him from a belated appreciation of the scholarship he had always been capable of handling.

*   *   *

Previously there had been a Sister Robert Vincent, she of the formidable Sisters of Saint Joseph, back in the eighth grade at Stella Maris. Fortunately, this was before Mike had discovered Elizabeth Pino, only a grade behind. There were, so to speak, three attractions in the class. One was the dominating figure of Sister herself, her cowl so enveloping that it all but hid her intense face, and her hand often clutching that threateningly long pointer, readily available under her desk. At times, Mike's father had been sufficiently annoyed to hit him with a belt across the behind. Yet it hardly conveyed the same sustained threat. The other two attractions in the classroom were the awesome breasts of Arlene Lamorggia (hopefully misspelled to avoid the retaliation of any ancient mariners still sufficiently ambulatory to defend her residual honor). They were enormous. Arlene was not only more amply endowed, but reputed to be significantly older than the rest of the class—and a favorite of sailors from the nearby naval base. She certainly wasn't dating eighth graders.

"I don't know what got into me that day," Mike recalls. Yes, he'd done some boxing and had been in on some schoolboy pranks, but when it came to girls, he was still the rather innocent, shy, and even nerdy kid his parents had raised. Yet here he was, directly behind awesome Arlene. Unable to restrain himself, he reached out and started pulling on her bra strap through her blouse. Mike must have gotten carried away. It broke, and the contents burst out, even though out of view, like Old Faithful. "You son-of-a-bitch!" Arlene screamed, demonstrating a grasp of invective then considered rare in one of her tender years. Then she turned to Sister Robert Vincent, confirming the obvious: "Mike Chitwood broke my bra strap!" Sister was on Mike like the Flying Nun, vigorously beating him with her pointer as he tried to escape, over, under, and all around his desk. Although having created the highlight of that semester, Mike was immediately suspended. Thankfully, his father was away. Somehow his mortified mother, as devout as any of the nuns, managed to get him back into school, although under very stringent circumstances. He was precluded from all activities, including C.Y.O. baseball, his favorite. Every day for a month, he had to go into the convent, kneel in a dark basement closet, and say prayers for an hour. At least Sister didn't keep beating him. Most important, he didn't lose a year of school.

One afternoon not much later, there was a knock on the front door of the Chitwood home. One of Mike's brothers answered it, telling him there were three sailors who wanted to see him. He rushed out the back door, figuring they must be angry because he'd messed with their Arlene, and didn't return for hours. Of course, that spontaneous bit of mischief seems rather harmless in retrospect, even if a bit sexist. Yet for years, Mike tried to reconnect with Arlene to apologize and reminisce about those times. Alas, he was never able to find her again.

* * *

With street after street of carefully maintained little row houses, many with picture windows facing the neighbors across the street, bisected by aptly named Broad Street, replete with immense churches, elaborate funeral parlors, noted ristorantes and cheesesteak joints, accepted illegal parking, and home of everything from Mummers to reputed mobsters (who only rubbed out each other), our image of South Philly seems eternal. Yet in its totality, nearly 10 square miles in area, it has changed profoundly since Mike Chitwood's childhood. The last great migration was African-Americans from the American South. A more recent influx came from Southeast Asia and Eastern Europe, although no longer in search of industrial jobs.

It would take a naturalist to explain it all, but even adjacent to the deep Delaware River and all its traffic, much of South Philadelphia was a swamp. It was landfill that made those expanding working-class neighborhoods possible. All that stopped when the postwar recovery phased out Philadelphia's matchless industrial base, sending its jobs first to the South and West and ultimately offshore. Initially, what is now South Philadelphia consisted of separate little townships like Moyamensing and Southwark, only urbanized with the mass immigration spurred by the Industrial Revolution, and only enveloped by the greater city of Philadelphia in the Consolidation of 1854. Hence South Philly, now gentrified on one end and depressed on the other end of its urban core, is still a place apart.

But the real change is in those areas that remained swampland—a sea of narrow islands and shallow inlets and channels. Mike's buddies were not really a gang. There was no crime or violence, certainly no guns or confrontations with others. They had naturally formed into their own regional neighborhood group of young males, based on their own little slice of geography, and were increasingly stimulated by young females. In the "neck" of the vast swampland where they played, each of these informal clubs had gradually established its own turf. There was plenty of room for all. No group even had a specific name beyond its home corner. Between Oregon Avenue and the naval base, the neck even had its early versions of hippies and the homeless. "Goat men" raised horses, cows, and pigs on more stable land that seemingly belonged to no one and everyone. It was like an urban frontier in a rural setting, too potentially valuable to stay that way for very long.

In 1957, the Walt Whitman Bridge had opened, making South Philly more accessible to South Jersey. Since 1926, there had been one vast stadium on the reclaimed portion of this extensive South Philly site. Originally called Municipal Stadium and later renamed for John F. Kennedy, it was rarely used except for the annual Army-Navy Game. Its more than 100,000 uncomfortable seats were ideal for such a spectacle, and its horseshoe shape permitted the dramatic entrance of midshipmen and the corps of cadets through the open end. However, the stands were so steeply banked that there was no such thing as a favorable vantage point from which to view the game itself. Furthermore, the isolated venue was wide open to the elements, and the game always seemed to coincide with the coldest day of the year.

Well, all that's gone now. Virtually the entire neck has been developed as the expansive site of a state-of-the-art ballpark, football stadium, indoor arena (already renamed four times), expanding entertainment complex, and thankfully a great deal of parking. Viewing it all from their front doorsteps, many residents must still question how and why their neighborhood had to be designated to border so much noise and congestion. There is also a lot of shopping technically within South Philly, from the venerable Italian Market to the new big-box stores along Columbus Boulevard, and a park with historic structures near the bridge, but the vast playground of Mike's youth has vanished as thoroughly as the Old West.

*   *   *

Young Mike Chitwood's last major lapse from his parents' strictures, seemingly little more egregious than his prior excesses, marked a watershed in his life. Hanging out on their customary corner of 10th and Oregon one Friday night, the group's spur-of-the-moment inspiration was, "Let's get tattoos." Mike was less than enthusiastic. But what the heck—at 18, his ties as one of the guys, even if becoming tenuous, still remained. They set out in two cars for a tattoo parlor named Sailor Eddie's in Camden, New Jersey. Mike recalls, "from ducks to doves," everyone got a different tattoo. His own spontaneous choice was a boxer on his bicep with the legend "Get 'Em Up" underneath. After all, he'd done some amateur fighting himself.

As soon as they departed, Mike knew he was in trouble. It was a humid August night, made steamier in the confines of South Philadelphia. He was wearing a sleeveless shirt, and the bandage on his upper arm was visible to anyone. As soon as he got home, Mike went quietly upstairs and, hot or not, put on a long-sleeved shirt and went immediately to bed. As the oldest son, he had his own room, although its dimensions were more like a large closet. The idea of air-conditioning at that time and place was still in the realm of science fiction. Window wide open, the heat in Mike's room only became more stifling. In his sleep he must have taken his shirt off. Normally, all three boys were supposed to be up promptly at seven to do their chores and then have breakfast. When he was home, Walter prepared it, the same cereal each day. This particular morning, however, the other two slept a bit late. Mike had just awoke, apparently forgetting his exposed arm. Just after he heard his father tell his mother, "I'm going to go up and wake them up," seemingly Chief Petty Officer Walter Chitwood was already in his room. Uncertain what to do, Mike pretended to be asleep. It didn't work.

Nor did it take long to lift the bandage on Mike's arm. The next exclamation Mike heard may have awakened the neighbors: "Marie, this son-of-a-bitch has got a tattoo! I was in the navy for 25 years and I never got a fucking tattoo!" Marie's response: "Oh, my God! I hope it doesn't say 'Mom'!" After he'd ripped the bandage off, Mike's furious father got even more incensed. At first it wasn't clear just who this guy with his arms raised was supposed to be. Sailor Eddie wasn't exactly Norman Rockwell. When the elder Chitwood finally read "Get 'Em Up" underneath the figure, there wasn't much doubt. His exhortations went from "What the . . ." to "Get 'em up, you son-of-a-bitch! Are you a tough guy? Put 'em up . . . I want to see if you're a tough guy." Fully awake now, Mike replied, "Dad, I'm not going to fight you," and tried to weave away. Furious, Walter hit his son square in the face, knocking him down. After that, it was simply "Get out of this house!" Father Chitwood kept cursing, and Mother Chitwood kept crying.

Mike left without even an extra shirt. The Pinos took him in. They had been like his second family since Mike had started dating Liz back at Stella Maris. There was never another girl for him. For two weeks he lived in the Pinos' basement, until Marie Chitwood finally convinced her husband to let Mike come back home. Nothing was ever said about the incident again, and to this day Mike Chitwood will still not show that faded tattoo in public. Except in the gym or at the shore, it is always covered.

Decades later, after the family had moved to Delaware County and his mother had passed away, Police Chief Mike Chitwood of Portland, Maine, would fly the 450 miles and back every weekend to help take care of his gravely ill father, any residual resentment submerged in a deeper affection and appreciation for the old man's standards, his own way of showing love. And it is worth noting that Mike insists that he brought up his own two "great kids" in the same way he had been raised—although I doubt that he was ever so provoked that he threw Michael Jr. out of the house.

His own departure, however temporary, hastened more permanent decisions. Many of his friends had already started taking drugs, even if only marijuana initially. Ultimately, in many cases, it led to methamphetamines and heroin as the organized drug culture took hold. As Mike observes, "It's amazing how the dynamic changed." He was never personally tempted even to try pot, not only because he knew his future lay in law enforcement, but because it simply held no attraction for him. Nor did he drink. Moreover, even as a senior in high school, he was more than ever focused on his coming career, sharing less and less in common with those childhood friends still rather aimlessly drifting along.

Similarly, fun-loving Liz Pino also possessed a sense of responsibility well beyond her years. They talked it over when Mike was a temporary resident in her basement. The following year, when she was only 17, a senior in high school, and Mike was 19, they eloped to, of all places, Wilmington, Delaware. There wasn't even time, let alone the means, for a scenic side trip to, say, the Delaware Water Gap. Neither family approved at first, although they were mutually fond of each other's kids. Still, these two were unusually young, even for a neighborhood with roots in European cultures. However, both sets of parents soon came around and were mutually supportive. It's with a smile when Liz Chitwood notes that she is still reminded that she was the first person of Italian heritage in her husband's family. This was no sudden impulse, however, but the decision of two young people who had long been attracted to each other—well, for four years, anyway. Four years of hanging out on the front steps together—along with ice cream, movies and going to Saturday-night school dances. Typical teenage times, but also getting to know each other better, to be certain of a future life together.

Of course, it wasn't easy at first. Mike was obliged to take any job he could find, largely construction work. Money was scarce. Things improved a bit after the following year, when, at 20, Mike was finally eligible to take the civil service written exam for the Philadelphia Police Department. Sworn in on April 6, 1964, he entered the police academy with about 200 new officers. Money was still in short supply, but from then on it was time that would be even tighter. Still, upbeat Elizabeth Chitwood recalls it all fondly today, even though she had to raise the two children who were to come largely on her own. Mike's days off "were the best . . . especially in the summer months. Packing a picnic lunch and going off to Valley Forge or the zoo or the shore or Holiday Lake for the day. On the go and trying to make up for lost time." Those customary nine-to-five fathers weren't having nearly as much fun with their families. Yet to this day, Mike Chitwood's greatest regret is that he couldn't spend more time with his children when they were growing up. Still, how close they all are today, each with their own families, even though Mike Jr. is down in Daytona Beach and Beth Ann is a busy mother raising two children in Greensboro, North Carolina. As for the golden anniversary couple themselves, Liz insists that they are still "'soul mates' in every sense of the word."

*   *   *

Mike Chitwood's first year on the job reflects the turmoil of the times, not unlike the truncated training period of new recruits during the early days of World War II. After only some three or four weeks at the police academy, the entire class was taken out and assigned to the 18th Police District at 55th and Pine. Their purpose was to provide safety and security for coeds at the University of Pennsylvania. Many were being robbed and even sexually assaulted by residents of the high-rise housing projects nearby. Our philosophy of what constitutes livable low-rent housing has gone through quite a transition since then. Moreover, in 1964, neither Penn nor many other major universities employed the sort of private security patrols they find it necessary to have today. Mike recalls, "We walked beats in uniform and plain clothes until the end of the school year."

He continues, "I was then assigned to the 18th District until September and was to return to finish the academy. However, that never happened. The riots of 1964 occurred in August. The rest is history." Mike Chitwood never returned to the police academy. As a result of his and the other students' practical experiences out on the streets, they were all graduated. In September 1964, Mike was assigned to the 22nd Police District at Broad and Montgomery Avenues. He computes that during that year he totaled only about 10 weeks of actual academy training. There was no lack of learning, however, including a practical exposure to the challenging neighborhoods of West and North Philadelphia. He was getting to know the whole city as he never had before—on-the-job preparation beyond any classroom curriculum. The escalating crime war couldn't wait.

3

Commendations or Condemnations?

T hat there would never be a placid period in Mike Chitwood's career was evident from its inception. The '60s, initiated with such bright expectations, had already dissolved into a time of turmoil by the summer of 1964. At only 20, Chitwood and his first partner, 27-year-old Anthony Kane, had been thrust with hundreds of other Philadelphia police into the midst of a short-lived but violent Philadelphia "race riot." One of the earliest major city riots, lasting only three humid August days, it was no less volatile than those of longer duration in other cities during a season of discontent.

What accumulated grievances caused them? The dynamic young American president elected in 1960 had vowed, however reluctantly at first, to advance the cause of civil rights, but John Kennedy was felled by an assassin in Dallas in 1963, horrifying the nation. His successor's intent was anything but gradual, an all-encompassing "Great Society" to not only assure equal opportunity for all Americans, regardless of race—to voting, housing, education, and jobs—but also to aid the elderly, advance health care, and wage a war against poverty itself. But Lyndon Johnson's ambitious domestic agenda would soon be overshadowed by the escalating demands of a controversial war in a small Asian nation thousands of miles away.

The most recognized and respected African-American leader in the nation, the Reverend Dr. Martin Luther King, Jr., speaking eloquently of a long-overdue litany of basic rights here at home, preached nonviolent means to achieve them. That smacked of gradualism to less patient voices, particularly when King's peaceful protests were met with raw violence in the South. To the militant and particularly the young, the time seemed overdue for direct action—even if only in impotent rage. In North Philadelphia, home to two-thirds of the city's black residents, the most visible target was "police brutality."

Although such tensions had been simmering for months, if not years, the immediate cause of the riot was an argument between a black woman whose car had been stalled at the busy intersection of 23rd Street and Columbia Avenue and two policemen who were trying to move it, and her. One cop was black, the other was white. Sensitive to allegations of bias, Commissioner Howard R. Leary had assigned patrols that paired policemen of each race, particularly throughout North Philadelphia. He had even agreed to have any accusations of police brutality submitted to a civilian review board. It can't be said that the Philadelphia Police Department was insensitive to implications of inequity. In any case, for whatever reason, the woman whose car was blocking traffic refused to leave it. When the two officers on duty tried to lift her out of the car, she resisted. A large crowd gathered, a man attacked one of the policemen, and eventually both the assailant and the reluctant motorist were arrested.

It all took off from there. Wild rumors circulated that a pregnant black woman had been beaten, perhaps fatally, by a white cop. For the rest of that day and the following two days and nights, mobs rampaged, particularly throughout the Columbia Avenue retail corridor. Another source of resentment was that most of the stores were owned by whites, many suspected of long-term exploitation. Whole blocks were burned out and looted. Despite the immediate police presence, its relative restraint in the wake of such rampant destruction drew a good deal of criticism from outside of North Philadelphia. One ultimate result of the riot was the rise of division captain Frank Rizzo, whose much firmer response to the rioters contained their destructiveness in the area under his direct control. Despite the brief duration of the overall riot, over 300 people were injured, over 700 were arrested, and well over 200 stores were destroyed or damaged. Fortunately, no one was killed. It took a very long time, however, for the already depressed area to recover economically. This was only hastened by the expansion of adjacent Temple University, with its own retail requirements. In the 1980s, much of Columbia Avenue was renamed for Cecil B. Moore, a prominent and controversial Philadelphia civil-rights leader—but no apostle of violence.

As it turned out, the riot's violence didn't engage young Chitwood directly, but it formed the backdrop for his earliest exploits as a patrolman. He was still technically on riot duty, although things had simmered down when in September 1964, he and his partner cornered a robbery suspect after a frantic, 15-block chase. That led to his first commendation. The second was won later in September, on the day he officially graduated from the police academy—after he helped to corner the three thugs who had been strong-arming a man in the street. Then, in November, Chitwood received his first award for actual "heroism," a higher level of commendation, for his dramatic rescue of a mother and her little girl from their smoke-filled home. The following November, with Kane as his partner, Chitwood earned a still higher commendation, for "bravery," when he kicked a loaded .38 out of a stunned assailant's hand and then found stolen money and narcotics on his person.

Both from South Philly and graduates of Bishop Neumann High School, Mike Chitwood and Tony Kane had hit it off from the start when they first met during the turmoil on Columbia Avenue. Consigned to the highway patrol in February 1965, they asked to be assigned to the same car. They would turn it into a sort of crime-seeking missile. To many of us, "highway patrol" implies the state police. In an urban context, however, it refers to a two-person police car assigned in particular to high crime areas that can be anywhere in the city. Most foot patrolmen work only one area, out of their district offices.

* * *

By the end of 1965, only his second on the force, Chitwood and Kane were being featured in local media virtually as Philadelphia's dynamic duo, "Batman and Robin." An article by Joe O'Dowd and Bill Malone in the *Daily News,* headlined "2 'Last Cops Out' Look for Trouble (And Usually Find It)," noted, "Since last February they've spent almost every night together, nights in which they've been punched, kicked, and shot at. . . . Apparently they can't stay out of trouble. But trouble is what they're looking for," working together as partners on "last-out" duty—11 p.m. to 7 a.m.—generally throughout neighborhoods where crime was concentrated. With their instinct for action, "they've steered more guys to a cell than Elliott Ness." Since nabbing and subduing three burglars in a West Philadelphia warehouse during their very first night on duty together, Chitwood and Kane had collared a murder suspect, four holdup men, and 29 burglary suspects. The article concluded with two questions: How did the two account for so many arrests? Their answer: "Hustle." And what did they do with their spare time? "We spend it in court."

Two awards were particularly relevant to the time. One was from the Veterans of Foreign Wars (VFW) for arresting six war protesters (termed "misguided" by the *Daily News*) who had publicly desecrated the American flag. Demonstrations against the Vietnam War were becoming paired more frequently with those for civil rights. The other was from the Philadelphia Retail Druggists Association, awarded at their annual dinner-dance, for catching a burglar at a drugstore. Drugs would become the next major emphasis of Chitwood's career.

He not only attracted trouble but could hardly avoid publicity, whether sought or not. From his first citation for heroism in rescuing that little girl, he also seemed unable to avoid conflagrations in his wide-roaming tours of the city. Chitwood's second commendation for heroism resulted from the rescue, in concert with three other policemen, of all 180 residents of Center City's Ritz Tower apartments, calmly leading them down to the street as a fire raged above. His third hero commendation came in April 1966, after Chitwood and Kane carried children to safety from the third floor of their burning home on Fairmount Avenue. Smoke inhalation had become an occupational hazard for the two highway patrolmen, who were rarely limited to highways.

As he approached his fourth anniversary on the force, Chitwood had accumulated a record number of commendations for so short a span of time, including those for heroism and bravery, and even "valor," the highest level of recognition. On December 5, 1967, the day before being interviewed by William Lovejoy of the *Bulletin*, Chitwood had helped nab two more suspects, in the process resolving four robberies. By now he had been elevated to colorful Captain Clarence Ferguson's elite special investigations squad. In one memorable raid initiated by Ferguson, Chitwood and three others were obliged to cross state lines, all the way to Cherry Hill, New Jersey, to arrest a pair responsible for $170,000 in burglaries. Asked by Lovejoy about his reaction to all of the accolades, team player Chitwood admitted it felt "great" but added, "and I guess I've been lucky . . . working with a lot of good men, good partners." Police work is "wonderful," especially now with "a great boss" like Captain Ferguson. It might no longer be last-out all night with Tony Kane, but it was still hardly a regular eight-hour job. "You work all hours. I like it that way." So long as you can do police work, protecting the public, "It's good."

Shades of that eighth-grade safety patrolman. Only Mike Chitwood no longer lived at 720 Oregon Avenue. He and his growing family, a daughter about to join his son, had moved into a larger home on Clarion Street. He'd longed to see more of Liz, Mike Jr., and now little Beth Ann. All those nights of last-out duty were bound to make him feel sometimes like a "last-in" father. People fortunate enough to love their work may appreciate an equally fulfilling home life even more than the rest of us.

* * *

That work would become more focused on the perils of narcotics—now more lethal and more organized than the earliest manifestations Chitwood had witnessed in his old neighborhood. It could be as dangerous and violent as any other form of crime, but because it combined both personal craving and potential profit, it could also take some pretty bizarre forms.

For example, Chitwood, still working with Kane and under the supervision of Ferguson, helped arrest four purveyors from one family who were also addicts, after finding heroin concealed in both a fireplace and an aquarium in their home and inside a woman's girdle in the house next door. He and other police then hung around to surprise a steady stream of patrons arriving for their regular weekly fix.

On another occasion, a tip that a large quantity of narcotics was about to be removed from a North Philadelphia location resulted in a quick-strike raid. The law dictated, however, that police were obliged to show a warrant and try to enter peacefully if possible. In these circumstances, it rarely worked. Chitwood had to tackle a man rushing outside, while a woman inside hurriedly swallowed some packets of white powder, spilling the rest. It would take a stomach pump to recover all the heroin. In the melee, Chitwood and another officer were punched and bitten. The ultimate defendants in the case would claim domestic invasion and destruction of their property, which was certainly true—as, on one side or another, was assault and battery. It is not always a simple matter to subdue a vigorously resistant and often armed suspect. It was only a short step, however, from so many such incidents to bringing back heightened public and media accusations of excessive force by the authorities. Over a decade later, this would culminate in charges of a whole pattern of "police brutality" that still rankle Mike Chitwood today.

*   *   *

A new word had entered the lexicon—"overdose," or simply "OD." Hard drugs injected into the body, feeding what had become a habit, initially intended only for a "high"—too often elevated the addict out of this world. In 1966, the recreational use of drugs was already widespread. Chitwood had seen it among his own crowd. But that year, there had been only 18 overdose cases reported in Philadelphia. By 1969, there were 118 drug deaths, with 39 victims under the age of 24, some only teenagers. And to Joe O'Dowd, who had written so extensively for the *Daily News* about Chitwood's exploits, in the 1970s it looked to be getting much worse. Each year, drug-related deaths would soar to a new record high. In the past, O'Dowd wrote, an OD case was "usually a junkie who had been hooked for a number of years." But now it was hitting the kids—throughout the city, rich and poor, black and white alike, "racing though the community like the plague." Of course, where there are users, there will be pushers, and behind it all, organized crime seizing a newly profitable opportunity. One recalls that scene in *The Godfather* where Don Corleone opts not to join in, which ultimately nearly costs him his life.

On a warm evening in South Philadelphia, O'Dowd joined Chitwood, now directly assigned to a new narcotics unit, to get some sense of "the world of drugs." Chitwood knew what corners to check out. The pushers generally had little money on them, since they were also addicts. They were only the foot soldiers of the trade and were generally in denial, always insisting they were about to quit. Burglaries were also up throughout the city because so many who had been hooked needed to keep feeding their addictions in any possible way. Typical users encountered by Chitwood and O'Dowd included a 20-year-old Vietnam veteran who had started with marijuana, but upon returning to the states, decided to move on to the "real stuff" because "everyone's using it." Now an admitted junkie, he had started "taking the cure" and was sure he was going to make it. Everyone seemed intent on recovery, at least when they talked with Chitwood. Another 20-year-old, Tony, with track marks all down both arms and his skin a yellow tint that made O'Dowd fear he might have jaundice, admitted to having sold as well as used heroin, but he insisted he'd never been able to keep any profit. A third addict, a Penn graduate, said he'd switched from marijuana "when the kicks ran out" and tried harder drugs, eventually heroin, while touring with a folk group in Asia. He visibly shook when being questioned. Hippie clothes and long hair were prevalent. Since Chitwood could find no actual drugs on any of them, he had each go to the local police station for routine questioning and observation, probably for neither the first nor the last time. Breaking the habit was no simple matter.

Chitwood's goal was bigger game. It was like fighting a many-headed monster. Somewhere between those kingpins who actually ran the drug traffic and these kids on the street were seemingly endless examples of middle management, some of whom combined virtually every form of legal and illegal business. The case of Raman M. Gaddis 2nd, of South Philadelphia, was a prime example. He advertised himself as a "consultant for physical disorders," but his second-floor bedroom contained loaded pistols, ammunition, film projectors, pornographic films, 50 cameras, $8,000 in numbers plays, two stolen doctor's bags packed with medical supplies, 35 credit cards belonging to other people, 50 blank Philadelphia Police Department identification cards, a great deal of untaxed liquor, and at least $10,000 worth of drugs. Following a tip, Captain Ferguson had obtained the customary search warrant and carefully prepared a raid. Gaddis, a longtime pharmacy employee, had obtained much of his extensive inventory of stolen merchandise from addicts who'd swapped them for prescription drugs. When Chitwood approached his house, the alarmed Gaddis, sitting on the front steps, drew a loaded revolver from his belt. Fortunately, he then tossed it inside and was collared by Chitwood. The resulting charges were as varied as Gaddis' cache, but at least they didn't include attempted murder.

Raids came in all sizes and varieties. One fairly extensive one, concluding two weeks of surveillance and investigation, targeted a supplier of narcotics for local college students and wound up confiscating some $150,000 worth. A typical young addict admitted to committing 31 burglaries to finance his $30-a-day drug habit. A raid in West Oak Lane resulted in the arrest of Philadelphia's "largest interracial narcotics ring" consisting of four men and two women, one only 19. Chitwood himself arrested a young Center City couple, non-users themselves, who sold dope to peddlers, who in turn sold it to users. Although technically unemployed, they drove a new Cadillac. It had taken a good deal of surveillance to nail them, which was generally the case. It could be a time-consuming business, the logistics of police work. A typical South Philadelphia narcotics raid on a "hippie-style" boutique netted 10 suspects, at the time all gathered in a circle, enjoying their own pot party. Their stock in trade was no longer limited to clothing, but more to marijuana and hashish.

Even some physicians couldn't resist the lure of drug-trade profits. In September 1970, Chitwood arrested a highly regarded, 85-year-old doctor and his aide on five counts of prescribing methadone, the purported heroin substitute. With so wide a field of skirmishes and battles, any ultimate victory in this intensifying drug war looked to be a long way off. It was an odd, insidious kind of war, trying to help victims who could technically wind up on both sides. Recruited and supplied, "hooked" by an enemy in the guise of their primary ally and friend, they might become pushers themselves.

*   *   *

By this time, Mike Chitwood no longer had Captain Clarence J. Ferguson to help him or give him advice. The old man died in November 1971, done in by diabetes. For years he had been the face of Philadelphia law enforcement, always wearing a porkpie hat and distinctive glasses, hands in his pockets, ready for action, his trusted investigative squad members waiting for his whispered word to raid another den of thieves. No one on the squad was more trusted than young Mike Chitwood. He was with Ferguson when he died, was one of his pallbearers, and had been almost like another son to "Fergy." Tom Fox of the *Daily News*, describing how so many of the captain's old friends lingered after his funeral, noted, "Mike Chitwood is in the narcotics unit now, but he learned the business with Fergy. He was a part of Fergy's squad for four years . . . always seemed to be at his elbow. . . . He made hundreds of raids with Fergy."

At West Park Hospital, as luck would have it, a major underworld figure had been placed in the next room. With that peculiar mutual regard of longtime adversaries, hoodlums stopping by would also look in to pay their respects to the old captain. But Ferguson, so drained by the diabetes, misunderstood and called Frank Rizzo, by then the police commissioner. "Frank, they're after me. Send a bodyguard," he pleaded. Rizzo replied, "All right, Captain. Who do you want me to send?" Fergy responded, "Send Chitwood. Get him up here right away!" And so, for the next three sleepless days and nights, Chitwood, who had previously kept the old man company, guarded his room from imagined assassins.

*   *   *

In a *Daily News* story headlined "His Name Is Chitwood. He's a Narc," Charles Montgomery and Jack McGuire provided an insightful picture of just how Chitwood appeared—and how he looked at things late in 1971. As usual, stressing his awards, commendations, and all the letters of appreciation from community associations and private citizens, the writers contrasted the emerging myth with the man. "Mike Chitwood is a quiet, soft-spoken 27-year-old. He doesn't look like a cop. But all six feet, 190 pounds of him is policeman." And not just an ordinary policeman. "Chitwood deals in one of the toughest areas in the business. He has been fighting the drug wars for the past 18 months."

The actual narcotics squad—a group separate from Ferguson's overall investigative unit—had been formed only four months before. It had already arrested some 150 drug pushers and had confiscated large caches of drugs of all kinds as well as firearms. Increasingly and ominously, they seemed to go together. In the article, the quiet, heavy-set Chitwood of 1971 became "visibly aroused" when he cited narcotics as "the biggest problem facing society today. . . . All crime is soaring because of it and people are dying every day from its effects"—over 200 in Philadelphia alone at that point in the year. "It used to be every neighborhood had its drunk, but now every neighborhood has its supplier, the friendly neighborhood pusher." Marijuana was the "starter drug," Chitwood stressed. "If I lock up 105 addicts, 104 have started with marijuana."

The ages of victims seemed to be declining. After a 16-year-old who had taken an excess of LSD broke away from medical personnel and plunged to his death from a fifth-floor window at Nazareth Hospital, Chitwood and two associates traced the original sales to three men in West Oak Lane. When there was no response to their announced arrival with a search warrant, Chitwood's men smashed open the door with a sledgehammer. A vigorous struggle ensued, this time fortunately without firearms, but it resulted in injuries to both a policeman and one of those inside. Among the variety of drugs discovered were 3,200 LSD tablets.

Local media monitored drug sales at specific corners, documenting that all the arrests simply weren't stopping drug trafficking, and that despite heightened police activity and frequent patrols, it remained easy to buy heroin in Philadelphia. In one North Philadelphia raid led by detectives Mike Chitwood and Frank Lombardo, which nabbed five suspects and an estimated $25,000 in heroin, some five telephones rang constantly. Chitwood and Lombardo answered them, counting at least 75 phone calls for "Pearl" and "Tammy," the contact names. Well, that was one distribution center shut down, but there was also a stolen gun on the premises, and one of the apprehended suspects had recently been released from prison after serving an abbreviated term for murder. Burglary, larceny, receiving stolen goods, and resisting arrest were becoming the less lethal charges for those arrested in drug-related cases. There was always the possibility of attempted murder.

*　　*　　*

Chitwood's new assignments were challenging, but his uniformly excellent evaluations were now being enhanced by specific suggestions for advancement. In mid-1971, his supervisor observed, "I have come to find that you are perhaps the most qualified investigator in the Philadelphia Police Department . . . outstanding in every category." In mid-1972, the reviewing supervisor added that he felt Chitwood "would make an excellent supervisor" himself. "You have shown judgment and maturity in your work, but more important you have shown common sense." Somehow Chitwood was finding time to start making occasional presentations and speeches throughout the community, explaining and promoting what he and his colleagues were doing and encouraging public interest and involvement. One that gave him special satisfaction was to students at Bishop Neumann, his old high school. This was just the sort of activity to enhance supervisory possibilities. He would not be characterized as shy much longer.

The special narcotics squad stressed action, but in his interviews and talks, Chitwood differentiated between pushers and users. Pushers, frequently guilty of crimes in other categories, should be jailed for as long as the law allowed. Habitual users should be rehabilitated, no easy task; addicts may have to be treated in step-by-step compulsory programs. Drug addiction is no less a sickness than alcohol addiction—and both require long-term treatment by trained, perceptive professionals. The use of methadone—weaning addicts from heroin by providing an ostensibly less harmful drug—was simply not the answer. Chitwood noted in one interview, "Numerous times we have arrested persons with methadone in one pocket and heroin in the other." Drug addiction is "communicable, like TB." Hard-core addicts must be taken off the streets and into treatment centers, "not as a punishment but as a help to society and themselves." Chitwood cited such recent experiences as witnessing a family sell their home, furniture, and car to bail their son out of jail for the 15th time, and seeing children of addicts go hungry because of their parents' habit.

One memorable photograph from May 1972 featured a newly mustachioed, somber, and suddenly much older-looking Chitwood, surrounded by five similarly hirsute officers, facing a table of assorted drug paraphernalia while holding up stolen firearms—the customary combination. Scarcely a month later, Chitwood and three fellow members of the narcotics squad made an 11 p.m. drug raid on an apartment in West Philadelphia. Knocking on the door and identifying themselves, they heard running footsteps after a peephole quickly opened and closed. As the police broke in the door, they were greeted by a blast from a double-barreled 12-gauge shotgun. Fortunately, it hit no one, but it left a gaping hole in a closet next to the entrance. Charles Grays, who had fired the shot, then quickly picked up a .38 caliber handgun, but it was too late. By then all four officers had their service revolvers leveled at Grays, who dropped his gun, exclaiming, "Don't shoot! I didn't mean it!"

In this instance, the heroin was between a mattress and a box spring. And, as usual, the phone rang constantly, people calling for "Pedro," Grays' professional name. Reportedly, he had previously served 18 years at Graterford Prison for murder. Again, that particular degree of murder didn't lead to life behind bars, but there seemed to be the potential for a fatality with virtually every raid made by the narcotics squad.

* * *

On May 14, 1972, a special ceremony took place at the Chapel of the Four Chaplains, then located at Temple University. This distinctive shrine memorialized the World War II chaplains—two Protestant, one Catholic, and one Jewish—who gave up their own lifejackets to save soldiers from the torpedoed troopship, the *U.S.S. Dorchester,* in 1943. Nearly 700 of the 900 on board perished. As the ship went down, each chaplain could be seen, arm in arm, and heard, praying in his own faith, an eternal symbol of solidarity and courage. And so it formed an appropriate setting for the Philadelphia Police Department's Legion of Honor Commendation Service for 1971. In all, 27 members of the department were honored for heroism, including 20 for bravery and 11 for valor. Chitwood was one of the 11. The handsome certificate does not specify the action. There is surely more than one possibility.

* * *

On November 17, 1982, Mike Chitwood received another certificate, far less ornate but even more welcome. It was from the City of Philadelphia by way of its police academy, informing him that, having "completed satisfactorily" the "prescribed inservice course," he was now officially a detective. It had taken only eight years, from uniformed foot patrolman to the highway patrol to switching to plainclothes as a member of Captain Ferguson's special investigations unit and then the narcotics unit, and finally to this coveted higher level. The *City Hall Paper* took note of "a big party for newly appointed detective Mike Chitwood, who has . . . gotten the big appointment—and raise." There was no accompanying photo in which he was actually smiling on that occasion, but one must surely exist somewhere.

Chitwood would be shifting his focus again from an emphasis on drugs back to combating the full range of urban crime, but now as a homicide detective. His well-publicized activities had already seemed at least remotely relevant to the hero of a highly popular motion picture hitting the screens at the end of 1971. *Dirty Harry* featured the taciturn Clint Eastwood as an unorthodox crime-fighter given to tight spots, swift action, and cryptic comments. There wasn't all that much resemblance to by-the-book Chitwood beyond a shared decisiveness, but back in the arena, to much of the local press and public, Chitwood became Philadelphia's popular personification of "Dirty Harry."

It didn't take long to earn that encomium. A night of panic began for a West Philadelphia family of six when four armed robbers invaded their home. Henry Watson, the young father, was forced by the intruders to surrender all the cash he had on hand and then go with two of them to his relatives to obtain their money, while the other thugs held his wife and children hostage. When the car containing Watson recklessly ran a stop sign and a police wagon forced it to the curb, the abducted father had the courage to blurt out a plea for help. Eventually, all four bandits were arrested, from both the car and home, in a complex operation led by Detective Chitwood. It would go easier on them if they surrendered, he reasoned—rather than challenging each to "Make my day."

Chitwood had ample opportunity to use both his persuasive and investigative skills—in everything from resolving a custody battle over a six-year-old girl to helping apprehend and arrest the robber of a major Center City savings and loan. But there was never a shortage of more violent assignments. In May 1975, an elderly woman was severely beaten and robbed in her South Philadelphia home by two intruders and was left in serious condition. Within a few moments of her neighbors' calling the local police station, the men were found, identified, and arrested. In subsequently praising the "wonderfully efficient men who were so sympathetic, considerate, and understanding," the recovering victim singled out their leader, "Detective Michael Chitwood, number 710."

Just as there were levels of commendation, to Chitwood there were also levels of crime. He had special contempt for those who preyed on the helpless or who seemed intent on senseless brutality. Yes, violence could be an inescapable part of his job, no less now that he was in a supervisory capacity, but he would use it only when and where he felt it was necessary, and certainly not on the defenseless.

* * *

A photograph in the October 18, 1975 issue of the *Philadelphia Daily News* shows a grim Mike Chitwood leading three other officers in carrying out the body of a shooting victim, one of two related deaths that day. It appeared that these fatalities and several others were very likely the result of a power struggle for control of what was being described as a "black crime cartel." Ostensibly a positive group organized originally to unify communities and resolve former gang rivalries, it had degenerated instead into a new conspiracy to try to corner the diminishing but still valuable heroin market.

Chitwood's immediate task was to find out who had killed this particular victim, 25-year-old Hershell Williams. Of considerable girth and six feet, six inches, he was known as the "Jolly Green Giant" and was one of those vying to lead the mob. But Chitwood also sought to get to the heart of the overall operation. Williams had been gunned down gangland-style as he emerged from his Mt. Airy home by as many as a dozen shotgun blasts from a passing car, possibly a Cadillac. Three men had been identified as Williams' possible assassins. They could well be rivals for power in an ever-changing situation. Chitwood would question each, one by one, in his small interrogation room within the police "Roundhouse," and try to obtain confessions indicting the others. The first, William Roy ("Rabbit") Hoskins, who seemed agitated, listened sullenly but then suddenly attacked Chitwood, hitting him wildly, and had to be restrained. The nature, degree, and necessity of such restraint would become the subject of considerable future controversy.

Chitwood later would try to describe the circumstances at a preliminary hearing for each of the men potentially accused of Williams' murder, but had no opportunity to do it in detail. During his earlier interrogation, Hoskins had initially denied taking part, blaming the two other "Black Mafia" members, Lonnie Dawson and Joseph ("JoJo") Rhone. It was when Chitwood said he would confront Dawson, who reportedly had driven the car, with this statement that Hoskins grew agitated and suddenly punched Chitwood in the face, knocking him to the floor, and jumped on him. By this time of shifting alliances, individual members of the mob may well have feared each other most of all. The other officer in the room then hit Hoskins several times with his nightstick. After he was put back in his chair, however, Hoskins came at Chitwood again, hitting him with his right fist. This time the detective retaliated. Chitwood recalled, "I hit him as hard as I could . . . with my fist in his face." So hard he fell backward into his metal chair, and was then finally handcuffed as quickly as possible.

A confession was obtained 15 minutes later. All three men were indicted and imprisoned, Dawson found guilty of first-degree murder. Williams had possibly been killed because of an unpaid debt of $2,000 for a cocaine shipment he owed to the current top man in this volatile organization. At the trial of the three killers, Dawson's attorney questioned Chitwood's ability to engage in such a fight and yet obtain a confession from Hoskins so soon afterward. Chitwood admitted that Hoskins was indeed injured, so much so that he would spend time in the hospital, but that he was still capable of recalling who was involved in Williams' murder and how it was done. Of course, in the police interrogation room, Hoskins had been the aggressor. No one imagined this debate had just begun when Chitwood was named one of two "detectives of the month" for June 1976, the Bicentennial year.

*　　*　　*

Supplementing Chitwood's responsibility in obtaining testimony was reading it in court, as he had in the Dawson case, and responding to those questioning it. One Andre Martin, only 16, had admitted shooting someone, but denied he knew it was a policeman. Housing Authority officer John Trettin, a bullet lodged in his head, died four days later. Two co-defendants with Martin testified that the youth had vowed "he was going to get a cop." Martin, however, in his confession, taken down and read in court by Chitwood, said he had actually aimed his rifle at what he thought were "three dudes from the Passyunk Avenue Gang." When one fell, "I didn't know he was a cop." In his statement, however, Martin added that after he had seen the man fall, "a whole bunch of cops came and . . . dragged him into 2508 Jackson Street and put him on a stretcher." Again, "I didn't know he was a cop." In fact, three shots had been fired, but only one hit its mark. In the tense courtroom, the youth's mother on one side and the officer's widow on the other, sometimes it appeared as if Chitwood were on trial. The lawyer assigned to Martin implied that the detective had led his client on. How was he certain whether the distraught teenager was coherent enough to give accurate testimony? How could he know Officer Trettin had been placed on a stretcher? Could he see through walls? It was known, however, that Martin was upset when a friend had been shot and wounded by police after robbing a South Philadelphia supermarket. Ultimately, there was no escaping Martin's guilt, only his age saving him from the maximum penalty.

There was no leniency for 31-year-old Thomas Whitaker, a loner who liked to sit on a bench and brood in Wharton Square. An escaped mental patient named Patricia McCloskey found him there, walked up, and told him, "You know you look like an ass." Whitaker went berserk. He leapt up and dragged her to the center of the park, started jumping up and down on top of her, bit her, and eventually raped and strangled her. "I got this bottle and I hit her," he told Chitwood. "I just snapped. Before I knew it, I was on her. I didn't see her sexually. I just saw her as something ugly." He often went to the park in the early morning, Whitaker confided. He liked to be alone. Thus the horrific result when two aberrant individuals happened to collide. His mental state didn't save Whitaker, convicted of rape and murder. But even steady Mike Chitwood, hardened by now to almost any category of crime, must have found such examples taking their emotional toll.

In 1977, a preview of Chitwood's future focus on hostage negotiations took place on the 10th floor of a Center City office building. In this instance, however, it was the hostages who were heroic. The circumstances were sad as well as scary. Yet another former mental patient, this one named Robert Bagley, had found his way to the offices of the Travelers Aid Society. He was homeless and also sought medication, more treatment, and a place to go. The three women in the office phoned around fruitlessly to try to place him somewhere. Realizing their efforts had been unavailing, Bagley pulled a switchblade knife from his pocket and barricaded the door. When a friend of office manager Anita Kolesa arrived on the ground floor, called up to have her come down to join her for lunch, and couldn't get any response, something seemed suspicious. A security guard in the lobby contacted the police. They quickly arrived, led by detectives Michael Chitwood and John Malone, and made their way up to the 10th floor. Unable to enter the Travelers Aid offices and fearing what might happen if they smashed down the door, they waited.

A five-hour standoff followed. Bagley became ever more agitated, his moods ranging from apologetic to menacing. Several times he threatened to cut his hostages' throats if he so much as saw a cop. Finally, as he was brandishing the switchblade, the three women managed together to grab him and pin him against the wall. Mrs. Kolesa got hold of the knife and threw it out the window. As Bagley ran wildly throughout the offices, Katy McDonnell, another of the employees screamed, "Help us!" And the police outside the door, led by Chitwood and Malone, battered their way in and rushed to their rescue. Bagley was quickly subdued. In a way, he had succeeded in his desire to find a place to stay. He was taken for observation to Philadelphia General Hospital. No charges were filed, but it had been a close call. The three women took the next day off.

*　　*　　*

The following week, Detective Michael J. Chitwood and three others were named by the Fraternal Order of Police as policemen and investigators of the year. Chitwood was awarded yet another commendation for apprehending a murder suspect and received the Valor Award, the department's highest honor, for subduing the man who had shot and critically wounded his partner during a drug raid. After 13 tumultuous years fighting both the drug and homicide wars, he felt ready to take on just about anything. In a letter dated April 4, 1977, Deputy District Attorney Esther R. Sylvester expressed her congratulations and her regret at being unable to attend the affair. "After seven years of prosecuting, I came to realize that few men in the history of the police department have the capacity of rising above their fellow officers. You have accomplished just that, because of the unique combination of courage, common sense, and an understanding of the law. We all admire you. The honor is well deserved."

*　　*　　*

Three weeks later, the roof caved in. Or so it seemed initially. The power of the press was still very potent in the 1970s. For four days, from April 24 through April 27, 1977, *The Philadelphia Inquirer* featured a major investigative report starting on the front page each day, titled "The Homicide Files." Written by Jonathan Neumann and William K. Marimow (a prominent journalist who today is serving his second stint as editor of the paper), it was an extraordinarily detailed account of a frightening pattern of police brutality. Typical headings of extensive examples included "How Philadelphia detectives compel murder confessions," "The only rights you get . . . are right fists," "How police harassed a family," "Why detectives are safe from prosecution," and "A police beating . . . and a decision to charge detectives"—this one directed squarely at the most honored detective of all, Michael J. Chitwood.

The most detailed focus, featuring a front-page photograph of Chitwood and fellow highly decorated homicide detective John Strohm, was on that interrogation of Roy Hoskins in 1975. The paper's lurid details were a world apart from Chitwood's own depiction of events. According to the *Inquirer*'s account, Hoskins first encountered an older detective named Bernard Carr, who had promised to "whip his ass." Thrust at 4:10 a.m. on November 5, 1975, into interrogation room 121, "a 10-by-10-foot cubicle containing three metal chairs and a table," Hoskins, "23, a slender, 135-pound black man with a record of four arrests in five years," asked to see a lawyer. "Do you think you're on television or something?" one of the detectives "sneeringly" replied. As far as the Philadelphia police were concerned, legal rights didn't enter into it. This was an accusation of murder.

According to his account, Hoskins was then handcuffed to the chair by both hands while a succession of detectives came in to question him. Chitwood entered with a blackjack and without provocation started vigorously beating Hoskins around his legs, ankles, and bare feet until the blackjack broke. He then returned with a table leg and bludgeoned the shackled Hoskins all over his body, while shouting vile racial and sexual slurs and threatening to kill him. The beating, with others taking turns, continued until 9:30 that night. Eventually, a criminal lawyer named Barry H. Denker, who had been called by Hoskins' family, arrived. He was appalled by "one of the most horrible sights I have ever seen," blood coming out of Hoskins' head and his whole body obviously battered and bruised. Shortly after 10 p.m., Denker called Judge Paul A. Dandridge to request that his client be taken to the hospital immediately. Denker noted that Hoskins was unable even to stand. He was kept in Philadelphia General Hospital for five days and was fed intravenously. His kidneys had been damaged, his face and feet were swollen, and his groin was punctured by a stab wound.

About the only agreements between the two accounts, Chitwood's subsequent one and the *Inquirer*'s reconstruction, were the fact that Hoskins had signed a statement implicating Dawson and Rhone as the killers as well, and that when momentarily freed, he had attacked Chitwood and had to be forcefully restrained again. Hoskins feared that when Dawson saw his statement, it would constitute a death warrant. Chitwood added, during the pretrial hearing, that at one point, emotionally upset and crying, Hoskins injured himself by hitting his head on the metal chair in which he was seated, damaging his eye. But Chitwood's testimony was limited to responding to questions. He never, in effect, had his own day in court.

In any case, within days of the interrogation, a team from the district attorney's office began their own investigation and decided that after so severe a beating there was sufficient evidence to prosecute four detectives, particularly Chitwood. However, District Attorney Emmett Fitzpatrick, City Managing Director Hillel Levinson, and Police Commissioner Joseph F. O'Neill decided not to prosecute. In this, not surprisingly, they were vigorously supported by Mayor Frank L. Rizzo, who would later take exception to the thrust of the entire *Inquirer* series. As noted, at the pretrial hearing on January 20, 1976, Chitwood and others testified under oath, but their own recollection of events was limited by the format. Apparently, the differing conclusions by assistant district attorneys and homicide detectives caused something of a temporary rift between the two groups. Police Commissioner O'Neill effected a face-saving compromise by transferring Chitwood and the three others to different districts for a time, but in a matter of months, they were quietly returned to their former locations and responsibilities.

Of course, this featured incident was viewed by the *Inquirer* as only one blatant instance of a veritable epidemic of rampant illegality. In preparing their four-day report, the editors noted that they had reviewed all 433 homicide cases from 1974 through April 1977, in which judges had ruled on the legality of police investigations. "In 80 cases, the judges determined that these interrogations were illegal." The newspaper's investigators also talked extensively with assistant district attorneys, defense attorneys, witnesses, judges, and defendants and sought to talk with homicide detectives in terms of these cases. Police Commissioner O'Neill, who "emphatically and categorically" denied all the *Inquirer*'s allegations of police brutality, would not permit the 31 policemen contacted by the paper by certified mail to testify, but the paper did claim to "interview a number of officers on condition that they not be quoted by name." Mayor Rizzo refused to comment specifically on the series, but he noted later in a telephone interview that although mistakes can be made by anyone, "The scales are shifting too much to the criminal. It's unfair to the law-abiding citizen." The Fraternal Order of Police issued statements similar to Commissioner O'Neill's.

On its front page on April 26, the *Inquirer* noted that Chitwood, at only 33, "The highest paid homicide detective on the force . . . last year earned $36,298.17, more than half of it in overtime pay." Thus he featured prominently in another of the paper's basic accusations, an emphasis on obtaining the maximum number of convictions through just about any means, legal or not—a sort of urban equivalent of a body count. As one of those unidentified policemen was quoted as bitterly recalling, in the initial article of April 24, "[Chief Inspector Joseph] Golden runs that place like a czar. . . . The rule down there: Convictions at any cost. . . . They know it doesn't matter how. . . . Beatings. . . . Yes, I've seen them. . . . Convictions is the name of the game. Not truth. . . . Police are breaking the law every day." You play the game, and you profit. Get out of line, and it's you who suffers, your career sidetracked and diminished. You're just not one of the guys. But that's nothing compared to the plight of the victims of police brutality. "Guilty or innocent, they are being denied even their most basic legal and human rights as Americans."

The same page featured a large photograph of Chitwood, poster boy for the entire series, next to one of Commissioner O'Neill. Later in this book, the same comparison is noted in a way both men found rather amusing, but here it is in a different context. Police overtime, based on how much effort it takes to methodically pile up the maximum number of convictions by exhaustive investigations, interrogations, and court appearances, resulted in some homicide detectives actually making more money than their superiors. Another chart illustrates how in 1976, six detectives earned more than Chief Inspector Golden. In those paired photos, the one on the left is captioned, repeating the earlier figure, "In 1976, this man earned $36,293.17. His name is Michael Chitwood. His title is Homicide Detective." On the right: "In 1976, this man earned $35,000. His name is Joseph F. O'Neill. His title is Police Commissioner."

By the end of their exhaustive analysis, with ever more outraged headlines, including overtones of racism ("Gun butts, fists and blackjacks and a suspect dies"), Neumann and Marimow concluded that so little has been done in part because, particularly when it's a question of taking the word of a policeman or, say, a murder suspect, a judge will generally rule in the policeman's favor. They quote defense lawyers who cite how unlikely it is that the Philadelphia police could obtain so many confessions, induce people to voluntarily waive their rights, and admit to crimes as serious as murder, without using illegal and often brutal methods. Judge Edward J. Bradley of Common Pleas Court, however, later pointed out that only "80 rulings of illegal interrogations since 1974, if accurate, indicated that the police acted illegally in only a small minority of homicide investigations." And if many of the suspects' claims were untrue, Bradley continued, "Here's a defendant fighting for his freedom. He might say anything to get off." It's not necessarily as much a result of police brutality or excessive pressure as it is of criminals trying to find excuses. Hoskins was badly beaten, but might he not have attacked Chitwood first? And who was first to use his baton on Hoskins? After being taken to the hospital, he had the advantage of careful coaching by a skilled defense attorney.

That pretty much summarizes Chitwood's views, as well. He had not been allowed to respond directly to accusations, beyond his testimony at the pretrial hearing, or to conduct his own post-series investigation or talk with the medical examiner. To this day, he resents his inability to frame a direct, thorough rebuttal of all those charges leveled against him, which he still views as essentially unfair, untrue, or biased. That he's had some subsequent and quite congenial conversations with William Marimow will never change that. As for the result of this highly touted *Inquirer* series, although it won the Pulitzer—probably a major objective of its prominent positioning in the paper—the effect of the revelations wasn't particularly long-lasting. It was no Watergate. As for Homicide Detective Chitwood, as indicated, he was transferred to West Philadelphia for a few months—hardly Siberia—and then was quietly returned to his former location and full responsibilities, and almost seamlessly to more action, arrests, and accolades.

The Hoskins case got considerably more complicated, however, as did the convictions of his two accomplices in the 1975 murder of Hershell Williams, himself a major heroin distributor. Hoskins' conviction was overturned by the Pennsylvania Supreme Court because his confession had been obtained by "illegal" means. Meanwhile, his lawyer sued the City of Philadelphia for three million dollars because of police "brutality." While denying all charges and reiterating that it was Hoskins who had originally assaulted Detective Chitwood, Commissioner O'Neill decided to settle out of court because it would cost too much to fight the case. Hoskins was awarded $21,000. In 1982, Lonnie Dawson, Hoskins' accomplice, who also had driven the getaway car, in a new trial was accused by a reluctant hit man of offering $10,000 if the hit man would kill a witness to the slaying of Williams. Guilty of so many other crimes in addition, Dawson, Rhone, and Hoskins were all convicted again of murder and conspiracy in their second separate trials. By the way, Roy Hoskins is *still* in jail. However, the odd circumstances of his being paid, like the Inquirer's series itself, would come back to haunt Chitwood in future years.

* * *

A veteran of the drug wars, the homicide wars, and now a survivor of the grand inquisition, Chitwood was ready to take on just about any challenge. Later in 1977, a fairly customary one, at least to a hardened law-enforcement officer, involved the arrest of a 19-year-old who already went by two names and had been a fugitive for two years. He was now wanted for two charges of murder and one of armed robbery. It had all started for Kevin Cargo (or Davis) with an argument at a party in 1975. Only 17 at the time, he went outside to settle some serious dispute with another guest, pulled a gun, shot him twice, and fled. Later Cargo and a companion robbed a man named Gerald Kramer of $700 outside his home. Cargo would have killed him as well, but his shotgun jammed. It turned out that Cargo had once worked for Kramer's beef company, but had been dismissed for stealing. A week later, Cargo's gun didn't misfire. As Kramer was leaving his place of business, a cab sped by. From inside, a shotgun was leveled. In a murder reminiscent of that by Hoskins and his accomplices, Kramer was struck by both blasts and fatally wounded. The stolen cab was later set ablaze. When Chitwood and Lt. William Shelton finally tracked down and caught up to Cargo, arresting him in the basement of his home, fortunately the presence of two armed officers induced him not to fire this time.

Random is a word well suited to the vagaries of crime. Precisely why there were so many violent incidents involving the Philadelphia Transit Authority in 1978 is difficult to discern. Perhaps the most tragic, even worse than drivers killed for no more than requesting fares, was the death of young Michael Gilbert, a recently returned air force veteran, on the SEPTA Route 56 bus. It took a while for Detective Chitwood to unravel the details. Driver William Bailey told Chitwood that, while boarding, Gilbert mumbled something about having had difficulty with other bus drivers. Gilbert then went to the back of the bus but soon returned to the front and lit a cigarette. Bailey asked Gilbert to put it out—and then events become confused. Bailey claims he felt pain in his nose and saw bleeding, but never actually witnessed Gilbert throwing a punch. At that point, with the door open at Torresdale and Harbison, Gilbert rushed out and ran away. The furious driver followed him. Gilbert slipped on the track of a trolley line and fell hard. Still upset, Bailey kicked him three times in the face. In the driver's subsequent statement, there was the familiar refrain, "I didn't think he was going to die." But he did. Somehow returning to his mother's home, Gilbert lapsed into a coma, and within 10 days he was gone. The autopsy revealed that an artery had been severed by some sort of severe blow. At that point the veteran's distraught mother still had no idea how it had happened. Mrs. Mary Gilbert offered a reward of $1,000, all she could afford, for any information. Three passengers on the bus eventually responded, and she contacted the police. Determining the driver's responsibility, Chitwood arrested him and obtained his confession. Bailey was ultimately indicted for murder. Of course, nothing could bring solace to the grieving mother, but she highly praised the homicide division, singling out Chitwood. "He's been marvelous throughout the whole thing," she said, "simply marvelous." Just another senseless tragedy, except to two stricken families.

Risking his own life may have been ordinary operating procedure to so committed a lawman as Chitwood. After all, his original motivation was the protection of others. Despite the attractions of his profession, he knew what he was getting into. But witnessing the results of such horrific crimes as the rape and murder of Patricia McCloskey was something no one could really become accustomed to. There was another such incident in 1978. As was often the case, mental illness figured in the crime. This time the sex was male on male. Richard Canady, 25, had a history of treatment, even if unsuccessful, for mental illness. The frozen body of a 16-year-old named Adolphus Talley was discovered in a vacant building. He had been burned, beaten, sexually molested, and strangled. Canady, on parole for a sexual assault on a 15-year-old boy, came under investigation for this new crime. In a confession obtained and read to the jury by Detective Chitwood, so reminiscent of others he had elicited, Canady protested, "All I wanted was sex with him. Maybe I squeezed too hard. I really feel bad about it." Small solace. Perhaps because of his mental history, a jury convicted him only of second-degree murder.

* * *

It was none of his customary investigative skills, however, that managed to land Chitwood a featured, if brief, role in solving Philadelphia's crime of the decade. Ultimately, it escalated into the crime of a quarter-century before being finally resolved.

Scruffy-looking, heavy-set Ira Samuel Einhorn seemed the personification of the "hippie guru" counterculture of the 1960s and '70s. Calling himself "the Unicorn," the well-educated, thirty-something LSD experimenter had parlayed his space-age theories, poetry, and philosophy into relationships with the most prominent of the avant-garde. Einhorn had a positive genius for attracting followers, resources, and reams of publicity. Operating out of a Race Street apartment, he helped organize Philadelphia's first Earth Day, and led peace protests and teach-ins, including a vast "Be-In" on Belmont Plaza in Fairmount Park. By 1971, he'd gone beyond the customary activities to embrace pseudoscience, exploring what he called the "planetary enzyme." He even ran for mayor of Philadelphia as a proponent of "planetary reformation."

In 1972, Einhorn met Helen "Holly" Maddux. A lovely young woman of 26 from Tyler, Texas, who had come east to study at Bryn Mawr College, she was captivated by the Unicorn, fell completely under his spell, and moved in with him. To the equally smitten Ira, however, such captivation also meant exerting his domination. Their tempestuous relationship lasted five years, punctuated by violent arguments overheard by their neighbors and fights that left Holly visibly bruised. Still she couldn't bring herself to leave Einhorn, so strong was his hold. Finally, however, she met another man on a trip to Fire Island, New York, who helped shape her resolve. Predictably, Einhorn reacted with fury to the news that she had decided to break off their relationship. However, he somehow induced her to return to pick up her possessions, which he had earlier threatened to destroy. Not long after Ira had lured Holly back to their apartment, the neighbors heard more than the customary arguments. This time it was piercing screams and loud thuds. Holly Maddux was never seen alive again. When questioned by police about her disappearance, Einhorn calmly told them that Holly had simply gone to the store and never returned. Later he reported that she had called him and said she was OK, but asked him not to look for her.

Holly's parents, who had always disapproved of her relationship with Ira Einhorn, had invariably received regular cards, letters, and phone calls from their otherwise still-dutiful daughter for holidays and family events. When, by Thanksgiving, these contacts had ceased, Holly's mother grew suspicious and hired two private investigators. They came to Philadelphia and wound up meeting, logically enough, with Homicide Detective Michael J. Chitwood. By then neighbors were reporting foul smells coming from Einhorn's apartment. A missing-person report had been filed and an investigation was launched, but the wheels of justice, like "the mills of the gods," can grind slowly. Finally, on March 28, 1979, 18 months after the disappearance of Holly Maddux and armed with a multi-page search warrant, Chitwood called on a still very composed Ira Einhorn. He expressed neither surprise nor any interest in conversation. Chitwood followed odors that had become ever stronger to discover the decomposing corpse of the murdered young woman in a trunk her onetime lover had stored in his closet. Facing him, the detective voiced the obvious, "It looks like we found Holly." To which Einhorn replied, "You found what you found." Then 41, he would face an indictment for murder. So much for Chitwood's moment.

With his $40,000 bail provided by an admirer and being represented by a noted former Philadelphia district attorney named Arlen Specter, Einhorn was released from custody in 1981. But just days before his trial was to begin, the unpredictable Ira skipped bail and fled to parts unknown, which turned out to be Europe. Reputedly, he had asked counterculture hero Abbie Hoffman for advice. Einhorn traveled from Ireland to Scandinavia, under assumed names, with no apparent shortage of resources, avoiding detection for the next 17 years. He married a Swedish woman and moved to the south of France under a new name.

Back in Pennsylvania, since Einhorn had already been arraigned, the state convicted him in absentia in 1993 for the murder of Holly Maddux. Since his guilt was indisputable, he was sentenced to life in prison without the possibility of parole.

Finally, in 1997, Einhorn was tracked down and arrested in France. After a complex give-and-take between the two governments to assure that the death penalty would not be invoked, and after Einhorn had unsuccessfully attempted suicide on July 20, 2001, the French finally extradited the fugitive back to the United States. In a new jury trial in which Einhorn insisted that the CIA had murdered Maddux and proceeded to frame him, it didn't take long to reach a decision. Convicted in 2002, Ira Einhorn will remain in prison for the rest of his life. From the time that he found the body of Holly Maddux to Einhorn's present incarceration, Mike Chitwood had served as police chief in two of his three separate localities.

*   *   *

Even as Chitwood's thinking evolved and broadened, for his first 15 years as a law-enforcement officer, his primary job was the apprehension and incarceration of criminals. "Scumbags" would always threaten those he was sworn to protect—the vast majority of law-abiding Philadelphians. The most violent criminals transcend considerations of race, age, or economic circumstances. Certainly, mistakes were made. Some innocent people went to jail, and still do. Hopefully, our criminal justice system can be vastly improved to overturn unjust convictions. Hopefully, the resources of society can do a much better job of rehabilitation. In the world as it is, however, good people can fall short of perfection.

The excesses attributed to Mike Chitwood in the *Inquirer* series went far beyond this. It remains all but impossible to equate the picture they projected with the real person, then or now. The candid recollections of his wife and children tell so different a story that it would take a Jekyll/Hyde transformation for both versions to be true. The Chitwoods' lives together were not always easy, but the overall picture, given the glow of memory, is simply too positive to discount.

In January 1980, Chitwood received an invitation of special significance. It came from Reverend Milton E. Jordan, S.J., president of Saint Joseph's Preparatory School, the outstanding high school Mike Jr. was attending. Father Jordan began, "For once I am writing to your home without any requests for money, tuition, special events or the like. I hope this does not come as too much of a surprise to you." The administrative council of the Prep had voted unanimously to bestow on Chitwood their highest honor, The Insignis Award. He became the first person from outside the school to receive it. It was given at a March assembly, attended by both beaming Chitwoods, father and son. For once, Detective Chitwood was not being commended for bravery or heroism or even valor but for his awareness "of the good in others," for spending "much of the day helping others," and for being "a dreamer, a darer, a worker who does not turn back from a challenge." In a way, it was even more a projection of his future than a recognition of the past and present. In his brief remarks, the elder Chitwood smilingly and not quite accurately recalled that as a "smart and upcoming" student in eighth grade, he had taken the entrance exam for the Prep but had failed. Patience is indeed a virtue.

Chitwood's greatest regret, often voiced, was not having had enough time to spend with his two kids when they were still small. But in their own recollections it doesn't seem to have been so harmful a handicap. Mike Jr. recalls, "As a child growing up, my father was my hero. I always wanted to be around him and be like him." Young Mike even read police reports and listened in on his father's official telephone conversations. The two were only 19 years apart, and as young Mike grew into a sports-loving teenager, his relationship with his father became more physical and highly competitive. Mike played no-holds-barred basketball with his father's friends, as did Mike Sr. with his son's. As Mike Jr. recalls, "I did my best to beat him as he did to beat me." However, this had followed years when his father was endlessly pitching in batting practice, tossing a football, and playing one-on-one hoops, all to perfect his son's skills. And jogging and biking, as well, as the older Mike was becoming more of a fitness fanatic himself.

"We never missed a sporting event in Philly," Mike Jr. adds, especially when their favorites were playing—Steve Carlton and the Phillies; Julius Erving and the Sixers; "the Broad Street Bullies," as the Flyers were known in the '70s; Dick Vermeil's Eagles, and the Big Five. How Detective Chitwood managed it all, despite his rigorous schedule, borders on the remarkable, but he was always skilled at timing. As Mike Jr. reflects, "I became a sports junkie because of him. It was our common bond."

But there were always rules. The elder Chitwood refers to raising his own children, as he and his two brothers had been raised by their own parents, with unquestioning authority from above. Although this was not nearly so rigorous a regimen as he had experienced, it was certainly far less permissive than the prevailing environment at the homes of the young Chitwood's friends. "Unfortunately, as I grew into my rebellious teen years," he continues, "we began to dislike each other's company. Today our relationship has come full circle. The adoration of a child . . . the rebellion of a teenage son . . . to our being best friends and confidants of each other." Of course, it doesn't hurt that both Chitwoods followed the same career, and through the same path, developed a unique perspective on both personal and professional grounds. Mike Jr. concludes, "Every success in my life and the person I am is because of my father."

With Beth Ann Chitwood (now Scannell, and the mother of two children of her own, a girl and a boy), the sports instruction may not have been as intensive, but she recalls her father patiently teaching her as well how to play baseball and throw a football the "right way." It turned out to be quite an advantage in dealing with her own son. More important, her father taught her to always stand up for herself, the importance of personal identity. After all, she was a Chitwood, and "as I grew up, the name meant lots of things to lots of people." Beth Ann, too, understood that there were standards of behavior. "I have always had a healthy respect for my dad. All my mom had to say was 'wait until your father comes home.'" Yet Beth Ann never really managed to get into that much trouble. The time-honored admonition was rarely necessary, in any case. Liz Chitwood was good at handling things on her own.

However, Beth Ann continues, "As my brother got older, things did get somewhat challenging. I had 'my Pop the cop' . . . and Michael Chitwood, Jr. I was 'Little Chit,' not always easy since everyone always knew who I was and what I was up to." Self-reliance was a valuable lesson. A memorable story comes to mind: When Beth Ann was old enough to start dating, her father told her with a straight face that he was going to ask any boy who came over to urinate into a cup just to make certain he was not a junkie. Serious or not, since "Pop the cop" was then working the 4 p.m. to 12 midnight shift, Beth Ann made certain that she was always picked up and dropped off while he was away. One story among many.

Mike Jr. adds that it wasn't prudent to send out his father for a Christmas tree, although he did go along in this instance. Perhaps because of frugality, the one they brought home had such barren branches that it looked like something from *A Charlie Brown Christmas*. "We both took loads of abuse from family and friends for this incredibly poor excuse for a tree. It took my mother days to make it respectable and my sister to stop crying."

A different kind of memory was recalled when Beth Ann's son made his First Communion. She remembered her father finding time to read her stories from the lavishly illustrated *Children's Bible*. It was a shared experience she thoroughly enjoyed. "I think he really enjoyed it, too."

Yes, it may all sound like *Rebecca of Sunnybrook Farm*, but these are typical recollections from a genuinely cohesive family. As recounted earlier, Liz Chitwood, when a young bride, had the toughest time of all. Only later did she realize that when money was especially tight, Mike would continue to wear his old high school clothes, investing any money he could scrape up into "something nice" for her—or later, a pair of shoes for young Mike. Raising two children, at least initially, largely on her own was more than challenging, but "I have the utmost respect for the work that Mike does" and his value system, which both parents passed along to their children. When, many years later, Liz was battling thyroid cancer, Mike would do everything he could to cheer her up, even starting off the day with such stunts as "dancing around the bedroom in his underwear and socks." Well, you had to be there.

And there are all the stories from his police work, only funny in retrospect. When once in the early days, Mike yelled, "Halt!" to a suspect he was chasing and then pulled out his gun, both the chamber and all the bullets fell to the ground. While warning the guy not to move, he was obliged to kneel down, pick everything up, and try to reassemble his weapon. Fortuitously, reinforcements arrived just in time to keep the farce from turning into tragedy. Then there was the time when he was the only officer in the unit in good enough physical condition to chase a suspected drug dealer, who fortunately didn't turn around to count the pursuing posse. And once, when he had just started playing racquetball and was practicing on an outdoor tennis wall, shots rang out. Chitwood was so certain they were meant for him that he made a mad dash for his car to check out the bullet holes. It turned out that it was simply rival gangs spending a warm summer day in their normal fashion. Well, perhaps not even funny in retrospect.

This book is the account of an extraordinary career, not a traditional biography. But in view of all those accusations of everything from insensitivity to sadism, some biographical input does seem relevant.

*   *   *

The ferocity of crime is only matched by its variety. Claiming he was Jesus Christ, 24-year-old Melvin White ordered his 19-year-old accomplice named "Truth" to behead 22-year-old Lynn Smith, the mother of his two-year-old son, because she was told to get out and didn't. Using a machete and two swords, the loyal White complied. When apprehended by Chitwood for this grisly murder, neither man denied it. However, White would sign nothing, claiming this time that Allah had told him not to. Police had investigated the home because of reports of a prior fight. Declared competent to stand trial, White received the death penalty. In another case, a young mother strangled her two-year-old son because in a dream "the devil" had come for him.

William Eichner was so upset that his former girlfriend wouldn't take him back that he held her eight-year-old son, Serge Stanley, hostage for two hours, using a six-inch folding knife to keep the police at bay. Eichner hadn't been at Sharon Stanicky's Fishtown home for two or three months when he suddenly appeared, tried to win her back, and beat her up when she refused. He then threatened to kill her but abruptly left. The next day, he broke back in to try again. When Sharon wasn't there, Eichner grabbed Serge. After neighbors informed her of the break-in, Sharon called police and tried to talk her former boyfriend into surrendering. While they were thus occupied, three policemen, led by Detective Michael Chitwood, quietly entered the house and overcame and disarmed Eichner just as Serge broke away and ran into Chitwood's arms.

Sometimes these troubled souls threaten only themselves. A young Manayunk man named Robert Rieser, claiming, "I can't take it anymore," threatened to kill himself by jumping off a 1,200-foot television transmission tower in Roxborough. Adding, rather obviously, "I've got a lot of problems," he had climbed up a narrow ladder to get near the top and had thrown down something visible called a marker-light cover. Thus alerted, police and firemen played searchlights on the structure but couldn't find Rieser, who was hiding among the girders. A negotiating team of detectives including Michael Chitwood and Frank Diegel decided to ride a small elevator up to try to locate him. "We're coming up," Chitwood yelled through a bullhorn. "Stay away from the cables. No one wants to hurt you." Then Chitwood added, "Nothing can be as bad as that. We'll get you all the help you need." Only a few minutes later, after nearly two hours aloft, Rieser apparently reflected and had changed his mind. "All right," he replied, "but don't let me fall." Back on the ground, he was driven to the Northwest Mental Health Center in Mt. Airy. For Chitwood, this sort of activity constituted another preview of things to come.

But despite every success and renewed acclaim, Chitwood was also still mulling over the too-recent past. To popular columnist Tom Fox, he reflected that he even sometimes considered a new line of work. "I'm still young enough to start over," he mused. "If the right proposition came along, I just might chuck it all and get into another line, because I've sure had my fill of tragedy." To the *Bulletin*'s Adrian Lee, he commented in early 1980, two years after the *Inquirer*'s series, "The people who wrote me up as 'brutal'—they never talked to me. People I used to see around, they didn't say 'hi' anymore. It got me to the point where I didn't talk to murder suspects for fear of jeopardizing the case; the prosecutor didn't have to prove his case; he only had to prove my involvement in it. . . . One day you're a 'hero,' the next day a 'bum.'" It still rankled. Thirty-three years later, it *still* rankles.

* * *

Of course, the sentiment passed. Chitwood was as much a lifer as those he'd helped to incarcerate for crimes that were beyond reason. He was just thinking things through, and now, whenever he could, he would try to substitute imagination for instinct. Take the case of Walter Ciz, for example, who had been in the Marines. Ultimately charged with kidnapping, burglary, simple assault, threats, and trespassing, Ciz had a three-hour standoff with police while holding his former girlfriend, Carol Stoner, hostage on the seventh floor of a Center City office building. Armed with a sawed-off 12-gauge shotgun, he claimed to have explosives on his body that he could ignite with a battery. It certainly appeared that he knew how to do it. Erratic as most hostage-takers, Ciz, desperate over his breakup, threatened to blow up the entire block and shoot his hostage and himself. But at other times he insisted that he only wanted to talk to her, perhaps even to win her back.

Enter Detective Mike Chitwood, only this time in the guise of a newspaper reporter. Before Chitwood's arrival on the scene, Ciz had said through the door to another policeman that he'd like to talk to a reporter to tell his story. This was all the break Chitwood needed. He simply borrowed the press credentials of Kevin Riordan of the *Camden Courier-Post,* whom he remotely resembled, and proceeded to talk things over calmly with Ciz, eventually persuading him to surrender. He was given three to 10 years, but with the stipulation of receiving psychiatric treatment. The editor of the *Courier-Post*, while insisting, "I don't condone policemen impersonating reporters," added that with lives in danger, "I cannot fault the reporter or the policeman for acting as they did." Colorful Jack McKinney, columnist for the *Philadelphia Daily News*, was more equivocal: "I have a ton of admiration for Mike Chitwood, whose controlled blend of courage and cool intelligence has earned him a unique record in preventing dangerously disturbed people from hurting themselves and others . . . but I wish he could have handled this last one without using that press card." In a later column, McKinney added, "The rumor spread quickly that the hostage-taker had surrendered to Detective Mike Chitwood, as they almost invariably do."

Such imaginative resolution wasn't much help when a mentally retarded woman was raped, robbed, beaten, and stabbed some 38 times. But even here, Chitwood led his homicide unit through an extensive investigation to find and peacefully arrest the two perpetrators. No beatings or intimidation. As usual, one of the youthful suspects insisted to Chitwood, "I didn't mean to kill her. I just wanted to get some money, that's all." After Chitwood's thorough testimony in court, the young killer got life, barely escaping the death penalty.

Reputed "mobs" encompass all origins. A series of murders involving rival groups in the '70s turned out to be motivated more by robbery than rivalry. It took eight days of digging, so to speak, for homicide detectives Dan Rosenstein and Mike Chitwood to uncover the truth and arrest the guilty, again without a struggle. The scope of their search put Chitwood in close contact with Delaware County criminal investigators, broadening his professional relationships beyond the borders of Philadelphia, contacts that would prove significant in the future.

By now Chitwood was being popularly acclaimed as Philadelphia's "supercop." *Philadelphia Journal* columnist Charles Brown, observing that three years had passed since all the accusations of "brutality," quoted the contemporary Chitwood as insisting that "you catch more flies with honey than you catch with vinegar." Now "Philadelphia's most respected detective," Chitwood could talk almost any barricaded criminal into surrendering without even a struggle. "Detective Mike Chitwood," Brown continued, "a tall, curly haired man whose life story could be played by movie tough Bruce Dern seemed unaffected by encountering another armed criminal suspect at close quarters." What happened to Clint Eastwood? And modest, too. As Brown added, Chitwood always gave credit to his associates, "the stakeout police and other uniformed officers. . . . I couldn't do it alone."

Another standoff meant just another job for the "supercop." Thirty-year-old Joseph Denofa, high on a variety of drugs, had a series of altercations with his Kensington neighbors and shot in one of their windows. Plainclothes officers rushed to the scene and attempted to arrest Denofa. However, leveling his shotgun at them, he fled into his row house and locked the door. Then he held them at bay for an hour. It happened that homicide detectives Mike Chitwood and Frank Diegel were in the area on other business. It took Chitwood 45 minutes to gain Denofa's trust. Standing on his front stoop and convincing the barricaded man that he would not be harmed, Chitwood gently carried away his loaded shotgun and took him into custody.

Sometimes a standoff couldn't be resolved without violence. Officer William Conroy, responding to the call of a loud disturbance coming from the South Philadelphia row house of burly Eugene Yannelli, was shot in the arm by Yannelli. Thankfully, the wound, while serious, wasn't fatal. As so often seemed to be the case, the man firing the shotgun was an agitated drug addict and former mental patient. It took Chitwood and a team of other officers and Yannelli's relatives some time to eventually get him to surrender. "I kept telling him that we wouldn't hurt him," Chitwood recounted. Once outside, having been the focus of so much attention, Yannelli raised his arms to a mixture of neighbors' cheers and jeers like a victorious prizefighter. Sometimes, at whatever cost, publicity is its own reward.

In acclaiming the work of Chitwood and his longtime partner Daniel Rosenstein, Philadelphia *Bulletin* writers Thomas J. Gibbons and Randolph Smith observed that over time, in hostage and barricade negotiations, they had played the role of a doctor, priest, rabbi, psychiatrist—and even a newspaper reporter. In a typical recent incident, "As usual, they played to an audience of one. As usual, several lives depended on their performance. Once again, they were a success." New challenges demand new methods, but to seasoned Mike Chitwood, Philadelphia's "top cop," his preoccupation was still the same perpetual war with the "scumbags" who blight our society and prey on the innocent. He may have been blindsided by such unexpected condemnation, but in overcoming it, he learned more about both the media and himself.

4

"Throw Your Gun Out!"

H ow was it that "Dirty Harry" changed into Mike the Mediator? By 1981, homicide detective Michael Chitwood had been in the Philadelphia police force for over 15 years. His popularity transcended all that controversy about using excessive force, which he would always vehemently deny. It was simply, necessarily, aggressive police work. His well-publicized series of crime-solving arrests leading to promotions, awards, and more than 70 record-setting commendations made him a personification of protection to a fearful Quaker City.

At 35, Chitwood bore only a passing resemblance to the rookie of 20. In the daily press covering his exploits, he could see two versions of himself. The Philadelphia *Bulletin* still pictured him in a file photo as he had looked then, heavier and clean-shaven, suggesting reduced visual resources at that venerable newspaper so soon to go under. However, the resurgent *Philadelphia Inquirer* prominently featured contemporary photos of Chitwood and described him as "a tall, slender, impeccably dressed detective," with a full mustache and reddish, fashionably "fuzzy hair." Hip or not, he still looked all business.

But something had changed. Or, more likely, something had been added. Firearms and fists had been pivotal to Mike Chitwood's police persona, even as he shed his uniform for plainclothes and then went on to heightened responsibilities as a detective in the narcotics unit and later to the action-oriented homicide division. By then he had seen just about everything. The life he laid on the line every day might depend on trigger-quick reflexes and on swiftly sizing up a situation and the means to resolve it.

Throughout the '70s, however, Chitwood had been questioning the role of his revolver in that resolution. One senseless tragedy particularly stayed with him. It had started as a case of simple burglary. A black male (as identified in those days) named Thomas William Martin had stolen 12 or 13 sheets of plywood from a construction site. Martin may have had some close calls during his 32 years of living on the edge, but he had never been arrested for anything. Apprehended and taken into custody without a struggle, he was driven to Roxborough's Fifth District police station.

Once inside, however, something in Martin simply snapped. "I just panicked," he recounted in his later confession. How would his wife take the news? "I wanted to get away. I was scared. I grabbed for one of the cops' guns. I got it from his holster and I just started firing wildly. I saw one of the cops coming after me and I shot at him." One bullet hit Officer James Griffin in the chest. Another struck his groin. As police closed in on the fleeing Martin, more shots were exchanged at point-blank range. A police station in one of the quieter neighborhoods of Philadelphia had suddenly become the O.K. Corral. Martin was hit before he could escape, but was not seriously injured.

As Thomas Martin continued in his confession statement, which wound up running to 11 pages, "I never been in trouble in my life. . . . The cops was treating me alright. I like cops. . . . It was just panic. I didn't want to get locked up. I hope the cop don't die. I don't need a murder rap. It's all my fault. I'm in enough trouble."

But the cop did die on the following day. In the trial, Martin's lawyer insisted that in such a melee, Officer Griffin might have been shot by a fellow policeman rather than by Martin. "No one can say for sure who fired the fatal shot." The jury didn't buy it. Nor did a somber homicide detective named Mike Chitwood, who had been called in to interrogate Martin and read his resulting confession statement in court. Yet such a possibility existed, friendly fire felling a fellow officer. Only the careless accessibility of guns had turned a frightened robbery suspect into a crazed killer.

*   *   *

As it turned out, during the following year, Chitwood was one of the Philadelphia police officers and detectives chosen by the local police academy to take an intensive FBI course on learning how to deal with hostage situations. It paid off almost immediately. In 1978, Chitwood was one of four detectives who, shedding their firearms, persuaded a gunman named Leon Rogers to end his siege of a Center City law firm. In a convoluted series of imagined slights, Rogers felt he had been misled by a partner in the firm. Storming their second-floor office, brandishing both a shotgun and a knife and unable to find the attorney he sought, Rogers took hostage the first lawyer he could find, young Gary Rose. Rogers' first demand was a face-to-face meeting with one of the firm's partners, Steven R. Arkins, and radio personality Mary Mason, who he insisted had defamed him. Frightened secretaries who had fled the building called the police. The four negotiators, including Chitwood, who were quickly dispatched to the scene, stationed themselves in a stairwell between the first and second floors, at close range to the well-armed Rogers. For more than five hours they took turns talking with him. Each offering to take Rose's place as his hostage, eventually they gained Rogers' trust.

As attorney Rose remarked after his ordeal, "They talked to him about anything and everything. They did a very good job of keeping him calm." Unable to provide either Arkins or Ms. Mason, the negotiators agreed to Rogers' back-up demand for a notarized memo detailing his charges against each of them, to go to the Justice Department's civil rights division, with a copy to Philadelphia's district attorney. "Okay, I'm ready to work out a deal," Rogers finally decided, and handed his rifle over to Chitwood. All that prior media exposure didn't exactly hurt in this new peaceful persuasion capacity. Virtually every account of Chitwood's involvement in a case began with "The most decorated policeman in Philadelphia history. . . ." As for the hostage in this case, Gary Rose could only conclude, "I'm just lucky to be alive."

*   *   *

Chitwood had evolved from accolades for apprehending murder suspects to crime prevention itself. As his area of activity expanded, the plaudits were no longer limited by locality. A letter to Philadelphia police commissioner Joseph O'Neill from the New York district attorney's office commended Chitwood for locating a key witness and obtaining a signed statement from him in an important homicide case. "I wish to congratulate you for having such a fine detective on your staff. He is a *credit* to the Philadelphia Police Department." At their annual dinner, the local F.O.P. named Chitwood one of their two "Investigators of the Year." Perhaps his most heartening of all to someone so recently accused of violating the civil rights of suspects, the Philadelphia chapter of the Southern Christian Leadership Conference unanimously chose Chitwood to receive its 1978 "Valor Award" for his successful hostage negotiations—a reciprocal affirmation of nonviolence. Although O'Neill insisted that Detective Chitwood carry a gun when not on hostage detail, it would take a clear and present danger to convince him to use it.

*   *   *

The front page of *The Philadelphia Inquirer* of January 8, 1980 featured a photo of Detective Mike Chitwood, captioned "Steel Nerves and a Gift of Gab." He had needed every ounce of that combination when confronting such a dangerous lunatic as Edward A. McNeill, the focus of the *Inquirer*'s dramatic and tragic lead story on that day.

A former mental patient who found periodic employment as an elevator operator and Rittenhouse Square doorman, McNeill, 34 and heavy-set, lived in a two-story southwest Philadelphia row house with his wife, Elaine, and their young sons, aged five and two. Later described by some neighbors as a "walking time bomb" given to erratic behavior, he had a penchant for hunting and collecting guns. His favorite was a 12-gauge shotgun. McNeill was also a heavy drinker and drug user, and he had served time at least once for assault. The words "Love" and "Hate" were tattooed across the fingers of both his hands. Opinion was divided about his shooting prowess, variously described as reckless or expert. An occasional target was the lamppost outside his house. However, some neighbors found McNeill "pleasant" or characterized him as "quiet" and "a nice, gentle guy." Perhaps it is closest to accuracy to conclude that none of them really knew him. McNeill had frequent loud arguments with his wife, a decade younger than he, but no one viewed his behavior as excessive enough to call the police about it.

That is, until the evening of January 16, 1980, when Elaine threatened to leave him and file for divorce. She'd had enough. Seeing her husband visibly troubled by that declaration, Elaine thought it best to take her two kids and leave that night for a friend's house. Hoping that Edward might have calmed down overnight, she returned the following afternoon. Instead, his anger had escalated to a state of rage. He had waited for them, all those hours, with his shotgun in his hands, and now he aimed it directly at his wife. As she grabbed her children, rushing outside and taking refuge behind a parked car, he began shooting wildly. Hearing the shots and Elaine's frantic screams to call the police, the neighbors no longer hesitated.

The first to arrive were William Washington, a former GI and nine-year veteran of the force who had just become engaged, and his partner, Edward Brinkman. They had been on plainclothes burglary detail nearby, and they were armed. At six feet two and 240 pounds, Washington provided the more obvious target. Approaching the house very slowly, he didn't know whether he was dealing with a single gunman or more than one. As additional police began to arrive and neighbors gathered, Washington cautioned everyone to keep down. A paddy wagon and K-9 jeep were being brought up to block the line of fire from the house. However, before they were fully in place, a single blast from McNeill's high-powered rifle rang out. This was no random shot. It tore into Washington's left cheek and ripped into the back of his head. Courageous fellow officers dragged the stricken patrolman into a vehicle and rushed him to nearby Misericordia Hospital, but there was no possibility of saving his life. Washington was pronounced dead at 5:20 p.m. in the presence of his parents and an anguished Mayor Bill Green. That Washington was black and McNeill white does not appear to have been a factor in the shooting. But there were no subsequent shots.

As the police, armed with M-16s, were thinking about storming the house, already raising ladders to its roof, a peculiar thing happened. McNeill called 911. A civilian police dispatcher took the call. A distraught McNeill told the dispatcher, "I just fired some shots at some people. I need help." Between sobs, he recounted the argument with his wife that had set him off. In his view, it was all her fault and that of her disrespectful father, who came over too often. McNeill warned that the police were not to shoot. He wanted to talk with his sister, Nancy Czechowitz, who lived nearby, and a Catholic priest. While the dispatcher kept McNeill on the line for half an hour, police administrators devised a strategy from their temporary command headquarters in a nearby house. The new police commissioner, Morton Solomon, knew what to do first. This was a case for his most skilled negotiator, a man with extensive experience on the police hostage team, homicide detective Michael Chitwood.

By the time Chitwood arrived on the scene, police had cordoned off both ends of the street, holding back hundreds of curious, apprehensive neighborhood residents. McNeill could see them from his second-floor window, but he made no threatening gestures. His fearful sister was on her way, along with the Reverend H. Thornton Kelly, pastor of the Most Blessed Sacrament Roman Catholic Church. Police were trying to find flak jackets for them. Dusk was giving way to darkness as their floodlights in the alley came on, bathing the street in light.

Crouching behind the stoop at the back door of the row house next door and then moving to the side fence of McNeill's house, the unprotected Chitwood yelled up to the barricaded man, "Nobody's going to hurt you, Eddie. . . . The priest is on his way. You got our word, Eddie. Now give us yours. We gotta have some kind of guarantee you won't hurt the priest when he comes in."

"Leave me alone! Leave me alone!" McNeill screamed, his mood having swiftly changed from fear to rage and back again. Then, from his kitchen window, he demanded that Chitwood come forward to prove he had no weapons. "Eddie! Eddie!" Chitwood yelled back, walking out as he did so and raising his arms. Then he implored, "Yo, Eddie. We want to help you. Throw out your gun. Come on out. Come on out. No one's gonna hurt you. It's not that hard, Eddie. . . . You promised we wouldn't holler and yell, that we'd talk like two men." McNeill yelled back, referring to all those crouching nearby cops, their guns obviously drawn. It was him or them.

"Why are you mad at the cops?" Chitwood yelled up. "What's the problem? I think you should come on out. Okay, Eddie?" Then Chitwood added just a touch of urgency: "I can't wait." And after a quick conference with the brass, "Whattaya actin' like this for? Whattaya want me to do to prove what I'm saying is straight?"

McNeill asked about his kids. Chitwood, now enunciating with more precision, responded, "They're all right. They're down the street with neighbors. They're just worried for their father, Eddie. I know how it is. I've got two kids of my own who worry whether their dad's coming home alive tonight. Stop and think what I'm saying. . . . You help me. I'll help you. I guarantee I'll let you spend some time with them. Eddie, my name's Mike. If there's anything I can do for you, let me know." Developing some rapport required a degree of deviousness. Chitwood indicated that he'd had similar problems in his own marriage, which was untrue, and he never revealed to McNeill that his shot had actually killed Officer Washington.

The priest had now arrived. He was fitted with a protective vest and was given a bullhorn to amplify his voice. He was also given an incongruous military helmet. "You throw the guns out and I'll come in by myself," Chitwood yelled back up to McNeill, whose response was a barrage of expletives. Then Chitwood announced that Father Kelly was with him and wanted to go inside, but "not with all those guns in there." At Chitwood's behest, the priest joined in: "Eddie, I'm still out here. . . . We want to help you. I can't hear you, Eddie. Come on out. Let me know what the problem is and I'll try to help you. I know you're upset." He continued, with biblical references. Then McNeill's sister, primed by Chitwood, added her voice: "Eddie, come out nice and slow. Keep your hands up. Nobody'll hurt you." Although Chitwood remained out in the open, both of the others were shielded by the bodies of policemen.

It was time for Chitwood to close the deal. The threatening policemen were asked to move back. "We want to give you a lot of room," Chitwood yelled up, "to make sure the priest and your sister don't get hurt. . . . What's that, Eddie? . . . You want to meet me? Well, I'd like to meet you too. . . . Now, I don't want you to come out yet, Eddie. The priest is going to walk up the end of the alley. You have to come out with no coat, hands up in the air. Now listen, your sister and the priest will come down." From the first, Chitwood had established a friendly, first-name basis with McNeill, however contrived. Before he came out, McNeill insisted, "Now make sure you're out there, Mike."

With that, at 6:44 p.m., Eddie McNeil's large frame emerged from his home. Seeing his sister, he broke down in tears. She and Father Kelly embraced him. A policeman offered him a cigarette. McNeill and Chitwood, finally face to face, exchanged a few quiet words. "I'm going to go with you, Eddie," Chitwood reaffirmed, "I'll be with you the whole time." Another police officer snapped handcuffs on the dazed cop-killer, gently explaining that he was obliged to do so by regulations. "Come on, pal," Chitwood continued in his reassuring voice, leading McNeill down the street into custody. The surrounding neighbors weren't so restrained. They had heard about the slain Washington. Shattering the silence, they yelled, "Shoot him, shoot him, shoot him!" as McNeil was led away and the cameras of all the assembled news media followed him. This was everyone's lead story.

Routinely returning for work the next day, January 18, at the Police Administration Building, Chitwood was greeted with a hero's welcome by his fellow officers of all ranks, congratulated even by those he didn't know. One top official insisted, "It's about time Mike gets the public recognition he deserves for the work he has done." Noting *The Philadelphia Inquirer*'s excessive coverage of those prior charges of police brutality, Pete Dexter, columnist for the *Philadelphia Daily News*, wrote that day, "In the time since, Chitwood has become the most decorated cop in the history of the cops. . . . It might be a good thing that the *Inquirer* can't put you in jail." A week later, the Philadelphia *Bulletin*'s Adrian Lee, in a column titled "Once Reviled, Now He's Hero," stressed how frequently "Michael Jude Chitwood" had put his life on the line. Yet he'd given up carrying both his old .38 and his .359 magnum. Lee quoted Chitwood: "God forbid I'd hit the wrong person, injure an innocent bystander. I hope I never come to the day I regret it."

Yet for all his heroism, he had arrived too late to save another police officer's life. It turned out that he had known well-liked Bill Washington for several years. Chitwood's skillful negotiations might well have cost his own life. He had been shot at before—luckily, as Winston Churchill once said, "without visible effect." A *Daily News* editorial put it plainly: "Detective Michael Chitwood, without guns or armor, talked the crazed killer into surrendering himself. These officers didn't just do what they did for money or glory. They just did it. They'll keep doing it. And we can thank God that they will."

Chitwood later remarked, having been involved in other major shootouts and hostage dramas, that he rather "enjoyed" confronting someone pointing a loaded rifle at him. The day after the McNeill incident, he told two *Inquirer* staff writers, "I like dealing with these [barricaded] people. . . . You have to have a level head, and you cannot let your emotions take over for you. . . . Our main purpose is to establish communications and have a good rapport with the man and find out what his demands are." Once you gain his confidence, "You talk about anything he wants to talk about. You talk sports, religion, or family."

As for Edward McNeill, he remained a man of swiftly shifting moods prior to his trial and of stoic silence throughout it. His defense attorney had asked the jury in Philadelphia's Court of Common Pleas to spare his client's life because of the mitigating circumstances of McNeill's having been a mental patient. He should be acquitted on the ground of temporary insanity. A psychiatrist called by the defense testified that an imaginary person named Buddy had told him to shoot his wife because she was a "horrible person" and to "scare police" when they had surrounded his house. The prosecution countered with their own psychiatrist, who testified that although McNeill obviously had some antisocial and emotional problems, he was not psychotic. Perhaps on the day he shot Officer Washington, he had been angered almost to the point of irrationality, but he knew what he was doing. He still knew right from wrong.

The defendant did not speak on his own behalf at the trial. He had done himself enough harm by talking to police interrogators beforehand. His testimony was read in the courtroom by Chitwood, something he was now accustomed to doing. In his hour-long discourse with the barricaded defendant on the night of the murder, Chitwood recalled, "He was determined he was going to kill the cops. He was ready to go down with the ship." When Chitwood shouted up at McNeill to throw out his gun and surrender, McNeill threatened to "kill any cop who comes in here. . . . I know I'm in trouble. I saw the cops out there. I shot somebody out there. . . . I got you in my sights. I can blow you away." It was all Elaine's fault, that "bitch" who had set him off. In his statement to police, McNeill reiterated that, after their violent argument and her threat to leave him, "When she came home, I just wanted to kill her. . . . Then the cops came. I figured I'd shoot them before they shot me." Although he had originally denied knowing he had killed a patrolman, McNeill expressed pride in his skill as a marksman. "I'm a hunter, and everything I shoot at, I usually don't miss." Later, however, he expressed remorse at the death of Washington. He hadn't wanted to kill anyone, even in his agitated state, except his wife. Despite everything, at the penalty hearing, she testified that he had been a "good father" to their two boys.

After deliberating, the jury found McNeill guilty of first-degree murder and aggravated assault but declined to impose the death penalty. Instead, McNeill was sentenced to life imprisonment. It was little comfort to Chitwood or to his fellow officers who had lost a comrade. The McNeill case was Chitwood's highest profile performance during his negotiating years, the media spotlight the equivalent of his finding the body of Holly Maddux during his prior role as a relentless police investigator.

Fortunately, his efforts at friendly persuasion were often in time to prevent tragedy. Only one day after Chitwood had induced McNeill to surrender, he was called to convince a lonely, middle-aged woman in fear of losing her South Philly home, suffering from cancer and threatening suicide, to come out of her barricaded house. She had only her cats for company and menaced only herself. As the *Philadelphia Journal* of January 18, 1980 put it, "No Rest for Weary Hero," describing Chitwood as "Knock-knock-knockin' on danger's door . . . all in a day's work": It was Josephine Black's front door in this instance, and yes, he assured her that she would not be evicted. She gave up her gun.

However, even Chitwood's attempts at conciliation were not always successful. His 95-minute effort to talk a rampaging, mentally ill killer named James Willis, who went by the name of "Lord Jimbo," to give himself up proved fruitless. "No one here wants to hurt you," Chitwood insisted, trying to establish his customary level of rapport. To which Willis, brandishing a knife, replied, "I'm Lord Jimbo. Nobody can hurt me, and I'm the only one who can kill." The standoff continued for two hours. Reportedly, a Taser stun gun to subdue Willis had failed to arrive. Ultimately, more than a hundred police were assembled, while perhaps a thousand spectators watched. Eventually, Willis was captured after a frantic fight, but he suffered knife wounds and in the melee, his chest was so compressed that he later died.

* * *

Interviewed in December 1980 by Maralyn Lois Polak in the *Inquirer*'s *Today Magazine* as the cop who "would rather talk than shoot" ("He's hostage negotiator Michael Chitwood, and he'd *better* be a good talker. The man doesn't carry a gun."), Chitwood elaborated on his conversion from a "make my day" equivalent of Dirty Harry to a patient negotiator. "They say I'm crazy; everybody says I'm crazy." He told Polak in their meeting at police headquarters, still known as the Roundhouse: "Everybody made such a big deal about me not carrying a gun. I never said anything to anyone. I just went about my business and did my job. I arrested a vicious murderer at the point of a pool cue once. The guy thought I had a gun. "Get up, don't move or I'll shoot, I told him. Like I say, I despise guns."

Described by Polak as "disco-thin in a bright blue suit and given to generous gesticulation," Chitwood, "the city's most decorated police officer," offered a variety of opinions and preferences that provide some insight into his next 30 years. He took this job, his only career choice since he was on school safety patrol, "to help people." Were he a woman walking the city streets alone at night, he probably *would* feel obliged to carry a gun. It's no fun going to a mystery movie because he can figure out the plot halfway through. He loves sweets and pies but counteracts their effects by running, racquetball, and working out in the gym. He's taking some criminology courses and could see himself someday in public relations, consulting, or even politics. During the past three days, he'd slept perhaps two hours. Polak wrote, "If he could choose his own death, it would be 'naturally and nice' at 90."

*   *   *

Earlier in the year, Chitwood had provided an equally penetrating self-analysis in a combination article/interview by Charles Brown. In *The Philadelphia Journal*, an ambitious but short-lived tabloid that folded at just about the same time as *The Bulletin*, it was titled "Top Cop." The featured photo was of a serious Chitwood at his desk, between two phones. As usual, "Det. Mike Chitwood is the city's most decorated officer. His skill at negotiating a safe ending to hostage situations is legendary in our town." Again, "[he] took this job to help people," but "super-cop" Chitwood added, "and every once in a while I get tired, tired of seeing people shot, stabbed, dismembered. . . . Cops have the same feelings, same needs as everybody else."

Chitwood recounted a typical recent work week. On Sunday, he talked a barricaded man out of his row house. On Wednesday, he talked Edward McNeill into surrendering. On Thursday, he dealt with potential suicide Josephine Black. Brown added "intense blue eyes" to the customary description of Chitwood as "a wiry six-footer with curly reddish hair." He quoted the "36-year-old father of two, a veteran of 16 years as a beat cop, highway patrolman, narcotics officer and detective," as observing, "One way or another, I figure I've been involved in about 1,000 homicides. I still get excited, but nothing can surprise me anymore."

He thought about no longer "packing heat" way back in 1971, five years before the murder of Patrolman James Griffin. Chitwood and three other narcotics officers hit an apartment in North Philadelphia. Once inside the building, the narcs spotted a guy selling "smack" to several people in a second-floor hallway. As soon as he saw the cops, the seller rushed back inside the apartment and locked himself in. "We're serving a search warrant," Chitwood shouted as he pounded on the door. The response was a bullet clear through the wood. It hit his partner, Officer Paul Taylor, in the chest. "It was a terrifying shooting," Chitwood recalled, "to see your partner go down and you're right next to him." Finally, the dope pusher, a man named Rufus Williams, came out, shielding himself with a two-year-old child. Talk about scumbags. Reliving it again for the article, Chitwood still seemed shaken. Aiming at Williams, he might have killed the child. Somehow he succeeded in disarming the pusher. Eventually, a judge gave Williams 10 to 20 years, the maximum penalty allowed by law, plus an additional three and a half to seven years for firing at Chitwood.

Fortunately, Temple University Hospital was nearby. Rushed to an operating room, Taylor nearly died at least once, a bullet lodged in his spine, but somehow the skilled surgeons revived him and he pulled through. The close call and his debilitating injuries, however, were enough to dissuade if not prohibit Taylor from a further career in police work. He decided to open a bar.

* * *

But not Chitwood. In one role or another, this would always be his vocation. "The longest I ever worked," he told Charles Brown, "was 48 hours straight. . . . from work to court to work and back to court again." Putting in so much overtime, as noted in the previous chapter, he made more money in at least one year than former commissioner Joseph O'Neill, which rather bemused both men. The two always maintained a mutual respect, until the commissioner's retirement in 1980. O'Neill remained a staunch supporter of Chitwood's work, even as the *Inquirer* excoriated his supposedly brutal methods. In each of his roles within the force, to Chitwood solving any crime, even a murder, "usually comes down to talking to people, neighborhood interviews, that kind of stuff." He knew that from his first days as a cop on the beat. The nerves of steel and gift of gab were in place early, his native tenacity only enhanced by experience and tempered by training.

Thinking back to his childhood in a tough South Philadelphia neighborhood, Chitwood mused that perhaps 80 percent of the kids he grew up with might now be selling dope or committing burglaries. Coming across them on the job, he'd been depressed by having to lock up old friends on drug charges. Brown concluded, "Only the hard stuff interests him, only the hard drugs, the hard crimes, and sometimes they make him mad." Chitwood noted, "Every time I see a face I recognize, I say hello. Who knows? It might be someone I've locked up." Smiling ruefully, he added, "I never know what their response will be. You can imagine the names I've been called."

But wherever the excessive epithets may have come from, over the years, institutional or personal, a seasoned Mike Chitwood had learned to transcend them, rewarded not only in rank and recognition, but also with the satisfaction of making a difference. By now, in 1981, as Chitwood said to Charles Brown, he was surprised at nothing.

Too soon, however, he would encounter a crime so revolting, so personally wrenching, that it would change his career path—and his life.

5

The Point of Departure

wo virtually identical photographs of a bright, broadly smiling, chubby, sweet, 12-year-old Catholic school girl with prominent glasses and abundant blond hair, parted in the middle and cascading down, dominated the local media for days as January 1981 turned into February. The only difference was that in one, Nicolette "Nicky" Caserta was wearing her First Communion dress. Hardened homicide detective Michael Chitwood couldn't get the image of that little girl from Kensington out of his mind. "She could have been *my* daughter," he kept thinking. Beth Ann was only a few years older.

"Bitch, why don't you die? You're supposed to die!" Henry Patrick Fahy had demanded after trying to strangle Nicky with an electrical cord. His own open-mouthed visage would soon also appear in the papers, looking disheveled and disoriented—one of Chitwood's prototypical scumbags. Indeed, everyone in this horrific case of rape and murder, save the innocent victim, seemed to be little more than trash. "Hank" Fahy, 25, was a familiar figure to Nicky, the child of the first marriage of her mother, Mary Piccone. For six years he had lived across the street, the common-law husband of Nicky's aunt, Rosemary "Cookie" Kelleher. Fahy, who drove a trash truck, was an independent scavenger who collected and sold discarded scrap metal and paper for a tenuous living. He was also a sexual predator who had long eyed Nicky—"stalked her," as one writer put it. At the time of the assault, he was already under indictment for the rape at knifepoint of another Kensington girl in 1979, but was out on $10,000 bail, free to target others. Later accusations against Fahy would include rape or attempted rape of a 17-year-old girl, a 13-year-old girl, and the sexual abuse of Rosemary Kelleher's own six-year-old son—a twisted pattern of perversion. How could Nicky's parents allow her to admit Fahy, however familiar to her, into their home when she was alone? Did they know nothing about even his first indictment?

But on that January morning in 1981, visiting Nicky proved to be no problem for Hank Fahy. After seeing Mary Piccone, whose husband had already departed for the day, go off to work around 7:15 and waving to her from across the street, Fahy crossed over and knocked on the Piccones' door. Nicky, whom he now knew to be alone, was about to go to a friend's for a preschool breakfast, but she readily let him in. Fahy asked if perhaps they had a pair of pliers he could borrow. Nicky quickly went upstairs to look. After locking the front door from inside, Fahy followed. Leading Nicky into her bedroom, he then told her bluntly to undress. When she protested, he stuffed some tissue paper and a white sweater into her mouth, fearful that she might cry out, and told her, "You talk too much." Finally, probably as astonished as terrified, she complied. Taking off only his pants, Fahy then tried to rape her, but as he later recounted, he wasn't sure he had achieved full penetration. He then calmly told Nicky she could put her parochial school uniform back on. By now so traumatized that she put it on backwards, Nicky still had the presence of mind to remind her attacker that she had to leave to go to her friend's house. Fahy had her turn the uniform around so that it looked normal. But then Nicky made a fatal mistake. As if suddenly awakening from a trance, she blurted out, "Why, Hank, why?"

Fearing how much she might reveal, Fahy panicked. He suddenly grasped Nicky as she headed for the front door and dragged her down to the basement. Her cries would be less audible there. She struggled as vigorously as she could, but soon Fahy, pushing her to the floor, was choking her with all the strength of both his hands. Yet she still kept kicking out and gasping for air. "She just wouldn't die," he later related. "I kept telling her, 'Bitch, you bitch, you're supposed to die!'" Wrapping a T-shirt around her mouth, he then ripped a cord from a washing machine and strangled her with it, pulling as hard as he could. Still uncertain that she was finally dead, he went upstairs to the kitchen to get a steak knife and quickly returned, stabbing Nicky in the chest with it "about seven times." The autopsy indicated it was 18 times. Concerned that somehow she might miraculously survive, Fahy placed a chair against the cellar door and fled. Wiping all the blood from the knife, he put it in a pair of rolled-up undershorts, which he threw in a sewer. Before long, as news of what he had done surfaced, death threats would keep Fahy in hiding, but his disappearance lasted for only three weeks.

Returning home, the Piccones found the house in disarray and at first feared that Nicky had mistakenly left the family dog indoors. Venturing into the basement, the slain girl's stepfather, Paul Piccone, found her body in a pool of blood. Exclaiming "Oh, my God, Nicky!" he rushed his horrified wife across the street to Cookie Kelleher's house—also the home of Nicky's killer—and called the police. Homicide detective Chitwood was among the first to see Nicky's mutilated body.

* * *

Cookie must have suspected something. Perhaps she eventually even came to know Hank's hiding place. Either she contacted him when she was called to appear at the Police Juvenile Aid Division, also known as the Sex Crimes Investigation Unit, or he had realized that flight was futile and decided to show up on his own. Homicide detectives Mike Chitwood and his partner, Sergeant Dan Rosenstein were alerted. They found Hank Fahy just outside the facility, on the prominent corner of Frankford and Castor Avenues. Whatever the state of his mind, he seemed resigned, as if expecting their arrival, when he was taken into custody. During a lengthy interrogation session on the evening of January 29, 1981, a seemingly depressed but coherent Fahy provided a gruesomely detailed description of each step in the crime. It was compressed into a 10-page confession of the murder of Nicolette Caserta, which Fahy signed with neither comment nor complaint.

On the advice of his court-appointed attorney, the highly regarded Daniel H. Greene (others had declined to defend Fahy, but Greene considered it his professional duty), Fahy waived a preliminary hearing. Why make his damning confession public prematurely? "What else is he going to say?" commented assistant district attorney Judith Frankel Rubino, who would prosecute the case. Fahy later contended that he'd understood that if he signed "some papers," he'd be permitted to go home, but a judge denied him bail this time. Later, his attorney predictably charged that Fahy's confession was not only "untrue but coerced." Apparently, some form of coercion would always be charged by the defense in any criminal case involving homicide detective Michael J. Chitwood.

Once she had recovered from the shock, Mary Piccone, sought out by the press, was highly visible. Fahy had volunteered to Chitwood and Sergeant Detective Rosenstein that the Piccones had always liked and trusted him. "I'm treated like family," he insisted, as indeed he might have been, as evidenced by that friendly wave to Mary as she went to work on that fateful morning. Both Mary and Paul Piccone were in their forties, almost a decade older than Cookie Kelleher, who was some years older than Hank Fahy. They may well have had little in common. While admitting that Fahy had been over from time to time for such chores as installing an air-conditioning unit and that Nicky had sometimes gone across the street to her aunt's home, Mary denied any particular relationship with the man of that house. "We did not socialize with Fahy," she insisted.

As for her daughter, Mary Piccone told *Daily News* interviewer Jill Porter how incredulous she was that Nicky would let Hank Fahy in and then so meekly follow his orders to go to her bedroom and undress. "She was a very spooky, scary child. She'd never let the gas man in. When he got in there, my daughter would have fought him." Which was precisely what Nicky Caserta did, to the limits of her strength—when she realized the full import of what was happening. As for Cookie Kelleher, the victim's aunt, she would be charged with failing to protect her own six-year-old son from Fahy's twisted sex drives. Chitwood pondered how any normally protective parents could fail to perceive so established a pattern of perversion.

As the lead investigator, Mike Chitwood was obliged to view Nicky's body again at the autopsy. It was hardly a new experience, but this time it only exacerbated his sense of identity with this particular victim and the image he'd carried in his head of her smiling face. Whenever he went home, he was reminded of it. Assigned from the outset to pursue the case with Rosenstein and members of the newly formed sex crimes unit, Chitwood had a long time to reflect.

The trial didn't start until two years later, in January 1983. In part it took so much time because, as Rosenstein pointed out, "There were a series of involved legal matters that had to be straightened out." Of course, Fahy had been accused of a number of other sexual assaults, even if only this one had resulted in a murder charge. Defense counsel's move to suppress his client's confession on the customary premise of coercion was denied by the judge, and the confession stood as originally recorded. Later, obviously coached by Greene, Fahy would deny even that he had killed Nicky Caserta, despite the grim clarity of the evidence, and said that he had confessed only because of mental coercion and implied physical threats by police detectives. Likely one in particular.

*   *   *

Finally the trial began. In the emotionally charged courtroom, Mary Piccone was an early witness. She broke down when describing how she and her husband had returned later on that day of horror, how she had seen on a table such ominous tokens of Nicky's presence as 50 cents, a house key, and a written excuse for a prior absence, before her husband made his terrible discovery in the basement. "My baby!" she sobbed. Presiding Judge Albert P. Sabo of the Court of Common Pleas ordered a recess.

Mary Piccone had departed before the late morning of January 27, 1983, when Mike Chitwood took the stand. He often re-read confessions as a preparatory reminder of specifics before his appearances in a court of law, but in this instance he hadn't done so. After all, there could be virtually no doubt that Henry Fahy was guilty as charged. His 10-page confession detailed it all. How often Chitwood had been called upon to read such confessions, some describing crimes of similar barbarity, to a judge and jury in a packed courtroom during his 18 years on the force, the past eight as a homicide detective. He started out, sitting erect and focused as usual in the witness box, the consummate professional. Yes, it was the rape and murder of a child, but describing it was the task of a typical day for Chitwood.

Only it wasn't. For the first and only time in a courtroom, after reading only a few sentences and long before getting to the most graphic details of Fahy's confession, Chitwood's voice began to tremble. Did he need water? Simply to clear his throat? No, he just couldn't continue. He was holding back his tears. When had he last cried? The hardened "supercop" was also a human being. Spectators were stunned. As Chitwood faltered, two women in the visitors' gallery, perhaps friends or relatives of the Piccones, began sobbing uncontrollably and fled the courtroom. There was also audible sobbing outside, and more quietly from the jury box itself. For the second time that morning, in this instance at the request of defense attorney Greene, Judge Sabo ordered a recess. They would return after lunch.

Thoroughly shaken, Chitwood went to the judge's chambers for some water. He couldn't believe what had just happened. He had seen it all, every kind of unspeakable crime, but this one had simply gotten to him. "There goes my macho image." Chitwood would later reflect, managing a smile. Defense attorney Greene, a friend across the lines of Chitwood's, reiterated that he'd never witnessed such emotion from this "first-class professional." Assistant District Attorney Rubino added her input. Chitwood had confided to her that he simply couldn't stop thinking about his own daughter, internalizing the case. To Jill Porter, who later interviewed Chitwood, it "had bothered him since the beginning," from the time he walked into the Piccones' house that night and saw the mutilated body of Nicky Caserta.

When the trial resumed after lunch, Chitwood returned and read the entire confession through, his voice "quavering" once or twice, according to Jill Porter. At last, she concluded, "After cross-examination by Fahy's attorney, Mike Chitwood was finally finished testifying. . . . It hadn't been just another day of work after all."

Defense attorney Greene did his best, including requesting that Judge Sabo instruct the jurors "not to be influenced by any display of emotion." After all, it was a highly emotional case. The judge complied. Greene could have called for a mistrial, but he took the high road—and in fact the most practical course in so challenging an assignment. His attorney described Fahy as a depressed, disturbed, confused young man who had been married and divorced as a teenager, whose own young wife had been raped, who still had difficulty relating to others, and who had attempted suicide more than once. Granted the "shocking" nature of the accusations against his client, what he needed most was professional care in a mental institution. Urging mercy, Greene told the jury, "I suggest to you that Henry Fahy is essentially a kind, decent individual who unfortunately did things and didn't know why he did them." However, for some reason, he let Hank Fahy take the stand. Fahy testified that not only had he feared coercion and brutality from the police in terms of obtaining his confession, but "I absolutely did not murder Nicky. I was more like an uncle, brother, father to her."

Of course, the Piccones were having none of it. Nor was prosecutor Rubino. After the jury took only an hour and a half to convict Fahy of first-degree murder, she remarked at the hearing, "If this isn't a case that calls for the death penalty, then I don't know if we'll ever see one." This time it took them four hours, but the jury determined that Henry Fahy should die in the electric chair. Taken to Graterford Prison, where he did in fact make several more attempts at suicide, Fahy was then transferred to Farview State Hospital for the Criminally Insane. On appeal, Fahy's death sentence was upheld by the Supreme Court of Pennsylvania and the U.S. Supreme Court. Eventually, however, he received a series of stays and his sentence was changed to life in prison.

*   *   *

After the trial, Chitwood was surprised to receive a gift from Nicky Caserta's mother and stepfather. When he opened the cardboard box, he found a little kitten inside. They had named it "Mikey" or "Chitty," or something similar. Perhaps it was all they could afford. Beyond the fact that Mike Chitwood is allergic to felines, it was still a touching gesture. Here were people Chitwood had already judged as something between scumbags and parents of appalling negligence. Perhaps his judgment had been premature. Perhaps they felt some residual guilt, or were simply appreciative. Whatever their means or motivations, they expressed genuine gratitude for Chitwood's efforts and those of his colleagues in convicting little Nicky's killer. They also sent a letter of thanks to the police commissioner.

But there is a postscript. In 2012, almost 30 years after this trial, Upper Darby Police Chief Michael J. Chitwood received an even greater surprise. One of Nicky's sisters, Phyllis Wilson, called him from out of the blue. She told him that their mother, Mary Piccone, had died in a household fire of highly suspicious origins. Phyllis believed it to have been set by one of Mary's grandsons. The young man, a habitual drug-user, had been thrown out of the house. Might Chitwood, who had helped her family so successfully in the past, look into it? Pointing out that from Upper Darby he no longer had the jurisdiction to pursue such a case, Chitwood nonetheless called the Philadelphia Fire Department and asked them to investigate further, as well as suggesting that Phyllis talk with a contact at the *Philadelphia Daily News*. Both concluded that the fire was most likely accidental, and any suspicions remain unconfirmed. Yet consider the circumstances. A new generation of tragedy. Perhaps no homicide case, even if resolved, is ever finally forgotten.

*   *   *

For Mike Chitwood, the Caserta case represented a watershed in both his career and his life. As a child younger than Nicky had been, Chitwood had determined he wanted to be a policeman to help protect the innocent (and he didn't even cry in those days). But in homicide he more often was called upon to find and prosecute the guilty after the crime had been committed. Nicky Caserta's bright smile still haunted him. Who could have been more innocent? He hadn't been able to protect her. He'd only heard of her after the awful event. Perhaps that is one reason Chitwood found hostage negotiations so much more satisfying. "You know," he said after being told he had to at least *carry* a gun, "I despise violence." The pressures in fighting crime are not unlike those of active military service and may result in the same psychological scars. Only in a supervisory capacity, working throughout a community, can one sometimes prevent the senseless waste of human life. Chitwood would care no less, but he could *do* a lot more as a chief of police, a supervisor on a larger stage. For some time, as detailed in the following pages, he had been pondering that possibility. But his applications for significant openings had been more or less spontaneous, little thought out, simply dropped off with a smile and a return address.

Now he would get serious. Chitwood possessed no college degree, increasingly a requirement for serious consideration as a police chief. That had to be overcome. Notoriety wasn't enough. It was time to get focused, start a full-court press, a campaign. Certainly, ambition played a part, but the prime motivation was still that sense of mission. Chitwood went to a professional personnel marketing firm and learned how to write an effective résumé, to anticipate questions in an intensive interview, to present himself forcefully as a logical candidate for any position, stressing the value of the experiences he did have. And in only a matter of months, it would actually work out.

*   *   *

The two years between the murder of Nicky Caserta and the conviction of Hank Fahy are not generally viewed as particularly productive for the Philadelphia Police Department, but for Mike Chitwood they were almost excessively productive. His highly publicized transition from tough to compassionate cop only heightened his visibility. Such a level of celebrity may in fact have handicapped his intention to be taken seriously as a contender for a major opening as a chief of police. As noted, normally the media mantra is "If it bleeds, it leads." In the 1980s, at least locally, that might be supplemented by "If it concerns Chitwood, we cover it."

It didn't matter much in what context. For one thing, as portrayed in the press, physically Mike Chitwood in his thirties little resembled Mike Chitwood in his twenties. Mike's new regimen included consistent, intensive exercise and much more attention to his appearance. A comparison of photographs, of which there is no shortage, is striking. Now Detective Chitwood was slender and dapper, with his neatly curled hair and trim mustache. His plainclothes were hardly plain, featuring Ivy "rep" ties and a distinctive raincoat that made him look more dashing, a lean and lanky urban equivalent of, say, Gary Cooper. He even smiled a bit more. All he needed was a distinctive nickname. As the program for his 1982 appearance at the Pen and Pencil Club put it, "Every decade, Philadelphia seems to spawn a larger-than-life cop, a hero. There was the 'Cisco Kid,' a.k.a. Frank Rizzo, then 'Fergy,' Captain Clarence Ferguson. Now we have Michael Chitwood." (Perhaps "supercop" wouldn't work.) Not only Philadelphia's most prominent law-enforcement officer, Chitwood was hailed in 1982 by a magazine called *Master Detective* as "National Police Officer of the Month." It quoted his longtime partner, Sergeant Dan Rosenstein: "There's no better man to have with you in a tough spot. . . . He possesses the most important quality—understanding of people."

As the *Inquirer's* Tom Fox put it in 1983, "I could never understand how anybody would call Mike Chitwood, who is 39, Dirty Harry. He is such a neat dresser and reasoned thinker, and, believe it or not, such a sensitive and nonviolent soul." And then there was the *Daily News* editorial of August 5, 1982, noting that *Playgirl* magazine had named "its 10 sexiest men, and not one is from Philadelphia." Why not? "After all," we have "the likes of Riccardo Muti, Mike Chitwood, John Murray, John White Jr., Manny Trillo, Dr. J. . . . " Was any city necessarily looking for a sexy chief of police? Lucky Liz Chitwood.

Detective Chitwood's first application had been to the troubled city of Camden, New Jersey, near the end of 1981. "One More Bridge to Cross" headlined a story by Jack McGuire in the *Daily News*. Technically, Chitwood was applying for the position of public safety director, in charge of both the police and fire departments. The prior acting police chief, Mario Ferrari, had resigned after only a month, accusing Mayor Melvin "Randy" Primas of interference. The layoff-plagued force was down to about 300 officers. It might seem peculiar that Chitwood would seek such a controversial opportunity had he not been determined to find "something that offers an exciting challenge." It wouldn't even equal his current pay in Philadelphia, including all that overtime, but his motivation was more than money. One likely reason why he lost out to Arnold R. Cream Jr., already a lieutenant in the Camden Police Department, is that Cream was the son of much-admired former heavyweight boxing champion Arnold "Jersey Joe Walcott" Cream.

However, now publicized on both sides of the Delaware—the supercop who had sought to improve a secondary city—Chitwood was lauded for such innovative successes as his use of that reporter's press card to talk a hostage into surrendering. But near the end, the articles would almost always return to those old "brutality" charges. Yes, the Philadelphia police chief had denied it all, but he had still settled out of court to save costs and had also paid off Roy Hoskins, just prior to his jail sentence. At the least, a questionable situation. It is known that Camden's Mayor Primus highly recommended Chitwood to the selection committee, that Chitwood was one of the finalists in their screening process, and that with his matchless record he might have seemed almost certain of selection. "I can't believe it's such a big deal," Chitwood said when local columnists put his application in the same league as Phillies manager Dallas Green's consideration of a million-dollar offer from the Chicago Cubs. But it also may be that Chitwood's very visibility intimidated some of those making the decision. Sad to say, it may also have been his color.

In any case, his Camden disappointment helped convince Chitwood that in the future he'd have to do a lot more than drop off some resumes and request an interview. He'd also applied for an opening in Houston, but it was rather half-hearted. As he said laconically when asked about the job by a friend, "They gave it to someone else."

Although Chitwood was looking to become a police chief, there was even more publicity of a possible political future, this time within Philadelphia itself. From time to time, of course, Chitwood had referred to tiring of dealing with so much tragedy. As sheriff of the city, a peculiar and redundant position that, as constituted, probably should have been phased out a long time ago, or more significantly as an at-large member of City Council, Chitwood would be faced with frustrations of a less lethal nature. He might have injected new life and direction into the sheriff's office. Or in Council, he might have managed to bring some refreshing decisiveness to the public arena. In either position, he'd get to spend a lot more time at home.

In August 1982, Chitwood was asked by Mayor Bill Green and other top city officials to run for sheriff on the Democratic Party ticket the following year. This time he responded realistically to reporters: "It's a flattering and interesting proposition." As someone already so deeply immersed in the law-enforcement field, it "could advance my career." But he continued, "Originally, it was suggested to me because of my alleged visibility. In my position, I lack administrative experience. I'm looking into it." Chitwood had learned that visibility, alleged or otherwise, could be a two-edged sword. A few handmade posters of "Mike Chitwood for Sheriff" appeared on neighborhood utility poles, and a committee was formed to draft him, but in the end he declined to run. Don Haskins, in his *Daily News* "Tipoff" column, ascribed this to Frank Rizzo's support of another candidate but added, "Personally, we think Mike Chitwood is a hell of a lot more valuable solving murders than he would have been serving writs." The paper's Tom Fox gave it his customarily whimsical spin, headlined "Politics Too Dirty for 'Dirty Harry.'"

Chitwood had also been approached by several Democratic leaders to consider a race to succeed prominent at-large City Council member Al Pearlman, who had resigned to run for the state senate. Chitwood seemed a natural for such an active political career, at least in the opinion of the *Philadelphia Observer*. Their unsigned article pointed out not only Chitwood's reputation for persuasiveness, but also that he had taken "nearly a dozen seminars" on subjects from negotiating skills to community relations during his 18-year career, many of relevance to working with any constituency. *Philadelphia* magazine's July 1982 issue weighed in, under a photo of Chitwood: "The heroic cop. He's ambitious and smart, and this could be his best quick shot at politics. His recognition factor goes right through the roof. . . . He needs fundraisers and some experienced pros to handle him—and a little luck." City-wide fundraisers held little attraction for Chitwood. This was no district council seat, but at-large, encompassing the entire city.

It is interesting that in 1983, Chitwood wrote a letter to the editor of *The Philadelphia Inquirer* protesting a proposed amendment to the city charter that would allow elected officials to run for higher office without resigning their current positions, but that would deny the same privilege to unelected city employees, such as policemen. He wasn't about to risk his entire career and the security of his family for a speculative political race, especially one involving raising sizeable sums, even for an office with appealing possibilities.

*　　*　　*

Meanwhile, Mike Chitwood was still a homicide detective, and crime takes no holidays. Even as he sought heightened responsibility, his final years in Philadelphia proper continued to demonstrate the wide range of all his previous experience. For example, there was a bizarre murder trial that proceeded despite missing two key eyewitnesses. It was based on a drug deal that went wrong. Efrain "Frankie" Flecha, a trigger-happy mobster, had gone to the home of Carlos Perez to buy drugs. Apparently, Perez reneged on the amount of money they had agreed to, and then pulled a gun. In the ensuing struggle with Flecha, however, it was Perez who was shot. Eventually he died. It gets more complicated. Distrustful of Perez from the start, Flecha had brought two associates with him. One of them had leveled a gun at the head of a Perez associate named Miguel Cordoba but had never fired it. A woman named Laura Bella was also in the room. It appears that both the buyer and seller of this particular drug deal mistakenly believed there is safety in numbers.

Assigned to what was now a case of murder, Chitwood could find no one willing to testify. Probably frightened of potential retribution, Cordoba had simply disappeared. However, Chitwood did track down Laura Bella and was able to take her testimony before she died of cancer. At Flecha's trial for murder, her words, as read by Chitwood, formed the foundation of the prosecution.

In another drug-related case, reminiscent of Chitwood's years of emphasis in this area, it had taken nearly a decade to put three "cold-blooded killers" (in the words of Assistant D.A. Richard Michaelson) behind bars. Throughout the 1970s, these three notorious kingpins had kept lesser drug dealers in line through intimidation and violence. They had also been involved in a series of holdups and murders dating back to 1973. One small-time drug dealer named Maurice Wilson, who had run afoul of the three, was shot and killed in a friend's apartment. Two women who witnessed the murder, despite threats to themselves and their families, were induced to testify at secret grand jury proceedings. It took all the persuasive power of Mike Chitwood to convince them that they would be protected, to overcome their fears and step forward, providing the key testimony to put the three killers away.

Of course, Chitwood had never been more persuasive than in the over 20 tense hostage cases he'd resolved during that subsequent stage in his career. Late in 1981, his counsel was much sought after in a hostage negotiation larger than any he had dealt with. At Philadelphia's Graterford Prison, Joseph "Jo Jo" Bowen, convicted of three murders, and two accomplices had failed in an escape attempt. However, they managed to obtain two shotguns and two pistols. Capturing three guards and three prison employees, they forced them into the institution's large kitchen. Then, joined by three like-minded inmates, they herded 32 other inmates into the kitchen as well, for a total of 38 hostages. The demands of these hostage-takers, who had all joined the Muslim faith, were based on fairly customary complaints in such situations, generally for better living conditions and more freedom of action within the prison's physical limitations. A team of professionals had been formed to negotiate with them, including prison officials, psychiatrists, and Chuck Stone, a well-respected African-American writer for the *Daily News*, who talked directly with Bowen.

Reviewing the "siege of Graterford" in a television interview, Chitwood characteristically stressed that in hostage situations, saving lives always has to be the primary goal. The negotiating team had "time on its side." They're doing what must be done: "Contain and talk . . . for as long as it takes." Only if the hostage-takers should start shooting and maiming people would a direct assault be justified. Keep everything working as normal—electricity, lights, heat. Talk seriously with the visible leader of the operation. He may view himself as a hero. Chitwood continued, "Everything is negotiable except guns, escape, and trading hostages. Some of these things have been settled with three cigarettes and a can of beer." Vintage Chitwood.

As it turned out, the siege of Graterford lasted only five days. Some modest demands were met. The hostage-takers were not held responsible for any damage to property. Any disciplinary time would be minimal. Some of the inmates were transferred to other locations, Bowen to the federal prison in Marion, Ohio. But a potentially dangerous situation was contained without injury to anyone—and without giving in to really significant changes.

*   *   *

Between 1981 and 1983, inevitably too many senseless homicides continued to remind Chitwood of the Caserta tragedy, to reinforce his combat fatigue. Here are a representative few.

It took two years for an investigative team led by Chitwood and Rosenstein to resolve the brutal murder of 64-year-old Dora DiFonzo, who lived alone. Her killer, young Jacqueline Massey, had ransacked her apartment but escaped with only a disappointing $20. DiFonzo, struggling and shouting "Leave me alone!"

denied she had any more. Angered and frustrated, Massey found a kitchen knife and stabbed DiFonzo with it repeatedly. "When she stopped moving," Massey recalled in her confession, "I said, 'Oh my God, what did I do?'" However, she later made the irrational mistake of admitting her crime to a relative. And then, as Chitwood put it, "They told somebody else, and somebody else told us." It often works that way in crime detection, but it can take time. The most persistent "somebody else" was DiFonzo's younger sister, Lydia Chiaoastri, who called Chitwood constantly, "pleading for us to solve the case. . . . She wouldn't let it die." Chitwood and Rosenstein worked 15-hour days, interviewing neighbors and relatives of the victim, learning a bit more each time until their suspicions pointed increasingly to Jacqueline Massey. The irony is that in a closely knit neighborhood, her own grandmother had been a close friend of the deceased. Again, a single moment of rage devastated two families. The only justification Massey could claim at her trial was, "I needed the money." She collapsed in the courtroom as Chitwood read her 12-page confession. The sentence was life in prison. Said Lydia Chiaoastri of Chitwood's efforts, "He cooperated with me" with patience despite her persistence. "He was the big hero."

A more complicated case combined murder, what amounted to attempted suicide, hostage-taking, and incest. A 51-year-old West Philadelphia man, Alvin Washington, described by the neighbors as highly intelligent, had made continual sexual advances to his attractive niece, Carol "Peaches" Warren, who had lived in his home with his wife and sons for 18 years. Finally disgusted at the increased intimacy of his intentions, the young woman moved out. Distraught at her departure, Washington stalked her for weeks, finally observing her entering a Thriftway supermarket. He ran after her, yelling, "I want you to come home!" Warren pleaded for help from passersby, screaming, "I don't know this man!" That only served to inflame Washington further. Coming up behind Warren, he shot her with his .357 Magnum and then, as she lay prone, shot her again, intent that she would not survive. He then returned home, supplementing his pistol with a rifle and shotgun. Stationed inside the front door, he kept his family hostage, vowing never to be taken alive, and started drinking heavily At one point, Alvin passed out and struck his head on a step, enabling his three sons and other relatives to escape. However, his wife, Rita, was still inside when he regained consciousness.

As police surrounded the house, leading to a four-hour standoff, and as neighbors gathered outside, three negotiators headed by Detective Chitwood, wearing a bulletproof vest, attempted to talk with Washington. This time it was to no avail. Having increased his arsenal, the barricaded man was especially dangerous. As police finally broke in through a basement door, Washington shot one at point-blank range. He was only saved by his flak jacket. Exchanging fire with the intruders, Washington got off some 10 rounds before he fell over, fatally wounded. One officer on the scene concluded, "He wanted us to kill him. He got what he wanted, but he almost took one of us with him."

"Detective Chitwood has never lost a defendant yet," said Municipal Court Judge Francis Cosgrove. Which sounds rather peculiar in that Chitwood's customary preoccupation was with the prosecution of the guilty. In this instance, however, the young "defendant" was South Philadelphia murder suspect Carmen "Joey D" D'Amato, who had evaded authorities for nine months. Charged with shooting to death three methamphetamine pushers, probably all mob associates, D'Amato was arrested by FBI agents, along with his girlfriend, Bernadette McFarland, in the small Ohio town of Newton Falls. Returned to Philadelphia, D'Amato was placed in special solitary protective custody. He certainly didn't seek bail. At his arraignment in the Police Administration Building, his attorney, Paul Sandler, had requested such protection, insisting, "I believe my client's life is in danger," and Cosgrove complied.

Chitwood, Rosenstein, and Detective Philip Checcia had picked up D'Amato from federal agents. He insisted that he had killed the three men because they were allied with hoodlums harassing his family and detailed his fears in a 37-page confession. Later his father was also arrested because, as Chitwood told reporters, "We have information D'Amato knew where his son was during the nine months he was a fugitive." In the lengthy statement read at his trial, the younger D'Amato readily admitted killing all three men but lamented what he viewed as the necessity of doing so. In the case of one, Anthony Bonaventura, whom he had known since childhood, D'Amato said, "I really wish it hadn't happened, from the bottom of my heart. I didn't want it to happen." The other drug-related homicides were of John Amato and Anthony Patrone. It's a convoluted story, but essentially D'Amato felt he was being set up—that Bonaventura was to kill him in revenge for the mob-authorized murder of Amato—so he struck first. It led to three separate trials and ultimately, whatever the circumstances, to a first-degree murder conviction of D'Amato. And Mike Chitwood's record of never having lost a defendant remained intact.

*   *   *

In all the violent history of the Philadelphia crime family generally known as the Mafia, 1980 initiated a period of unprecedented internal warfare. Like any other tightly structured organization, a mob needs one unquestioned leader to function smoothly. Under Angelo "Gino" Bruno, the "Gentle Don," appointed by the five families who oversaw Mafia affairs, the Philadelphia mob enjoyed two remarkable decades of relative serenity, prosperity, and internal peace. Certainly, this was unusual for an enterprise based entirely on illegality and under constant surveillance by law enforcement. Bruno, well-respected throughout the network of mob fiefdoms, expanded into resurgent Atlantic City, and unlike other bosses, adroitly avoided excessive periods of incarceration. Generally, he was available, like any corporate executive, to oversee the scene. His fatal undoing, presaging the end of his unquestioned power, was his firm refusal to get involved in the burgeoning field of narcotics.

Greed knows no limits. Gambling, loan-sharking, labor racketeering, and extortion weren't enough for the impatient lieutenants and foot soldiers of the Bruno family. Moreover, their New York associates wanted in on Atlantic City. On March 21, 1980, Angelo Bruno was murdered in his car by a shotgun blast, launching a period of violent competition for power, extreme even by Mafia standards. Antonio "Tony Bananas" Caponigro, who had ordered Bruno's murder, was killed on the retaliatory orders of Vincent Gigante. Others from both factions were dispatched in short order: Alfred Salerno, Frank Sindone, John Simone, John Calabrese. In 1981, it was the turn of Bruno's short-lived successor, Philip "Chicken Man" Testa. Many more were murdered at the instigation of new boss Nicky Scarfo. The established order of the Quiet Don had descended to the chaos of a series of subsequent pretenders.

And, of course, homicide detective Mike Chitwood was in the middle of trying to deal with it all. Few years were more violent than 1981 and '82. For a time, it looked as if no likely leader would survive long enough to attain more than temporary power. In January 1982, Frank "Chickie" Narducci, who had been a close associate of Bruno, was shot "gangland style" 10 times as he opened the door of his Cadillac Seville around the corner from his South Broad Street home. As the *Daily News* team of Joe O'Dowd and Mike Freeman put it, Narducci, "chief of gambling and loan-sharking for the local crime family and a charmer who reveled in his role as the ward leader for friends and neighbors," was the eleventh recent fatality "in the blood-soaked story of the Philadelphia mob."

They quoted Mike Chitwood, who had been dispatched to the scene of the slaying: "Whoever did this was right on top of him. It's strictly an organized mob hit." At least, he must have reasoned, they tend to murder only their own. Of course, no witnesses could be found who had seen anything. There is a memorable photo of Chitwood holding a flashlight under a burned-out streetlight so that a priest could deliver the last rites, with Narducci's hand visible under his car. He had been at a court hearing that day on a racketeering charge but was in good spirits. "God is the only judge," the priest intoned, and then went to console the Narducci family, members of his parish.

"One by one, they keep falling," Mike Leary wrote in the *Inquirer*. Among all the Italian names was an Irishman, the recently deceased John McCullough, a close Bruno associate who had been the leader of Local 30 of the roofers' union. Organized crime transcends national origins or ethnicities. In American history, there had been various nativist gangs. There had been an Irish mob, a Jewish mob, a Greek mob, Asian crime families, and now a "Black Mafia," with a Russian mob,

Middle Eastern terrorists, and a Hispanic drug cartel to come.

Leary concluded his Mafia summary with a quotation from Chitwood: "There's not many more left," said Michael Chitwood, the tall, lean homicide detective who has become a fixture at the crime scenes. Starting with Bruno's killing, the string of mob-related deaths had wiped out nearly the entire leadership of this Philadelphia crime family. Indeed, a joke making the rounds was that it should be called the "Rodney Dangerfield Family" because it no longer got any respect. Chitwood later suggested to reporters that perhaps because organized crime was simply being cleaned out, there soon might not be a coherent Philadelphia mob at all. He could not have been happy with the Mafia's South Philadelphia identity, his own home turf. Bruno, Testa, Narducci, and the others were all murdered within its confines, most of the others only a few blocks apart.

With so few people coming forward, actually convicting someone for any of these killings was a daunting challenge. Rocco Marinucci, for example, had probably been involved in the Testa murder. Chitwood and Rosenstein interrupted longtime Bruno associate Raymond "Long John" Martorano during his dinner at Cous' Little Italy, renowned as the gastronomical haunt of mobsters, and took him in for questioning. He may have ordered Marinucci to murder Testa. With so little loyalty in any direction, any remnant of honor among thieves had died with Bruno. But nothing came of it.

Perhaps someone, anyone might cooperate with authorities to save himself. Or herself. Despite death threats, Lucy Mangeri, who had seen her son Thomas shot from her own window, screamed at Salvatore Scafidi, "You're my son's murderer! I will never forget the face of the person who shot my son." Chitwood and Rosenstein had used her testimony to put her on the stand "as the sole eyewitness" to the crime, but now they had to preserve her life, as well. At least they were putting mobsters on trial, and breaking in just a bit on "omerta"—their code of silence.

It was rare that a mob hit was solved. However, Chitwood, who had investigated almost all the gangland killings since the death of Bruno, told the *Inquirer* that despite the lack of community cooperation, "Someone will get arrested on an unrelated offense and will work some kind of deal for immunity. Information will be supplied . . . and then everything will start to come together." There at least were some glimmers of hope.

Eventually Nicodemo "Little Nicky" Scarfo, based in Atlantic City, came the closest to taking over the Bruno mantle in Philadelphia. Cutting a deal with the New York mob helped secure his tenure. His ruthlessness, however, was no less than his predecessors', perhaps worse. Of him, Chitwood would say in the *Inquirer*, "I think he's living on borrowed time. The only reason he's alive today is because he's under constant state and federal supervision. It's tough to get near him. . . . If you live by the sword, you die by the sword." That might summarize Chitwood's own surveillance of the Philadelphia mob. It was tough to get near them, but what remained of their own code made them vulnerable. Being so consistently under federal scrutiny, most of the mobsters spent considerable time in jail on a variety of other charges, even if rarely for murdering each other. Near the end of his tenure in the city, this was probably the most frustrating assignment of Mike Chitwood's career—just as his hostage negotiations were likely the most satisfying.

* * *

At the same time, however, he was making more public appearances than ever, in demand to speak before groups of all kinds. Besides the Pen and Pencil Club, they included everyone from the Saint Gregory's Holy Name Society, the St. John Neumann (formerly Bishop Neumann) Alumni, American Society for Industrial Security, Armed Robbery Conference, Judicial Secretaries Association, and Philadelphia Boosters Association to the Greek Orthodox Church of the Annunciation, State Sheriffs' Association, the National Association of Banking Women, Marconi Senior Citizens, American Legion, Department of the Navy, Temple University, St. Monica School, Big Brothers, and even a group espousing Transcendental Meditation.

* * *

As it turned out, Mike Chitwood's first opportunity to actually head a police department, one he'd pursued with all his native vigor and newly developed personal promotional skills, didn't come in a city the size of Houston or even of Camden. He began work on August 2, 1983, as the police chief of less than 20-square-mile Middletown Township in Bucks County, adjacent to Philadelphia, boasting a population of some 35,000 and a police force of only 45. Of course, chief township supervisor Robert J. Brann insisted, "We have the top police force in Bucks County. It is young and well-educated." Perhaps that's one reason why 116 people applied for the job.

Eventually, after a seven-month nationwide search and evaluation period, it was narrowed down to three finalists. At least in the minds of township residents, Chitwood, despite his glowing record in Philadelphia, wasn't even the favorite. The five-man board of supervisors, its most prominent member future governor Mark Schweiker, made the decision. The township had grown immensely from its bucolic origins with the construction of Levittown after the Second World War and all the subsequent commercial development. It was and still is overwhelmingly white. Its only police chief had retired after 30 years, and popular former Middletown chief of detectives James Duncan had been named interim chief, serving seven months. He, Chitwood, and a recently retired police captain from White Plains, New York, were the finalists. Duncan was viewed as the local favorite, particularly by the rank-and-file policemen currently on the force, who at least knew him. However, the supervisors split two-to-two between Duncan and Chitwood, with chairman Richard Scott breaking the tie. "There's nothing wrong with Jim Duncan," he noted, but "I leaned towards Chitwood." If he accepted their offer, Chitwood would serve a one-year probationary period, as stipulated by law, and be expected, not unreasonably, to move to Middletown Township within 18 months or so.

Duncan declared himself "disappointed" but "relaxed" about the supervisors' choice (and perhaps was more than a bit surprised). "He's getting a good department," he told the *Inquirer*, and "He seems like a likeable guy." Apparently word leaked out prematurely. Joseph Grace of the Bucks County *Courier Times* had reported on July 17, 1983, that "informed sources" had confirmed the narrow choice of Philadelphia's "well-publicized, highly decorated" homicide detective.

To Chitwood, it wasn't the size of his new domain that mattered but the opportunity it presented. "It's hard to leave" Philadelphia after 19 years on the force and his lifelong residence in the city, Chitwood told Lacy McCrary of the *Inquirer*, "The men and women I've worked with, and the job, and even the people I've dealt with (during police cases) have been good to me." But it was time to advance his career "in the area of administration and apply the knowledge and experience I've gained in a new and more challenging way. I want to round out my career." He added, "How long can I be a detective and a member of the hostage team? I want to be an administrator. Hopefully, what I've learned I can put to use for Middletown Township." Certainly his communication skills were helpful in the interview process. All three finalists were also put through extensive physical and psychological testing, as well as a lie-detector test before the five-member board took a straw-poll vote.

If Chitwood wasn't certain which two had voted against him, he was left in no doubt by the investigative skills of Joseph Grace of the *Courier Times*. It had been Schweiker and Thomas Kearns. During the interviews Chitwood surmised that they might object more to his lack of academic credentials, for example, than the other members. These three—Raymond Mongillo, Robert Brann, and chairman Richard Scott—simply seemed more friendly and down to earth. However, after the decision, Schweiker and Kearns insisted they were never anti-Chitwood, just pro-Duncan.

Grace reported, "Mongillo and Scott both said they based their decision in large part on results from a battery of tests the three candidates took. Brann said he supported Chitwood throughout." According to Grace's "well-placed sources," Graham was eliminated from contention when he failed his lie-detector test. Chitwood suspects that Schweiker and Kearns also felt that, coming from such an urban repository of possible corruption, Graham would be the candidate most likely to fail. One board member suggested that "the results of Duncan's psychological test showed his decision-making ability was lacking," but that view was not confirmed by others.

Agreeing to go with the results of their straw poll, they had offered the job to Chitwood even before there was an official vote. The "lanky, curly-haired detective" accepted immediately and promptly tendered his resignation from the Philadelphia Police Department. According to Grace, Chitwood added after the meeting, "I just want a chance to prove myself and gain all of their support. I'm not worried about any factions or splits." But the new environment might take some getting used to. As Grace put it, in hiring this 19-year Philly police veteran, "The board selected a policeman accustomed to headlights, spotlights, and controversy." This compact little township was bound to seem a bit tame. But that's not the way it worked out.

From Chitwood's former employers there were only positive reactions. On July 25, 1983, then Philadelphia Police Commissioner Morton B. Solomon sent Mike Chitwood his "personal congratulations" and expressed his willingness to help him in the future in any way possible. Frank Rizzo weighed in: "He's a very fine young man, and I've known him all 19 years he's been with the force. He's an excellent officer, very heroic, very courageous." Interestingly, shortly after Chitwood's arrival, some Middletown policemen anonymously expressed to, yes, Joseph Grace less than glowing accounts about the actual prior working environment within their ostensibly top-flight organization. As Grace put it, "Tension, dissent and open antipathy" had "cloaked the 45-man department in a dark, brooding cloud." Apparently, their new chief potentially represented, in one patrolman's opinion, something "like a new dawn."

For his part, after being sworn in, Chitwood stated, "I'm proud to be in Middletown." Holding a series of meetings during his first long day on the job and anxious to start off by setting the right tone and clearing the air, he added, "I don't know anybody. . . . We start from ground zero. . . . I won't be working 16 hours a day six months from now, but . . . I'll keep busy." So would they all.

What Am I Doing Here?

Shortly after Mike Chitwood had accepted his new job, a woman from Trevose told *Bucks County Courier Times* columnist Joe Halberstein a story that ties together both the big city and small township versions of Chitwood. Her 61-year-old husband, Robert Smith, a former navy pilot, had been the victim of an attempted mugging in a Philadelphia parking garage. However, he managed to snatch his assailant's pistol away, and after a wild chase, the two wrestled to the ground, where Smith suffered a gash to the head. The first Philadelphia police officer on the scene, off duty and on his way home, was none other than future Middletown Township police chief Michael Chitwood. After the mugger had been taken into custody, Chitwood drove Smith to the hospital for treatment and then all the way home to Trevose. Subsequently, he also went to the hearing in the case and attended the trial, as well. "My husband and I can't say enough about what he did," Mary Smith told Halberstein, "I just thought people would like to know what kind of a person Middletown Township has picked to be its new police chief."

There might be fewer muggings in Middletown than in Philadelphia, but Chitwood never bought into the premise that his new locale would be a repository of relative serenity. His tenure in the township, ostensibly so different from its neighboring metropolis, would reflect everything he had experienced in Philadelphia—with, of course, one significant difference. During the previous 19-plus years, he had always been on call. Now he was in charge. In distance, Chitwood's move to this compact Bucks County community measured only a few miles. In responsibility it was a world apart. Yes, he might now be faced more with burglary than homicide, but the variety of crime changes little. And as Middletown Township had evolved into a much more populous suburb of Philadelphia, the boundaries became more blurred. As Chitwood would reflect many years later, whatever the size of his domain, the "scumbags" he faced still seemed so similar that they might have been the same people he'd encountered in Philly. Only Chitwood's responsibilities had changed, starting in 1983, when he arrived in Middletown Township, Bucks County, Pennsylvania.

* * *

The modest but well-maintained home in which Mike Chitwood had grown up reflected a restless generation of "baby boomers," initiated by the ambitions of their parents. Not since the great migration west had mobility been on the minds of so many Americans. It came home with millions of young veterans after the Second World War, enabled by the GI Bill to attain educational levels unimagined prior to the conflict. So many could now realistically contemplate launching their new families to earn a share of the nation's broadening prosperity. For many it led from a row house to a new home carved out of the countryside. Their dreams reflected upward mobility in all its dimensions. Develop your skills. Reach your potential. Go wherever opportunity takes you. And the interstate highway system, initiated during the 1950s, combined with the immensely increased percentage of American families owning their own cars, would make every corner of the nation more accessible in the succeeding decades.

Of course, it was career, not geographical mobility, that had brought Mike Chitwood to Bucks County, but for the prior 18 months, he had sought such an opportunity *wherever* it might develop—from Camden to Houston. As he told Kurt Heine of the *Philadelphia Daily News* after accepting the Middletown job, "There comes a time when you have to move . . . in my career, when I wanted to enhance myself." Chitwood admitted to knowing little initially about the community he was coming to. He had driven through it, and visited its administrative offices, but had actually met only those who had interviewed him and then offered him the job. But no worries. Chitwood was a quick learner. And what he hoped to accomplish as a police chief was based less on where he settled than on how his ideas would be received.

What qualities, Heine asked, would he bring to this new challenge, this "whole new realm of police work"? Chitwood replied, "I think the greatest thing I've got going for me is my ability to know how to treat people the way they should be treated. . . . I have something of a "Dirty Harry"–type image, but that's not the kind of image I want. I just want to come across as a guy who's semi-intelligent, who's compassionate, and who has common sense." However confident a person is, a bit of self-deprecation, particularly when embarking on a new venture, never hurts. Heine wrote that at Chitwood's swearing-in ceremony, he was grinning like "a kid at Christmas." An ebullient Chitwood had vowed to "make it the best police department in the whole country." Its motto would be "professionalism, courtesy, and service." Careful not to offend his long-term predecessor, there was a lot of "if it's not broke, don't fix it" rhetoric, and he named Jim Duncan, the candidate he'd beaten out, as his second in command. But Chitwood's most telling comment was, "I'd like to open up the police department." He could hardly wait.

For the first six months, however long the hours, Chitwood commuted daily to Philadelphia, at least 45 minutes each way, depending on traffic. When he finally sold his South Philly home and bought and moved with Liz and Beth Ann to a Levittown condo, 19-year-old Mike Jr. didn't join them. He had his own conception of mobility, but also of independence, instilled over the years by his parents. Of course, it was no easy decision for either child, but they were comfortable where they were, each within a circle of their own friends.

As Beth Ann Scannell recalls it today, despite her parents' affection for Philadelphia and reluctance to sever family ties, they were never about to limit their children's horizons. "When I was growing up," she reflects, "my parents talked about education and college, even though at the time neither had their degree. I always knew I would go to college because of the things they stressed. My dad never talked to me about moving from South Philly, but he was determined to show me other places, even places not very far away. Although we belonged to a parish in South Philly, we would go to New Jersey for Saturday night mass—and pizza. Sometimes we even went to a Burger King all the way 'over the bridge.' That was something my friends could never figure out. It sounds funny, but as an adult I get it. I guess you could say they showed us it's OK to leave home, that home will *always* be there."

Mike Chitwood's father had been transferred to Philadelphia by the United States Navy. But beyond their families' original migration to this country and their settling in South Philly, Liz and Mike Chitwood were the first to move away. Initially, it was not that far, but distance was not the dimension that mattered. Five years later, a new opportunity would develop hundreds of miles farther away. In later years, Mike Jr. would move to Oklahoma and then to Florida. Beth Ann would move to California and then to North Carolina. And yet the family would grow ever closer, even as its mobility increased. "It's OK to leave home," Beth Ann said, "home will always be there." And, in effect, those we love will always be with us.

*   *   *

Centuries before there was a Levittown, there was a Langhorne, the established "borough" of Bucks County, named by William Penn for his home in Buckinghamshire. Were you to ask the average Philadelphian even today for his or her impression of Bucks County, their response would likely center not on any community within Middletown Township, but on a slender, scenic, and not very representative stretch along the Delaware River, encompassing creative New Hope and bustling Doylestown, the county seat. Overall, its idyllic image combines the enduring charm of country roads and covered bridges with historic inns, theatre, arts, antiques, fashionable restaurants, and the luxuriously secluded weekend retreats of New York–based celebrities. However, that image presents only one small segment of Bucks, and not remotely the environment Mike Chitwood found when he became the second police chief in the history of Middletown. The township name is apt yet misleading. Indeed, it is located in the middle, but not of the entire county but only of what is called "Lower Bucks"—the southern end of an elongated entity stretching some 600 square miles to the north. In both proximity and postwar growth, Middletown Township has more in common with the "Great Northeast" of Philadelphia than with the rest of Bucks County.

The period of expansion of both areas coincided. The Northeast, with the mass migration of residents from older, declining neighborhoods of the city to endless streets of new row houses—a contemporary version of the sort of neighborhood the Chitwoods had grown up in—became a city within a city. And all municipal employees were obliged to reside somewhere within the city, no matter how far from its center. In Middletown, it was tracts of mass-produced single homes. One popular song of the time satirized such developments as "all made out of ticky-tacky . . . all look just the same," but the song missed the point. Such congenial communities represented a promising way station to these young families, not their ultimate destination.

Although it stretched over four townships, the growth of Levittown was largely responsible for expanding the population of Middletown Township by over 400 percent in one decade. Boasting some 35,000 residents when Chitwood arrived, it has more like 50,000 today. The difference is that as the population of Philadelphia's Great Northeast became far more ethnically diverse, many of its upwardly mobile earlier residents moved with their families out to the suburbs. Already living within a suburban community, many upwardly mobile residents of Middletown Township chose rather to relocate to larger, personalized homes within its confines, making it more visually and economically diverse. And new families found it attractive to move in. Why lengthen your commute to Philadelphia or Trenton? Moreover, already situated within a network of good roads, the township supervisors managed to balance its growth by retaining hundreds of acres of public parkland, many farms, and orchards; sustaining an excellent school system; and welcoming the establishment of great shopping centers and even a popular racetrack-casino, not to mention Sesame Place! It had everything.

However, all that growth also tied the township more closely to Philadelphia, making Chitwood's task more challenging than it might have been a decade or two earlier. The crime rate was still low, but he had to function with only those 45 policemen, backed by a support staff of a dozen. With the possibility of sharing more of the overlapping law enforcement concerns of Philadelphia, Middletown wouldn't be all that quiet an assignment for Chitwood—just as he had predicted. And he wouldn't have wanted it any other way.

*   *   *

Starting his first day on the job, as Mike sat in solitary splendor behind his new desk, before assembling all those staff meetings he'd planned, for just a moment or so, Mike Chitwood's customary confidence faltered. Here he was in an enormous office. It looked to be a lot bigger than the Philadelphia police commissioner's office in the "Roundhouse." Previously, the Middletown Police Department had shared space with the township's other administrators. However, in 1982, they had purchased and moved to an expansive new building and had given their old facilities on Levittown's New Rogers Road to the police department alone. It would be 20 years before they were all reunited again in a handsome new municipal center.

As he looked around his spacious domain with its huge, conference table surrounded by a dozen chairs, Chitwood's initial reaction was, "Wow! It looks like I've arrived." He needed only a platform under his desk to duplicate the setting of a Mussolini.

However, his next reaction, only a second or two later, was, "What do I do now?" Chitwood had gotten the job because at least a majority of the board members wanted a younger, more vigorous chief who could lead the department into the future—so to speak, a fresh face. But the man attached to that face had never even balanced a checkbook. Now Chitwood's first major assignment would be to put together a three-million-dollar budget for the department he was to lead. As he recalls it, he didn't quite yell "Help!" into the phone, but he reached out to the consultant who had assembled his résumé and prepared him for the interview. "Now that I have the job," Chitwood asked, "what do I do?" It may be more accurate, since Chitwood already knew what he wanted to accomplish, to suggest that what he really needed to know was "*How* do I do it?"

All his experience had stemmed from basic police work on the streets. From that perspective, even as he'd graduated to homicide investigations, narcotics, and hostage negotiations, by now he had a Ph.D. in practical policing. But in terms of any administrative capability, he was still as inexperienced as on his first day as a patrolman.

After the consultant laughed, he offered Chitwood some very direct and seemingly simple advice: "Find the sharpest and smartest officers in the organization, reach out to them for direction and assistance, and make sure you thank them for everything they do." As Chitwood was to discover, many members of Middletown's police department, feeling underappreciated and relatively leaderless, were more than willing to be asked for their opinion—and more than appreciative of being thanked for offering it. Chitwood concludes, "Over the next several years I did just that."

One might amend this to refer to the next 30 years. Encouraging the experienced input of others became not only a vital ingredient in enabling Chitwood to master this, his first administrative responsibility, but he would take such commonsense counsel with him to help shape his leadership style and his management skills for all his future success.

By Chitwood's third day on the job, the dimensions of his office may have seemed a bit smaller, but he was still getting acclimated when another challenge arrived. Fortunately, it was somewhat less serious, despite its size. A large delivery truck had arrived in the driveway. Two men got out and opened its rear doors. They laboriously unloaded six enormous planters, each about five feet tall, containing different types of colorful floral arrangements. And then they brought all of them directly into Chitwood's office. "Are we to become the viewing site for a funeral?" he pondered. No, as the planters were arranged around them, Chitwood's new administrative assistant, Carol Theobald, came in and announced, "These are for you." All that the accompanying card said was, "Congratulations!" To this day, Chitwood doesn't know who sent the flowers, but for the next several years, he and Carol tried to keep them alive. Alas, like most fragile flora, eventually they passed on.

In time the very size of the building became an asset. Chitwood had the former public auditorium turned into a records room where all crime reports were filed and microfilmed, with retrievals processed by a computer. The former stage area became a center with a terminal connected to the state computer, surrounding municipalities, and the National Crime Information Center. The site also housed Chitwood's newly formed Accident Investigation Division. Eventually, as Chitwood announced in the *Middletown Township Newsletter*, when completed the facility would be "the most modern in Bucks County."

*   *   *

To the Philadelphia media, colorful Mike Chitwood, whether in terms of "most decorated" or "most dapper," would be much missed. So they simply continued to cover him as if he'd never left. Nothing was too trivial. By mid-September, a feature piece by Tom Fox in the *Inquirer* was headlined, "Mike Chitwood Is Feeling the Heat." After noting that magnanimous Mike had frozen his pension to assume his less-compensated new duties, Fox pointed out that Chitwood was continuing his practice of jogging three miles every day, wherever he might be located. On a recent 95-degree scorcher, returning bathed in sweat from a circular track he'd found at a school not far from police headquarters, Chitwood was delighted to find a shower in the basement of the building. Unfortunately, after soaping up, he found that the shower contained only scalding hot water. With little time to get to a dinner in Langhorne, Fox notes, "He finally had to take a bird-bath in a wash basin." However, Chitwood reflected to Fox, "If that's the only headache I run into," this new job "ought to be a piece of cake." Still, he planned to have the shower fixed, as well as the air-conditioning system, which shut off every day at 5 p.m., evocative of a more relaxed administrative regime in the past.

At that point in the interview, Carol Theobald, whom Tom Fox described as Chitwood's "pretty blonde secretary," came in and said softly, "Oh, Chief," to which Chitwood was slow to respond. Finally, smiling, he said to Fox, "I just can't get used to being called 'Chief.'" He'd only been dreaming of it for some 20 years. "It's crazy," he concluded.

Well into his new tenure, even as Chitwood implemented his reforms, Philadelphia writers still speculated on why this quintessential street cop had traded all the visibility of the big time for such a relative backwater. What they failed to appreciate was that for an ambitious professional, not yet 40, this was likely to be only the first necessary step, a preparation for the future. As Chitwood pointed out to Tom Whitaker of the *Inquirer*, he'd made this commitment to "round out" his career, his own launching pad. It also enhanced his upward mobility by enabling him to add the vital educational component he still lacked. Despite the long hours, he managed to get back to Philadelphia two evenings a week to take courses at Antioch College. Eventually, he would earn two degrees there.

Moreover, as Chitwood stressed to Whitaker, mastering the administrative requirements of his new responsibility would enable him to carry out long-held convictions about the relationship between people and power. Asked about his first priority as Chief, Chitwood replied, "People unconsciously despise authority. I want to find out how to break that down . . . learn to establish police-community relationships." His second priority? "Police and press relations" leading to "an open-door policy." The press should not only report to a deserving public when "the police were out of whack," but also "let the people know just how hard the police officer's job is out there," overcoming "inherent mistrust" with two-way communications throughout the community; consensus replacing confrontation. It may sound simplistic, but Chitwood had some experience with the power of the press.

The new style started in Chitwood's own office, where his door would always be open (and the air-conditioner on). However extended his hours, Mike could always make the time to listen to a citizen's complaints or suggestions, no matter how seemingly trivial. "Anybody who walks in can talk to me," he told reporters, especially if they had called to reserve a time. Within the department, well beyond his honeymoon period, Chitwood was almost excessively active in instilling a more positive attitude. Dick Tracy may have had his two-way wrist-radio. Chitwood added a personal "radio-quip" program. Once each hour, every police car would get a cheerful reminder about courtesy, professionalism, or safety on the job—a kind of pep talk from the top. It may have seemed a bit hokey had it not been based on his other innovations.

Chitwood handled all personnel problems personally. Previously, they had been sent up to the impersonal attention of the township's board of supervisors. And his offer to hold individual talks extended to police officers. As business owners noted, there appeared to be more patrol cars, more police on the street, simply more visibility; a new, more positive attitude. Chitwood instructed everyone pursuing an investigation to leave their cars and talk to people personally, more confident and concerned about finding a solution. One of his first decisions was to create a table of organization indicating precisely who was responsible for what, and when. Henceforward, no tenured lieutenant would sit back and loaf at headquarters while patrolmen pounding their beats took all the risks. As promised, particularly in terms of administration, Chitwood listened and learned.

Of course, it worked both ways. Beyond the department, Chitwood started making personal appearances just about everywhere, a visibility not previously noted from Middletown officials. This, after all, was an area in which he was already comfortable. A typical early response was a letter from the Middletown Senior Citizens Center thanking Chitwood for his "very informative talk" and adding, "We do hope you will have many years here in Middletown and love it here just as much as all of us do." He also established information sessions within police headquarters for residents of all ages. For example, some 2,000 students from the Neshaminy School District were asked in to be fingerprinted, explaining just how that program aided community safety and security. It certainly beat a dry lecture. In a typical community gesture, Chitwood was able to get the price of Phillies tickets reduced for an outing of some 400 handicapped residents. He also provided a police escort for their buses to the game and free gifts for all, and he set up a personal performance by the Philly Phanatic to enhance their enjoyment of the experience.

* * *

No community is immune to crimes of violence. On June 17, 1983, Middletown patrolman James Kane, heading home after an uneventful shift, heard this message on his police radio, "Armed robbery. Shots fired." Kane rushed to the scene, a friend's drugstore in Levittown. He found his friend, Richard Sharp, lying on the floor, surrounded by paramedics no longer able to help. Sharp had been shot in the head. Putting this horror aside, Patrolman Kane went outside to calmly interview eyewitnesses. Eventually, the killer was found and indicted for murder. But in such circumstances, how did Kane manage to keep his composure? Because, said Joseph Grace in the *Courier Times*, "He is a cop." Grace quoted another township patrolman, Jon Edgar: "The public expects the supermacho cop image. So we maintain it."

But what if the stress becomes too great? That is why Chitwood would bring in two prominent Philadelphia psychologists, becoming perhaps the first suburban police chief to provide his officers with stress-management counseling. By October, after only two months on the job, he turned his focus to this concern that had long been on his mind. Grace quoted Chitwood: "Cops have a closed mentality.

It's tough to get inside. I know. I was the same way." The constant stress leads to higher than average percentages of suicide, divorce, and alcoholism.

The psychologists conducted an eight-hour stress seminar. It was voluntary, but 41 of the department's 45 officers chose to take it, learning techniques for recognizing and alleviating the job pressures they all faced daily. Chitwood followed this up with a similar program for officers' wives, so they could better appreciate an area in which their supportive efforts could be essential. Among the other benefits, in Chitwood's view, such counseling led his officers to develop more of a team mentality, peeling away the "police veneer" that each one has on his own. Communication should not only be external—with the community they all served—but also internal, within the force itself.

As the *Courier Times* put it, "Chitwood's ability to relate to the problems of the officer on the street bodes well for the direction of the Middletown Police Department, where relations between the rank-and-file and the leadership have not always been the best."

*   *   *

Of equal importance to the improved performance of police officers was simply acknowledging it. Again, Chitwood recalled his consultant's advice. An article by Joseph Grace in the *Courier Times* of October 12, 1983 was headlined, "For Once, Cops Hear More than 'Thanks.'" During the prior month, three patrolmen had apprehended four robbery suspects in a drive-in movie theatre, arrested them, and brought them to headquarters. In the past, all this would have led to was filling out an abundance of paperwork and then getting back on the street. As Grace put it, "Big arrests, little fanfare." One of the three officers, Patrolman Patrick McGinty, added, "The way it always was before, you never got told when you did a good job, only when you did a bad job." But not this time. The three patrolmen, six other township police officers, and five civilians basked in the glow of TV lights, the applause of family and friends, and public commendations read by the board of supervisors—all instigated by Chief Chitwood.

Joseph Grace continued, "The public ceremony, replete with engraved invitations, gold bars, and bright TV cameras, is part of Chitwood's new policy of rewarding his force—and the citizenry—for exemplary law enforcement. 'When I was a city policeman and I did something right, I was proud to be recognized for it,' said Chitwood, who had contacted the TV crew, 'I think these guys appreciate it too. It's a morale booster.'" And another form of visibility.

Others honored that evening reflected the township's fortunate prevalence of crimes like burglary over homicide. Citations went to a patrolman who had broken up a flimflam operation and fencing ring in a department-store chain, to the extended investigation by five detectives that led to the arrest of a man charged with several home break-ins, to four employees of a township apartment complex who were able to wrestle a burglary suspect to the ground and detain him until police arrived, and to a local resident who for 12 years had voluntarily trained police dogs for the department.

*   *   *

Early in Mike Chitwood's tenure, there was a particular incident that underscored his constant concern that the growing interrelationship between Philadelphia and Middletown Township would present problems. Even though it did not result in serious injury, it still drew his ire. The benignly named Bensalem Youth Development Center, actually a detention center, housed juvenile offenders from throughout the area, particularly Philadelphia. About half of the 178 inmates between the ages of 13 and 18 who lived at the center were considered sufficiently reformed to be eligible to go to supervised outings. One night, 11 of the youths were taken to see a drive-in movie (ironically, *48 Hours,* involving a released criminal working with the police). However, on this occasion, the supervision was less than thorough. Four of the teens, all of whom had records for prior convictions involving burglary or robbery, wandered away. (One of the youths, only 15, who was six feet two and weighed 228 pounds, had been convicted of armed robbery.) Later, an embarrassed supervisor said he thought the four had gone to get some popcorn. Instead, they headed for a restaurant where they tried to rob an employee, who managed to run away, and later accosted a young couple, stealing the woman's purse. Her boyfriend chased the four back to the drive-in and called the police, who apprehended them there. Apparently, a lot of casual crime seemed to center on drive-ins, but it might lead to something far more serious.

Chitwood was outraged. "It's a breakdown of the whole system when something like this happens," he said in a statement to the press. "These guys are court-committed . . . They're out doing a robbery while they're in the program. . . . They are not Boy Scouts. They all have extensive records. . . . It could have been a murder. It could have been a rape. It could have been anything." Chitwood told the Camden County *Courier Times* that he was particularly incensed that red tape prevented the police from charging the youths immediately, but instead had to release them to the same people who had failed to supervise them. "It is not fair to the public. It is not fair to law enforcement. I just don't see where the system is working when something like this can happen." Referring to Philadelphia, he added, "The same cast of characters that are up here are the same cast of characters that commit murder down there."

*   *   *

Increasingly, there would be new incursions, some quite dramatic, that would both evoke old memories and again underline Chitwood's prediction that outside crime was bound to intrude into his suburban setting. Combating the narcotics trade had been a major part of Chitwood's Philadelphia career, but this time it came from the sky to a private airport in Middletown Township in the form of a "mystery plane." The twin-engine Piper Aztec landed, took off, and then landed again in quick succession three times during the middle of the night at the Buehl airport near popular Styer Orchard. When it came down the third time at around 4:30 a.m., again without benefit of landing lights, the airport's owner became more than suspicious and called the police. His field had shut down officially at 2:00 a.m. A car nearby had been observed using headlights to signal the aircraft. Chitwood immediately suspected drug drops. Middletown officer John Kelly, first on the scene, found the plane still on the runway. That must be it for the night. He also observed a man standing nearby, who upon closer investigation reeked of marijuana.

Why had they chosen to land at this location? Perhaps because of its obscurity? But surely they would be observed by someone. Soon a car arrived, as did Chitwood and more police. Both the driver and the other man, ostensibly the plane's pilot, were taken into custody. It turned out that the aircraft was indeed involved in delivering drugs for local distribution. It was equipped with extra fuel tanks and sophisticated radar-jamming equipment, and five of its six seats had been removed to accommodate more cargo. The car was bringing back the missing seats.

Sometime earlier, a plane that landed at a small field near Doylestown had contained 912 pounds of marijuana. That pilot-purveyor had disappeared, at least for a time. This one, named Philip J. Destaven, was a fugitive from North Carolina, already under indictment there on smuggling and theft charges. Apparently, all the drug shipments had come originally from the Caribbean, later conveyed from way stations to locations throughout the eastern United States—in this instance, Bucks County. After consulting with the FBI and U.S. Customs, with total bail from both Pennsylvania and North Carolina now totaling four million dollars, Destaven was eventually extradited back to Union County, North Carolina, and local drug distribution returned to its less exciting conveyances.

*   *   *

Mike Chitwood's memory bank had been jogged earlier by a case more similar to his experiences in the big city. Well, he had predicted that his new job would be no quiet sinecure. This case had just about everything he was most familiar with—a barricaded fanatic, family turmoil, violence, firearms—and, at the end, although fortunately no one was killed, he would be sued for, yes, "abuse" of the defendant.

In the words of *Philadelphia Inquirer* writer Lacy McCrary, "It was a situation made to order for Chitwood [who] left his spacious, neat office, immaculately dressed as usual," and drove to the scene of action. It was September 15, 1983, less than six weeks after Chitwood had been sworn in as chief, still trying to bridge the initial "trust gap," as he put it.

A frantic woman named Helen Singer had called Middletown police headquarters to report that her husband, William, after beating her and her stepdaughter following a vicious argument, had thrown them both out of their Penndel home. "He's armed with weapons, a lot of weapons," she added. Not only armed but also dangerously erratic. Both women were sufficiently battered to be taken to the hospital for observation. It turned out that Bill Singer, an unemployed insulation installer, was a militant tax protester affiliated with extremist anti-government organizations, including one called Posse Comitatus. Several officers were already on the scene. Chitwood deployed them around the house and then walked to the front door. All the doors and windows had been locked. Chitwood tried to talk to Singer, as he had so often done in prior situations, actually shouting for about an hour, telling him that if he just came out, they could talk things over. Finally, Singer replied, "You can't come in. If you do, you'll be sorry." Chitwood then broke a pane of glass in the front door with his nightstick and calmly reached in. It turned out that Singer was unarmed after all, but he kicked the door hard, and flying glass cut Chitwood on his hands and face.

A moment later, officers broke in from the back of the house. As Singer rushed in that direction, Chitwood and other police came through the front. They had to wrestle a truculent Singer to the floor, where he finally gave up, insisting, "There are too many of you." Although Singer was unarmed, Chitwood's men found—concealed in a false ceiling over a second-floor closet—weapons of all kinds, from pistols to shotguns, and even a five-foot blowgun with wire darts, plus between 8,000 and 11,000 rounds of ammunition. The only ones hurt in the melee had been Chitwood and a second officer, neither seriously.

Singer was removed from his home and bound over for trial on assault charges against both his family and the police. When finally his trial began, he acted as his own attorney, although flanked by two other men, probably supplied by one of his organizations. They remained silent, but Singer repeatedly disrupted the proceedings. He refused to offer a plea, insisting that the court had no jurisdiction over him. Later he filed a $23 million lawsuit against Chitwood and a host of others, claiming that his rights as a homeowner had been violated, that there had been excessive violence in subduing him, and that Chitwood had also intended to smash him in the face with his nightstick. Nothing came of it. Found mentally competent to stand trial, Singer was ultimately convicted in December 1984, on three counts of assault. The sentence was relatively light, a total of 90 days to two and a half years in county prison. The judge, still uncertain of Singer's mental state, added the stipulation that he should undergo a further full psychiatric evaluation and, before sentencing, must stay away from the women he'd assaulted.

For Chitwood, the Singer episode represented an early validation by those whose opinion mattered most to him. The headline on Lucy McCrary's *Inquirer* article announced, "The Chief Has Taken Charge." Its first paragraph began, "Michael J. Chitwood officially became the police chief of Middletown Township, Bucks County, on Aug. 2. But he didn't really become *the chief*, in the eyes of his men, until Sept. 15" when that call came in from Helen Singer and he personally responded. McCrary went on to quote a number of Chitwood's patrolmen. "The turning point for a lot of us was the barricade," said Lloyd Patton. "He's our leader." Sgt. Leroy Anderson said the incident in itself had boosted the department's morale. "He's the same as us. He's not in some ivory tower . . . not a desk jockey." Lt. Frank McKenna, a 27-year veteran of the force, agreed: "The barricade situation enhanced his position here. It's one thing to tell men to go out and do a job and another to lead them. The guys saw in him an example of what he wants them to be." Putting himself on the line, even should it turn out to be the line of fire, won a lot of hearts and minds that day.

*   *   *

And so it didn't take long to remind Chitwood of his more perilous past, justifying his prediction that his present post would reflect just as great a variety of challenges. Some of them would not end as peaceably as William Singer's barricade.

Middle Management

A s Mike Chitwood crossed the chronological divide that used to constitute the onset of middle age—that is, 40—he was appropriately in mid-career and presiding over the police force of a place called Middletown Township. The media consensus continued to portray him as a genial workaholic with many interests but few hobbies, protective of his family's privacy but not averse to personal publicity. After all, shouldn't what was good for Mike Chitwood be good for Middletown?

He viewed himself as both teacher and student, pursuing those Antioch degrees that would enhance his credentials for future opportunity, while working extended hours on other nights or attending community meetings where residents voiced their continuing concerns with theft, drugs, and vandalism. Chitwood had been in Middletown for only three months when Lacey McCrary had announced in his *Inquirer* feature article that he'd "taken charge" and won the respect of many of those he supervised. But he still had a lot to learn. As he told McCrary, he already knew that "this quiet suburban community is not quiet anymore." With his open-door policy, Chitwood heard all the complaints. But what if *you* need advice? McCrary asked. Chitwood replied, "If I've got a problem, I don't hesitate to call Philly and talk to legal or management experts" before making a decision. After all, he'd made that call to his consultant on his very first day on the job. "Managing manpower is my biggest challenge," Chitwood continued. If he could make "75 or 80 percent of the force happy . . . I'll be all right."

And so he continued to publicly commend his most deserving officers and civilians who supported their efforts through periodic award ceremonies. At the one in January 1984, amidst a cheering, standing-room-only audience, three residents and an assistant district attorney were praised for helping to apprehend and prosecute suspects in the murder of pharmacist Richard Sharp, the crime that had motivated Chitwood's stress-management program. Recognition was also extended to those who had foiled burglaries and arrested drug suspects, as well as to all the winners of the township's annual shooting competition. There were so many that supervisor Richard Scott was moved to assert, "Anyone thinking they can commit a criminal act in Middletown Township had better think again."

After more than eight months on the job, while acknowledging that 1984 marked the third year of overall crime reduction in the township, Chitwood also noted that burglary and car thefts, the most prevalent crimes, had declined in the past year. Characteristically, he directed credit to others, although in the context of programs he had personally initiated. Writing in the *Middletown Township News-letter* of April 1984, he singled out the efforts of Lt. Frank McKenna, the police department's primary liaison with the township. Apparently, a much more receptive attitude among young people in terms of reporting criminal activity had been developed, at least in part stemming from Chief Chitwood's emphasis on parental involvement as well as McKenna's meetings with students. McKenna added, "It is the kind of police-community relationship that will continue to have a positive effect on our ability to make Middletown Township among the safest places to live."

* * *

Perhaps even in such seemingly serene surroundings, the increased humidity of spring and summer is apt to bring out some pretty bizarre incidents. Well, hadn't Chitwood observed that things in Middletown weren't quite so quiet anymore? In May 1984, a Levittown man who had kidnapped the same woman, a neighbor, twice within four days was arrested in a car he had stolen from her home. He had threatened to kill her husband had he tried to intervene. The first kidnapping had also been intended to initiate a nationwide tour. The kidnapper was 23; his victim, 52. Apparently, the young man had become friendlier with this woman after his disappointment over breaking up with her 21-year-old daughter. Not your normal Middletown arrest.

In another incident, three truckloads of stolen property were discovered by Middletown police and taken to their fortunately quite spacious headquarters building. All had come from a series of thefts at a remarkably insecure local public storage facility. At least 30 lockers had been tampered with or broken into. Lt. James Duncan expressed pride that this discovery came as the result of "extensive police work," not an outside tip. The problem was how, without receipts, any of the many customers of the facility could prove precisely what belonged to them. In any case, everything was put on display every Saturday from 10:00 a.m. to 4:00 p.m., a sort of garage sale in reverse—bring an honest face in lieu of cash.

"Dog bites man" is not as unusual as "man bites dog," but what if the man is a police officer working with trusted police dogs, prized members of Middletown's K-9 corps. Patrolman James Edgar was feeding all six of the force's dogs when he was suddenly attacked by one of them, a 90-pound German Shepherd named

"Midnight." Edgar suffered bites on his arms and chin that required 40 stitches. When the canine, which had shown no prior indication of antipathy to any handler, refused to let go, Edgar had to shoot it. Chitwood suggested that it might have been a result of the 90-plus-degree temperature, commenting, "German Shepherds despise the heat." Later, however, another dog, 100-pound "Bandit," attacked and mauled another policeman during the 10-week training course at the Philadelphia Police Academy, where all the dogs were initially trained—a program Chitwood loyally praised as the "most rigorous in the area." He suggested that perhaps a future "one man, one dog" system, training together to familiarize both, might limit any future problems. But he also put out a call for some promising male German Shepherd pups to join the K-9 corps in the future.

Then there was the case of another eccentric "survivalist." This one, intent on finding the thief or thieves who had stolen his car stereo, was found wandering around an apartment complex adjacent to his apartment, wielding a 9-mm. Uzi semiautomatic carbine. For some reason, he handed ammunition to each of a terrified group of women he ran into—and asked them to hold on to it. One called the police. Chitwood was already aware of the man, Edward Butler, because of some prior instances of aberrant behavior. Butler had vowed that after killing his prey he would not be taken alive. After police took him into custody, they went back to his apartment, where they found a cache of firearms and ammunition. It was all held legally, although "terroristic threats" and "reckless endangerment" were of enough concern to justify his arrest.

Unusual challenges extended into the fall and winter of 1984. At a local K-Mart, a robbery of the day's receipts, some $120,000, was foiled by some courageous clerks. With their accomplice in a truck, the two masked robbers, waiting for the store to close, ran into some unexpected opposition when some employees spotted them, and deciding they looked suspicious, started asking questions. In the resulting confusion, one employee broke free and yelled "Robbery!" Outnumbered if not outgunned, the two panicked and fled. A 19-year-old clerk and junior college student named Robert Reinecker, over in the auto department, thinking it was shoplifters, ran after one of them to the parking lot. When he was hit in the chest by pellets from a shotgun, he realized this might be something a good deal more serious. Fortunately, his wounds were superficial, but he had slowed down his prey. While organizing a search for the foiled robbers, Chitwood referred to Reinecker, "I don't know whether he's a hero or crazy, but the bottom line is that a well-planned, well-organized holdup scheme was aborted by sheer luck."

Concerns about vandalism reached their height at the end of the Christmas break, to the likely delight, even if temporary, of thousands of public, private, and parochial school students. Two teenagers, one suspended from the local high school, and the other a dropout, managed to slash or puncture some 303 tires on 75 school buses, disabling the entire fleet for two days. Chitwood estimated the damage at $60,000. The two suspects were apprehended near Neshaminy High School's gymnasium. Neshaminy's assistant school superintendent, Bernard Hoffman, unlike his students, didn't appreciate the extended vacation. "I don't call it vandalism. Terrorism is a better word. . . . We are just infuriated about it."

*   *   *

Burglary continued to be a constant concern, and it didn't always originate in Philadelphia. A cat burglar who had broken into and robbed over 30 Levittown homes came all the way from New Hampshire. He was arrested after a cooperative effort by three New Jersey townships, where he had also been active. In another series of home invasions, the ringleader came from New Jersey but was arrested in Middletown. Perhaps it was Chitwood's very public emphasis on coordination between community and police, stressing residents' surveillance, that helped to break up such burglary rings. At least the public perception was that there seemed to be a high percentage of local arrests.

Between the ceaseless but challenging variety of such relatively mundane matters as charging a "nuisance" but popular after-hours club with serving liquor illegally after 3:00 a.m., determining just who was guilty in an arson attempt at the I-95 Marketplace, concluding that a publicity-seeking girl of 13 had made up her story of being raped, and putting extra patrols around the area's major shopping center, popular Oxford Valley Mall, Chitwood also faced the reality of the kind of senseless violence he had seen all too often in Philadelphia.

At 2:00 a.m. on an October morning, driving his patrol car only a mile north of Oxford Valley Mall, Patrolman John Bender stopped a pickup truck for running a red light. Just after he approached the driver's open window, saying "Good morning," a shot rang out. Deflected by his badge, which probably saved his life, the bullet from a .38-caliber revolver, aimed at Bender's chest, lodged in his shoulder. Although severely injured, Bender was able to draw his pistol and return fire at the fleeing truck. He shattered its rear window but had no idea whether he'd hit anyone. His bullet-proof vest was still in his vehicle, from which he was able to radio an alert before passing out. A recent weight gain had made the vest difficult for him to get on.

After an intensive eight-hour search for the truck, all four of its occupants, three boys and a girl, were arrested. Two were escapees from a Tampa, Florida, prison, and the other two were runaways. All were teenagers, only 13 to 16. The truck had been stolen in Florida. Jurisdiction would have to be resolved between the two states, but with its more recent incident, Pennsylvania prevailed. Each of the four served jail time, the oldest for attempted murder.

To Chitwood, this narrow escape confirmed his long-held belief in the importance of physical fitness. Out-of-shape officers could be a danger to everyone. In such a small department, Chitwood pointed out to John Martellaro of the *Courier Times*, he could only strongly recommend but not enforce specific weight and fitness standards. However, "physical fitness is vital to a cop's job performance." Patrolman Bender concurred. After being released from the hospital, he vowed to combine a fitness program with his recovery. His aim was to lose enough weight to allow him to fit securely into his uniform, including its bullet-proof vest, and just maybe also get a bigger badge "if I can find one." Next time he might not be so lucky. Shaping up could be a life-saver.

Drug dealing also had deadly overtones. Fugitive Peter David Yannes was wanted in Middletown Township on a series of charges, from failing to show up in court on three occasions to trying to run down two policemen with his car. He had already been convicted of dealing drugs. He was found dead in a Northeast Philadelphia hotel room. Reportedly depressed about a failed romance as well as his future prospects, he left several notes before hanging himself by a drapery cord tied to an overhead beam in his room. In the trunk of his car police found methamphetamine, cocaine, and heroin worth more than $100,000. "He was tired of running," Chitwood concluded, but it was another reminder of the proximity of Bucks County to Northeast Philadelphia.

When not presiding over such events as Crime Prevention Month, Chitwood continued to lead his men personally, particularly on drug busts. After an exchange of meth was observed in a parking lot not far from Middletown's police headquarters, both easily observed participants were arrested. Obtaining a search warrant for one of their apartments but unable to enter, Chitwood's associate used a sledgehammer to knock down the door. They confiscated not only a variety of drugs and extensive paraphernalia, but also a substantial amount of cash and two .22-caliber automatic pistols. There was the same disturbing relationship between drugs and firearms as in Philadelphia—perhaps generally the case. Two days later, another drug raid resulted in four arrests. Shortly thereafter there were three more, based on a tip that "speed" was being sold at an adult bookstore on the edge of town, additional reminders of the necessity for constant vigilance against all the ills of contemporary American society. Middletown was hardly immune.

*   *   *

Nor was it from any of the other perils that afflicted mainly the young. One poignant episode that stayed in Chitwood's memory was only a crime of neglect. An investigation into the apparently accidental deaths of two children, ages six and eight, at the Woods School for mentally and physically handicapped youth considered the possibility of criminal negligence. Both children had been left alone for relatively short but critical periods of time. One had apparently choked on some food; the other had drowned, found face down in her bathtub. There were no arrests, but some suspensions of employees and a program stressing more intensive supervision were put into place.

A growing national concern affecting adolescents, related to both drugs and dangerous driving, was the upsurge in teenage suicides. In 1984, throughout the United States, 14 adolescents a day were committing suicide. Nationwide some 5,000 young Americans killed themselves each year, triple the figure of three decades previously. In June 1984, Chitwood participated with other professionals in a new group organized to prevent teenage suicides. It might not yet be an epidemic in Middletown, but as with crimes like auto theft or home invasions, periodic instances of multiple incidents could be alarming. In November 1983, for example, six Bucks County youths took their own lives, and there were two additional attempts—all apparently related, the "copycat" effect. There had been only two teenage suicides thus far in 1984, but prevention is always preferable to post-tragedy analysis.

Chitwood pointed out that his experience indicated that in nine out of 10 teen suicides drugs or alcohol are involved. He observed, as reported by Gail Hawraney of the *Courier Times*, "That's how they work up the courage to do it," and added that in his experience many auto accidents also are caused by suicidal tendencies. Particularly concerned with potential "clusters" of suicides involving even high-achieving teens who've simply run into some unexpected obstacles, the group put together a coordinated crisis-prevention service. It included presentations to students, parents, teachers, and counselors. Naturally, Chitwood took the lead. In both family conferences and student sessions, he didn't hesitate to show grim slides of what actual suicides looked like. To parents, he also stressed the importance of child safety, wearing seat belts, and not drinking while driving. Thankfully, he didn't yet have to deal with using cell phones or texting.

Another perennial subject was highway safety. As Chitwood pointed out, "Traffic is a big problem in the suburbs." Yes, Middletown was blessed with good roads and major highways, but with so much growth, they were increasingly overwhelmed with traffic, and most roads had been constructed over 30 years before and were in urgent need of maintenance and repair. During 1984, Middletown police investigated 1,824 accidents, some 152 a month. The way things were going, it might someday exceed domestic disturbances as a reason to contact the police. Chitwood formed an Accident Investigation Division to deal with the ongoing problem more efficiently, the first step toward pursuing funds to modernize the entire area's infrastructure.

*   *   *

After having witnessed Chief Chitwood's "very professional" slide presentation on hostage negotiations, the editor of the *Pennsylvania Detective and Police*

Journal pondered in print, "How are they going to keep a guy like Mike up in the farm district?" But then he added, "Only kidding. He loves it." There was no doubt of that. Mike Chitwood had come to feel very comfortable in what was hardly a "farm district" and would be reluctant to leave. Even today, Chitwood reflects on it as not only a fond memory of great relationships, but also "a time of tremendous professional and personal growth for me." However, his aim was ultimately to head the police department in one of the nation's major cities, and he had in mind from the outset staying no more than five years in Bucks County.

An essential objective was gaining those increasingly necessary academic requirements. By commuting to Antioch University's new Philadelphia location two evenings a week and on Sundays, he was able to earn his bachelor's degree in human services by January 1985, and his master of arts in administration in June of 1986. In 1987, they would be supplemented by completion of an 11-week course at the FBI National Academy for police administrators in Quantico, Virginia, and later by postgraduate work at Harvard and Temple Universities.

Educationally progressive Antioch had no "gut" courses, but they took into account all the relevant prior programs Chitwood had attended and his impressive life experiences—to the tune of allowing him 50 credits to enhance his intensive college curriculum. Antioch was particularly strong in the social sciences and was very receptive to accommodating the schedules of hard-pressed men and women intent on overcoming any obstacles to further their ambitions. Most of Chitwood's classmates were women, a high percentage of them African American, and many were single mothers who worked full time while raising a family and running a household. How could they possibly manage to pursue a college degree? Chitwood recalls: "While at Antioch, I learned some very important life lessons. One in particular stands out. . . . I would listen to their stories in utter amazement and I would shake my head and wonder how they did it all."

At his master's graduation, Chitwood was asked to deliver the commencement address. It came from the heart, and drew more than a few tears. He had learned as much from his fellow students as from his professors. In awe of their character and achievements against odds, he could only say that he "shared in their strength and their commitment." The subsequent applause and standing ovation made that address as memorable and meaningful as any Chitwood would ever deliver, buoying his resolve to apply what he had learned in order to improve his own performance.

Mike Chitwood had never forgotten the narrow three-to-two vote of the Middletown supervisors that had won him his current opportunity. As he recalled, the three who had voted for him were a salesman, a plumber, and an elementary school teacher. The two who had voted against him both had master's degrees and vehemently protested entrusting the safety of their community to a "humble homicide detective" lacking even a B.A., who possessed only the "trivial experience" of nearly 20 years of practical policing. Well, at the next interview, wherever and whenever it might be, his academic credentials would no longer be an issue.

*   *   *

In the midst of all this, Chief Chitwood received an impressive reminder that "you can take the man out of the metropolis, but it never quite lets you go." He was named by *Philadelphia* magazine in its 11th annual "Best of Philly" issue as "Best Honest Cop." What that implies about the thousands of other still-active Philadelphia police officers is best left to conjecture. In 1984, when the issue came out, Chitwood had already been in Middletown Township for the better part of a year, but here he was, still honored as "The Best of Philly," placed somewhere between "Best Hoagie" and "Best Facial." As editor Ron Javers put it in a note to all the winners, accompanying their handsome plaques, "Congratulations! After much tasting, testing and deliberation, our panel of judges for the 11th Best of Philly competition has decided that you're the best. Of all the people who do what you do, we consider you the top . . . and keep up the good work." It pays to be an "honest cop."

Not much later, Chitwood would get another unexpected accolade, reminding him of those great days (and endless nights). Detective Carol Keenan, 35, also from South Philly, became the first woman permanently assigned to the homicide unit of the Philadelphia Police Department. There was as yet no woman in Middletown Township's modest police force. As Joe Clark put it in the *Daily News*, she "has been in and out of the . . . homicide unit for five years, but now she's 'going home' for good." In her first homicide case, Keenan had worked with Chitwood on the rape and murder of Nicky Caserta, the case that had changed his life. Now she would actually wear his old badge, number 710. "He was more than helpful," Keenan said of Chitwood. "I am very proud to wear his badge. I hope I can be half the cop Mike Chitwood was. Then I hope someday I can help someone the way he helped me."

*   *   *

Too soon the memories of mayhem would intrude in a more ominous way. However, for the immediate future his focus remained on the job at hand. In *The Law Officer's Magazine-Police* of June 1985, "The Beat" column by Franz Serdahely, entitled "Switch to the Suburbs," ended with observations by and about Mike Chitwood's experience in Middletown Township. "Chief Chitwood believes he has focused the direction of his department in a positive, helpful way" while "broadening his own law enforcement career experiences . . . his own psychological attitudes and objectives," building credibility and trust with his officers and the entire community. "Chitwood's shift to the suburbs was perhaps the most important step taken in his law enforcement career."

Throughout 1985 and into 1986, Chitwood continued to cope with and try to contain crimes not unlike those his department had faced in 1983 and '84. Some of his activities including the following:

Warning residents and businesses alike to review their security procedures at a time when terrorism was on the rise.

Giving protective advice to the growing senior-citizen population or people dealing with mental-health problems.

Advising what to do in hostage situations.

Rescuing a woman who had been kidnapped and raped by a would-be suitor.

Responding to increased drug and alcohol abuse, especially among the young, including a crackdown on teen drinking.

Determining how to deal with a threatened homeowner who had used an Uzi semi-automatic to kill a robbery suspect.

Having yet another private plane intrude into local airspace, carrying a drug smuggler from the south, this one killed when his aircraft crashed just short of Buehl Field.

Disarming a man threatening others with what turned out to be a toy gun.

Combating new instances of random vandalism, the most destructive being the smashing of car windows.

Closing the notorious Club Demi, a nightspot that had previously enjoyed police protection.

Coordinating a drug bust that arrested the major suppliers of narcotics to students in the Neshaminy School District.

Catching an intrusive five-and-a-half-foot boa constrictor that had slithered into a local home from parts unknown—a new experience.

Inevitably, the police sometimes were too late, as when a deranged gunman sprayed bullets into a Levittown home, killing two residents and injuring one before killing himself. The customary cause—rejection by a young woman from her family. There had been a number of prior complaints, but there could be no legal arrest of 26-year-old Robert Martin in the absence of a specific threat. The "what ifs" of such senseless violence are bound to haunt any conscientious cop.

Near the end of 1985, Chitwood denied that he was under active consideration for the job of Philadelphia police commissioner. In a telephone interview with George Mattar of the *Courier Times*, he remarked, "I have not been considered, nor am I actively seeking the position." He did not deny, however, that he had talked with Philadelphia Mayor W. Wilson Goode, the city's first African American mayor. Reportedly, morale in the city's police department was low, particularly in the wake of the historic MOVE debacle. Having been on the scene in 1978, when members of that well-armed black separatist movement had been evicted from a house in a gunfight that left one policeman dead, Chitwood was certainly well situated to offer advice. Respectable families in long-established, predominantly black neighborhoods were particularly anxious to not have these disruptive, confrontational, unsanitary, law-breaking MOVE members as neighbors. However, in another attempted eviction in May 1985 that went terribly wrong, 11 people were killed and 61 homes were destroyed by fire as police dropped a bomb on the MOVE block of Osage Avenue in West Philadelphia. The memory would stay with Goode long after his tenure as mayor had ended.

It wasn't surprising that Mike's name would come up. Nor that rumors would surface about other job possibilities, such as in Lower Merion Township. Chitwood insisted to Mattar that were he to consider leaving Middletown Township for any other job, he would "give plenty of notice to the supervisors," while agreeing that it was his position as its police chief that had "given him the opportunity to be considered." However, his protestations that at only 41, he was still too young to be commissioner of a police force the size of Philadelphia's was somewhat less than convincing. This was hardly the last time he would be considered or promoted for the Philly job by the local media.

*   *   *

The most horrifying crime in the whole of Chitwood's experience, prior or subsequent, was not committed within Middletown, but wound up there in July 1986. Even though he had left Philadelphia three years before, Chitwood had the momentary suspicion that perhaps this might have been intended as some sort of murderous message for him personally, stemming from some previous confrontation.

The bodies of two unidentified men (at least, seemingly men, although remnants of women's clothing had been found—both dismembered and sexually mutilated) had been stuffed into plastic trash bags, their separated legs included, and then apparently transported from some unknown location, deposited, and set on fire off Trenton Road in Middletown Township. What looked to be a brush fire was noted by passing motorists, who called the local fire department. After finding the body bags, they contacted the police. Surveying the victims, Chitwood described the scene as "the most gruesome I have ever seen" and termed the murders a "well-planned, animalistic, sadistic act . . . premeditated, cold, calculating . . . [by] somebody who is filled with hatred . . . some kind of sex-torture murders for whatever reason." The decomposed condition of the bodies made identification especially difficult.

Chitwood had come to view his domain as a kind of still largely safe citadel, its ramparts constantly under assault from outsiders bent on mischief. But this was something beyond burglary or drugs. In his years of dealing with crime in all its dimensions, he had never encountered anything more horrifying. Despite the size of the victims—the larger one was six feet three and weighed about 190 pounds— the remains of women's clothing led to at least the possibility that both men were homosexuals or transvestites. Autopsies concluded that one victim had been shot, and the other suffocated. All the physical evidence had been sent to the FBI. Chitwood reached out to Mark Segal, publisher of the *Philadelphia Gay News,* to run a description of the two men and also to contact gay newspapers in New York, asking them to call in if they had any idea who these two might be. At least there were still fingerprints and the potential for forensic reconstruction.

Remarkably, by July 20, one victim was identified—Faustino Arroyo, 27, of Camden, New Jersey, a male prostitute with a lengthy record for burglary and car theft in Philadelphia, Camden, and New York. In a joint news conference, Chitwood and Bucks County District Attorney Alan M. Rubinstein said their investigation would now center on the Locust Street strip in Philadelphia, frequented by male prostitutes.

By mid-August, police were able to identify the second victim, Jonathan Streater, 31, who also had an extensive record of prior arrests. Chitwood announced that the FBI had matched Streater's prints with those previously taken by the Philadelphia police. Moreover, there had been numerous phone calls about both men. Both were African Americans who, dressed and made up as women, engaged in prostitution, particularly in Center City Philadelphia. Streater had been known to many acquaintances as "Tanya Moore," and Arroyo as "Tina Rodrigues."

Bob Bowers of the *Courier Times* explored the often dangerous world of such transvestites. "The men who would be females . . . take a fatalistic view of their lot in life. Theirs is a world in which convention is shredded and thrown to the wind." Tanya, according to one who had lived with her, "was very clean-cut. She went to church and visited her mother. But Tanya would travel to different places all the time because she was boy-crazy. . . . Basically, for transvestites that leads to prostitution. . . . We already have three strikes against us. We have to deal with society . . . the cops . . . and the tricks. And now we have to deal with a madman." But who was he? And why would he, or others, want to so brutally murder these two "men who would be females"? Might they have tried, as Chitwood surmised, "to rip off the wrong guy? That's certainly one scenario." Both Tanya and Tina were known to have been in South Philadelphia in late June.

By mid-August, there were two suspects, at least in terms of composite drawings assembled by police, both white and both male, between 25 and 35. Several other prostitutes had come forward to say they had seen the two victims enter a light-colored, medium-size car in Center City in the early morning of June 30. When the car had pulled up to the corner of 13th and Sansom Streets, Arroyo hollered out, "Does anyone want to party? The money's good." Other prostitutes gathered around; the two potential "johns" selected Tina and Tanya, and drove off with them. It is not known if either man was aware that both of their passengers were transvestites. None of the others had ever seen these two men before. Their car headed north on 13th Street. Their passengers would never be seen alive again. Chitwood was not yet clear about what had motivated the murders. Might there have been an attempted "rip-off" in either direction?

It took a long time to find the murder suspects, both of whom, it turned out, had been involved in criminal activities of their own, including armed robbery. However, both had to be released for lack of specific evidence in terms of these murders. It is one of Chitwood's abiding regrets that he was unable to solve this most horrible crime in his entire career, even though it took place out of his jurisdiction.

*   *   *

The highlight of Mike Chitwood's 1987 was completing that 11-week, highly coveted training program at the federally funded FBI National Academy. His classmates included several attorneys, a colleague with a doctorate in political administration, and the number-two man in the Guatemalan police force. The highlight of 1988 was being inducted at a luncheon in Pittsburgh into the International Police Hall of Fame. His former rival for the Middletown post back in 1983, and still his second in command, Lt. James Duncan, was gracious in his observation that Chitwood's coming to Middletown represented little in the way of transition: "The guy came along and fit like a glove."

In between, fortunately, there were no more startling incidents like the uncovering of the two transvestites, but much that reminded Chitwood of what he'd encountered and participated in since 1983, enhanced by the community involvement he'd developed:

Stopping drug trafficking at a home in a working-class neighborhood, where neighbors alerted police to an unusual amount of daily and nightly traffic.

Chasing a highway toll evader, resulting in the crash of three cars and an injured officer.

Expressing pride in his officers giving seminars to police across the commonwealth in accident-investigation techniques.

Increasing drug arrests, with confiscated drug money used to finance undercover operations.

Suggesting that the training of constables be enhanced and supporting two of his officers when they had been sued for using unnecessary force—a familiar complaint.

Observing more firings at the Woods School, the site of earlier tragedy.

Forging an amicable pact with the police union.
Involvement in attempts to improve local roads.
Setting guidelines in terms of dealing with infectious disease.
Assuring a safe Halloween.
Retaining school buses for local children in view of so much increased traffic.
Talking another barricaded gunman into surrendering.

That so much of this involved activities not directly or even remotely related to normal police work may well have enhanced Mike Chitwood's qualifications for greater responsibility elsewhere. In 1988, he was in his fifth year as police chief of Middletown Township, the time frame he had originally envisioned. He saw an ad in a professional journal, soliciting applicants for a larger position. It wasn't in New York or Boston, let alone—at least this time—even the seemingly obvious location of troubled Philadelphia. It was "Down East," or, in reality, due north, up in Portland, Maine. Although the largest city in the state, it boasted a population of only 65,000, not all that much larger than Middletown's, and covered some 23 square miles, only four more than Middletown. But its police force numbered 153 officers (Middletown's was now up to 47), with a support staff of 50, and an annual budget of $4.6 million. Although neither the state capital nor the home of the principal state university, Portland, situated by a scenic shoreline, was and is the center of everything else in the state, business and cultural—a major city in all but its physical dimensions. The job would pay initially somewhere between $44,000 and $57,000, likely in the higher direction, which would total at least modestly more than Chitwood's current $47,000. But money was never his major motivation. He thought it over and decided to apply. Nearing 45, he was no longer the youngest of the four applicants ultimately selected to be finalists. But on his trip up to be interviewed, they must have forgotten to tell him about the weather.

From stocky, dedicated patrolman in the 1960s...

to dapper detective in 1981, the most decorated
policeman in Philadelphia history.

Courtesy of the Philadelphia History Museum
at the Atwater Kent. Photo by Neil Benson.

Still at it today.
Upper Darby Police Superintendent Mike Chitwood with his drug-busting team.

Philadelphia magazine, March 2007. Photo by Chris Crisman

It takes hours of daily conditioning...

to keep up the pace.

Upper Darby Police Department files. Photo by Charles Peatross

A moving symbol of peace.
Portland Police Chief Chitwood joins a group of international runners.

Portland Press Herald, August 13, 2001. Photo by Jill Brady

The personification of preparedness.
Upper Darby Police Superintendent Chitwood with the spoils of a gun battle.

Delaware County Daily Times, December 21, 2010. Photo by Robert Gurecki

Personally on the scene,
from working with victims of sexual abuse...

Portland Press Herald, December 7, 2004. Photo by John Ewing

to joining his men in investigating a murder.

Delaware County Daily Times, April 9, 2012. Photo by Eric Hartline

But sometimes community involvement includes some clowning around...

Delaware County Daily Times, November 1, 2005. Photo by Pete Zinner

or even "arresting" the Phillie Phanatic

Upper Darby Police Department files. Photo by Joann DiMauro

Crime crosses city lines.
Even as criminal activity has fallen nationally during the past decade,
it has risen in such "inner-ring" adjacent communities as Upper Darby.
A major reason has been the proximity of Philadelphia—the immediate
source of a disproportionate percentage of Upper Darby's crime.
To combat the rise, Police Superintendent Chitwood stresses community
involvement and high visibility. Here he appears with civilian liaison
officer Nashid Furaha-Ali outside a community police station.

Philadelphia Inquirer, April 23, 2012.

A unique legacy in crime prevention:
the two Mike Chitwoods, from Florida and Pennsylvania, as they appear today.

Daytona Beach Police Department files.
Photo by Nigel Cook.

Upper Darby Police Department files.
Photo by Charles Peatross

"Media Mike" Meets Maine

Emerging as a finalist for the Portland job, Mike Chitwood had not only survived an extensive background check, but had also talked several times over the phone with his potential employers. Now they wanted to meet with him in person. On a Thursday afternoon, Chitwood set off for Maine. It was to be only an overnight stay, the Friday morning session including both his interview with the city manager and some concentrated psychological testing, enabling him to fly back on Friday afternoon. Continuing to follow his mother's admonition to travel light, Mike packed little more than a toothbrush and some clean underwear.

The news was already out. In mid-February 1988, both the *Portland Press Herald* and the *Bucks County Courier Times* had the same lead story—the identity of their police chief. In Maine, who would be coming? In Middletown, would Mike be leaving? The prior Portland chief, less than universally admired, had departed to head a state drug bureau. Chitwood felt a sense of déjà vu about the selection process. There always seemed to be three or four finalists, culled from a great many applicants, and at least one would be local. This time two of Chitwood's competitors came from the immediate area, but now both were younger than he. The other finalist, the former police chief of Springfield, Illinois, eased out by a new administration, was a decade older. Moreover, there was the same emphasis on psychological evaluation, only this time unaccompanied by a lie-detector test.

Asked with the others by the Portland paper to summarize his experiences and outlook, Chitwood stressed themes familiar in Middletown. "Crime," he pointed out, "is a community problem. It is not only a police problem." In terms of auto theft, Portland's most prevalent crime, he would supplement visible cops on the street with a highly trained undercover team. In conjunction with a fully involved, informed community, "I don't think there's any problem that a group of professional police officers can't address." Chitwood went on to express his complete confidence in the Portland psychiatrist he was soon to meet. Indeed, he later told Ted Cohen of the *Press Herald*, "I believe all police officers should have psychological evaluations.... Society demands professionalism from its police officers. You wouldn't want someone in police work who could be a sociopath."

Of course, there was also that vital new element in Mike Chitwood's résumé. As the *Press Herald* summarized, "Chitwood said he offers Portland a blend of police and management skills, with a bachelor's degree in human services and a master's in administration as his educational background." No matter how much he had learned on the streets and in harm's way, and how cognizant he was of such enlightened adjuncts to professional police work as psychology, Chitwood had come to understand how essential academic credentials were to advancing his career.

His plane arrived on time, and soon he was settled into a downtown hotel. That night he had a vivid dream. He was in Hawaii and waves were crashing against the shore. As he woke, he realized the sound was real. It was actually the wind blowing against his hotel room window. He looked out to see snow hurtling sideways against the building. It was a storm of more intensity than he had ever before witnessed. Yet when he rose the next morning, people in the lobby seemed to be taking it pretty much in stride. Although the snowstorm had scarcely abated, there was a cab available to take him to his interview.

Tiptoeing through several inches of snow to keep his pants and shoes reasonably dry, Chitwood made it to the interview and completed the testing as scheduled. In fact, everything appeared to go quite well. However, by the time he emerged, snow having accumulated all day, the airport was already closed. Even by the standards of the region, this was a major storm. As it turned out, no planes would take off until the following Tuesday. Eventually there were 23 inches of snow on the ground. Shoveled and plowed, the banks piled up outside his hotel reached five to six feet in height.

After multiple days indoors, although the hotel restaurant remained open, Chitwood was feeling a bit claustrophobic. The concierge was good enough to lend him a pair of boots and an overcoat so that he might emerge cautiously to look around, stop for coffee, and get his bearings. By the time he was finally able to arrange to take the first plane back to tropical Philadelphia, Chitwood had resolved that there was no way in the world he could live, let alone run a police force, in so inhospitable a climate.

* * *

Upon reflection, Mike changed his mind. A series of phone calls from the city manager didn't hurt. Weather was simply a fact of life and, climate aside, Portland had been (and still is) frequently cited as one of the most "livable" cities in the United States. Beyond offering a challenging opportunity in line with Chitwood's career goals, Portland's history and amenities were undeniably appealing. Indeed, its very extremes in weather stemmed from its scenic seaport setting, on a coastal peninsula in Casco Bay, leading to the Gulf of Maine and the Atlantic Ocean. Its humid summers might sometimes soar into the 90s. Its winters, including fierce nor'easters, could dip below zero. But most of the time it merged moderation with precipitation. Chitwood finally decided that a few degrees of volatility shouldn't dissuade his decision, if it came to that.

He got the job. And in time he fell in love with the place. Leaving Middletown Township was not only Mike Chitwood's "most difficult" decision, but a reluctant recognition of reality by those with whom he had worked. They understood that this was never intended to be his final destination. Just before getting the news, Chitwood told Donna Shaw of the *Inquirer*, "People say, 'Are you nuts? You've got it made where you are.' I don't think there's another police chief in the county who's gotten the kind of support I've had." Middletown Township supervisor Robert J. Brann referred to the great void they would now have to fill. "[Chitwood] gets along with everybody. . . . He's a good listener, very perceptive. . . . I can only wish him luck."

There was a special commemorative ceremony in Langhorne, this time with Chief Chitwood on the receiving end. His tenure was bookended with a second letter from those senior citizens who had welcomed him originally, "We will not only miss you, but remember you kindly." Just about the only person who demurred was his long-term predecessor as Middletown chief, who suggested that Chitwood had used the job as a stepping stone in his career. Well, of course. Doesn't any ambitious person's career imply a progression to bigger things?

Leaving for Maine in March, Chitwood mused about the past quarter-century. Sometimes, after all these years, he still missed the excitement and unpredictability of patrolling a beat, one reason he always wanted to be out there with his troops as events unfolded. It helped his morale as well as theirs. Well, he later suggested to a reporter from the *Press Herald*, "If things become too quiet, I can always get up and go out."

To be sure, from what he'd been told, Portland's crimes, like Middletown's, tended more to auto theft and home burglary than to violent homicide or hostage-taking. But such apparent similarities can be misleading. Although not all that different in physical size or population, in regional significance Greater Portland was the polar opposite (no pun intended) of a Middletown Township. Chitwood's prior posting was a suburb. The central city of Portland is a hub, surrounded by an expansive metropolitan area of over a half-million residents, more than a third of the state's population. Even in bureaucratic terms, this represented new territory for the new chief of police.

*   *   *

We can sometimes make too much of differing regional characteristics throughout the United States—from the supposed reticence of frigid New Englanders to the warm hospitality of those in the sunny South. However, it's fair to conclude that the residents of Portland had never previously encountered a public servant quite like the man they soon came to call "Media Mike."

"There will be no overnight miracles," Chitwood projected at the outset to the Portland media. "It'll be a process of the police officers learning to trust me" and of getting to know one another. "My ability to lead," he added in his favored alliterative mode, "is based on principle, professionalism, participation, and pride . . . consensus-building, not confrontation." In an interview with Ted Cohen of the *Press Herald*, Chitwood reflected back to the incident in his Philadelphia days that had affected his outlook only a little less than the rape and murder of Nicky Caserta. In his prior career, he had to defend himself many times and had been obliged to shoot at and wound a number of suspects. But he had never actually killed anyone. During the course of that running gun battle with a drug suspect 12 years before, Chitwood's partner had been shot through a door. He still bore the crippling effects of his near-fatal injury. When, using a sledgehammer, Chitwood broke down the door and the scumbag emerged, his gun blazing, he was carrying a two-year-old as a shield. "But for the grace of God I did not fire my weapon," Chitwood recalled. "I would have killed a small child." Somehow he managed to subdue the drug suspect without shooting, at the risk of his own life. Carrying a gun can be a necessity in police work, particularly in such perilous times, but that incident cemented Chitwood's personal reluctance to do so. As Portland's police chief, it was still a last resort, and prudent gun control would be a pervasive theme of his tenure in the job.

*   *   *

Mike Chitwood was sworn in on April 11, 1988, and set about decorating his new office wall with rows of photographs, commendations, and decorations for merit. He didn't mind exhibiting his previous accomplishments. It couldn't hurt. His first day, characteristically from 8:00 to 8:00, involved meeting as many city officials as possible and concluded with a freewheeling interview. Dennis Hoey of the *Press Herald* described Chitwood as "a straight-from-the-hip" fast and free-talking, hands-on administrator with expressive gestures, an answer for everything, and a ready wit. He had been boning up on the Maine driver's test and wanted to know if there were any cheesesteak sandwiches in Portland. He knew there'd be pizza. As always, Chitwood stressed the vital importance of openness with the media. He said he was originally drawn to police work for its "excitement" and that he had accepted the job in Portland for two reasons—"career advancement and quality of life." He also noted that he continued to work out strenuously and ran two miles every day. Soon there would be a prominent photo in the local press of this still slim, trim, neatly mustached, grimacing, middle-aged man doing rigorous weight exercises. He was a media godsend.

Chitwood's style hadn't really changed since Middletown, nor had the nature of his earliest confrontations. Once again, he was upset by the lax administration of the local juvenile detention facility. Chitwood quickly concluded that on any given day, 20 to 25 percent of the residents from the Maine Youth Center in South Portland were AWOL and that these runaways were a major cause of auto theft and home burglaries. He organized a group of city officials to pressure the state legislature to tighten their juvenile justice system. Might a security fence around the facility, for example, really inhibit rehabilitation? Then he assembled a meeting of a new group called Citizens Against Auto Crime, wasting little time in taking charge. He also launched a program of public education to convince owners to take such practical precautions as not leaving valuables in their cars. A *Portland Evening Press* editorial welcoming their new police chief noted that 25 cars had been vandalized on the very day he had been sworn in. Chitwood had already shown "he understands that a problem of small crimes can loom large in the lives of a community's residents. So far so good, chief."

*　　*　　*

While pushing for long-term solutions to the juvenile crime problem, such as more security guards and regional centers to help relieve crowding in the South Portland facility, Chitwood was also visibly alert to any assaults, verbal or physical, on the members of his new police force. When an officer was violently attacked by three men while investigating an early-morning auto accident and all three were quickly released from jail, Chitwood was furious. Three passersby, one an off-duty policeman, had come to the officer's aid. While commending them for doing "a brave thing that may have saved a man's life," Chitwood assailed the bail commissioners for so quickly releasing the assailants after they had been apprehended. At the same time, however, he determined to improve his own department's reporting procedures. It was classic Chitwood—vent your spleen, but suggest solutions.

Also important to Mike was finding any conceivable way to involve and then commend both his officers and the community. When there were difficulties in developing a bank's surveillance-camera film after a robbery, Maine Video Systems quickly got involved and developed the film for Chitwood. After seeing the pictures, an enterprising policeman spotted the suspect, a fugitive from New York, and arrested him a few blocks from the bank. "It's just what I've been talking about," Chitwood told the *Evening Express*, "the need for community-police cooperation."

After only a matter of months, the new chief seemed not only to be in the news with unusual frequency, but also to assist in manufacturing it. What is more comforting to residents than the symbolic significance of mounted patrolmen looming protectively above them? Moreover, they can get to places police cars can't. But, although the five horses in Portland's mounted unit were all donated, they did consume a lot of hay and grain. While recognizing some sentiment for phasing out the patrol, Chitwood decided in favor of keeping it. In terms of crime deterrence, he noted, "There is something about an officer on a horse." And while "cruisers have their place, I'd rather pat a horse." Of course, it all lent itself to endearing visual coverage in the press and on local TV.

Long-term planning was also initiated. In July, Chitwood launched the first recruiting campaign in the history of Portland's police department, anticipating the retirement of some 60 personnel in the next five years. After a collision of two police cars in which three officers were injured, Chitwood tightened the policy on wearing seatbelts at all times and set up a driver-training program. Even while planning to teach his new officers about the techniques of hostage and crisis nego-tiations, Chitwood seemingly couldn't avoid getting personally and very publicly involved. Jogging on a Sunday morning, he heard on the portable radio he carried a police dispatcher's call for officers to investigate a report of someone threatening to jump from the top of the 200-foot Maine Medical Center parking garage. Get-ting there about the same time as two of his men, Chitwood found another patrol-man already on the scene, trying to talk the despondent 23-year-old out of leaping to his death. The four then took turns trying to reason with him. Eventually, his girlfriend was brought to the scene, and the young man agreed to come down and be taken to a psychiatric hospital for evaluation. Although so highly experienced in dealing with would-be suicides and hostage-takers, Chitwood expressed to the local media that he didn't plan to make it a regular part of his personal responsibili-ties in Maine. He just kept running into incidents.

Perhaps it was not quite a presidential parallel, but the *Evening Express* evalu-ated on its front page of July 19, 1988, the first hundred days of Mike Chitwood's tenure in Portland. He was pictured smiling, something he seemed to be doing a lot more as he got older. It is interesting that in the very first paragraph staff writer Bob Niss pointed out that Chitwood was "still committed to serving at least five years and unruffled by the attention he has attracted so far." Chitwood had rarely been ruffled by attention, but he had never revealed so specific a time frame while at Middletown. There should be no surprises this time, when and if he left for the next big step.

Chitwood described his first hundred days in Portland as "frantic ... the fast-est period in my life." Having so quickly reacted to the deluge of car break-ins and vandalism, the collision of police cruisers, the youth detention problem, and many other challenges, Chitwood expressed his appreciation of the work ethic he'd found throughout Portland and the degree of cooperation within and beyond the department. He still tried to get out of his office as much as possible, even reluctantly conveying demonstrators at the demolition site of an historic building to a paddy wagon. But when in his office, he also still liked to take calls from the public personally. Overall, he pronounced himself "very happy here."

Still, Chitwood saw a cloud just over the horizon. "Portland's an exciting city . . . on the move. But it is an urban city with growing urban crime problems," perhaps less a relatively secure haven than in the past. Drugs in particular and the crimes they cause are the greatest potential concern, a subject with which he had some acquaintance. Chitwood added a plea for local law enforcement officers to be compensated more in line with the pay scales of other major cities and noted the excessive workload of the local DA's office. In his limited free time, Chitwood was enjoying "acting like a tourist," with so many inviting attractions to explore, from Kennebunkport to Castine.

When there were two bank robberies in Portland within a single day, a rare occurrence, Chitwood rushed back from Lewiston, while hastening to assure the public that 90 percent of local bank robberies had led—and would lead—to arrests, maybe someday 100 percent. In August, having thought it through, he reorganized the police department into two separate divisions to improve cooperation between those who respond directly to crimes and those whose responsibility it is to solve them. Later that month the first group of officers "graduated" from Chitwood's refresher driving course. As he had pointed out, Portland was not immune to even the most bizarre phenomena afflicting larger cities. In the first such incident in the city's history, two men wearing Ku Klux Klan robes and hoods were arrested outside a housing complex partially occupied by members of the city's modest black population. Later, when local "skinheads" assaulted members of Portland's gay community, Chitwood was quick to react, vowing, "We will not tolerate hate groups in this town."

As in Middletown, Chitwood continued his policy of talking with local groups as frequently as possible. To legislators he urged stiffer drug and theft penalties as well as attention to ostensibly victimless, quality-of-life crimes such as loitering, disturbing the peace, public intoxication, and prostitution. The past would never quite disappear. In October, he returned to Philadelphia to reenact for a TV show his brief but dramatic role in the infamous Einhorn case. What bothered Mike most, beyond the fact that Einhorn had not yet been apprehended, was all the makeup he was obliged to wear. An accidental shooting by one of his officers (for which he was later cleared) brought back to the fore Chitwood's ambivalence about guns, and a Portland appearance by George H.W. Bush rekindled his concern with security. Some welcome and meaningful recreation came when Chitwood led the 27-mile AIDS "Bike for Hope" bikeathon from Portland to a nearby connected island and back. It was nothing new. He had the experience of pedaling a stationary bicycle nearly every day for years as part of his rigorous regimen. Chitwood was involved in everything, even going to "jail" ("Celebrity Jail 'n' Bail") to raise funds to fight birth defects.

*   *   *

With the end of his first year in Portland, however, so many memories of past challenges had recurred that Chitwood may have felt he was in a time warp. Much of it involved his perpetual concern with the use and misuse of firearms, which put him in conflict with powerful pressure groups. As Nancy Grape reiterated in the *Sunday Maine Telegram*, "There are days when . . . Chitwood must feel he traveled farther than from Philadelphia to Portland when he took the chief's job. . . . Otherwise, how is it that he keeps ending up a Wyatt Earp shooting it out with the Sportsman's Alliance of Maine and gun-totin' lawmakers in Augusta?" Beyond that escalating dispute, he tried to achieve a sensible balance between law and order and his affirmation of civil liberties.

Chitwood had already instituted a peer-support-team counseling program within the police department, just as he had in Middletown, to deal with the inevitable stress of the job. It differed little from one locale to another. So much of what is now termed post-traumatic stress syndrome was work-related, and much of it was gun-related. There had been a number of incidents that summer, from the results of that patrol-car collision to the accidental shooting of a civilian and the brutal beating of a policeman on duty. Not to mention everything officers ran into on a daily basis. As he had before, Chitwood reminded the public, "Just because someone wears a uniform doesn't mean they aren't affected by tragedy." Simply when dealing with violent and dysfunctional families, "without the sophisticated training of a psychologist, [police] need tools like this peer group to keep their own equilibrium."

As in Middletown, reaction to Chitwood's very public posture was mostly positive, as indicated in this letter to the *Express* from the public relations officer of the AIDS project: "The people of Portland, in my eyes, have the greatest police chief of any major city in the country. . . . A man who would get involved with the AIDS project's bikeathon and pedal a bike 27 miles has to be extraordinary. It takes a man of strong courage and leadership to perform all his duties in so many ways." And for the first time in recent memory, Portland and its police benevolent association settled on a labor contract before the old agreement had expired.

Sometimes Chitwood's duties were not so pleasurable. Part of Portland's appeal was its wealth of historic and attractive old buildings. In the absence of a preservation ordinance, one after another of these structures was being demolished to make way for commercial development, as in so many other communities. When a group of citizens headed by "the Portland Seven" vainly attempted to interfere with the legal demolition of an Italianate mansion by confronting the bulldozers, Chitwood had been obliged to arrest them. Eventually, criminal trespass charges were dropped, to which he responded that the matter had always been more a social issue than a crime. Although, as noted, Chitwood had personally headed the operation, privately he sided with the preservationists.

*　　*　　*

Increasingly, Chitwood was preoccupied with establishing a practical, balanced policy to deal with the possession and potential use of guns. From the start, in this area, he courted controversy. It escalated when he campaigned for tougher concealed-weapons permit laws by enforcing an old 19th-century ordinance that made it a crime to carry firearms in the city from sunset to sunrise. Hunters had always been a sizeable and influential constituency in Maine. In that regard, Chitwood stressed that conscientious sportsmen were not the people he was worried about. But did it make sense that someone seeking a hunting license had to demonstrate proficiency while the laws governing permit applications for concealed weapons allowed the police to check the background only of people in psychiatric institutions? Meanwhile, Chitwood could point to progress in other areas. In the year he had been at the helm, the persistent problem of thefts from Portland's motor vehicles had been reduced by over 1,200. He must have been doing something right.

Chitwood's relations with sportsmen and gun enthusiasts remained an issue. Echoing Nancy Grape's column, Clark Canfield in a *Press Herald* article headlined "Chief Faces 'High Noon'" quoted officers of the Sportsman's Alliance of Maine and the National Rifle Association. Inevitably, despite Chitwood's popularity in Portland, focus returned to his past. "Philadelphia is not Portland," a pistol range owner insisted in the same article. "We don't have big city problems here yet." That they were bound to come was Chitwood's essential premise. He raised the stakes by joining with Portland's city attorney to file a challenge with the state supreme court to declare the current statewide law on gun permits unconstitutional. In one of the milder reactions from opponents, an NRA representative called the case "frivolous."

Chitwood gathered facts and figures, citing permit-holders who had run afoul of the law. The issue received national attention. Howard Kurtz wrote in the *Washington Post* that at a time when other states were also moving toward more sweeping gun restrictions, Maine's debate might seem "tame by comparison." There had been only four homicides in Portland during all of 1988. "But any suggestion of greater police control cuts deeply into the fabric of Yankee individualism." Chitwood, who knew what guns are about, told Kurtz that he realized that many people in Maine might view him "as a meddlesome outsider." But he also had become, as

Kurtz pointed out, "a local celebrity who takes solace when people stop him on the street to voice support for his cause."

In the process, Mike Chitwood had also become something of a national celebrity. On April 12, 1989, his first anniversary on the job in Portland, Paul Clancy vividly described this unique police chief in *USA Today*. A lawman whose whole purpose was protection didn't carry a gun. As Chitwood, who had investigated hundreds of murders, put it, "Knowing what one small projectile can do to a human being, my focus is public safety." Clancy characterized Chitwood as being prepared, if necessary, to enforce stronger laws for the possession of handguns, and to fight his case all the way up to the Supreme Court of the United States. What were his plans to celebrate this first anniversary? "I'm being taken to lunch," Chitwood replied, grinning, "but not by the NRA." He had also been interviewed on NBC and was drawing mail, pro and con, on this hot-button issue from throughout the nation. Overall, he concluded, "It's been a great year."

*   *   *

In the meantime, Chitwood was going forward with other innovations. He not only made the wearing of seatbelts mandatory for all of Portland's cops, not a standard practice at the time, he turned "guns into plowshares" by auctioning off weapons confiscated in connection with crimes (only federally licensed dealers were permitted to bid) to purchase bullet-resistant vests, new shotguns, and repair parts for the use of his police force. Teddy bears were provided by a local radio station for police to take to children in the local community who'd been traumatized by crime or catastrophe. He championed new regulations requiring towing-company operators to charge uniform rates, contact police prior to towing away any vehicle, and in general stop ripping off the public. That was popular even with gun owners. An ominous development at this time was the first appearance of crack cocaine in Portland, a harbinger of the escalation in drug-related crimes that Chitwood had predicted. Drug busts were already becoming common.

At the behest of one of his captains, Chitwood had this "Mission Statement" placed on a wall in the lobby of the Public Safety Building: "The Portland Police Department is dedicated to the enhancement of the quality of life throughout the city of Portland by working cooperatively with all of our citizens to preserve the peace, enforce the law, reduce the perception of fear and provide for a safe and caring environment."

The very infrequency of murder tended to underscore Chitwood's concern with its unpredictability. In April 1989, the first killing of a Maine state trooper in 25 years shocked law enforcement professionals across the state. The trooper was investigating reports of child abuse at a trailer home in rural Leeds. He was shot to death by one occupant, who then turned the gun on himself and his live-in girlfriend. To Chitwood, the Leeds case, as well as a double murder-suicide in Scarborough, further underscored the necessity of a state licensing procedure for firearms. He renewed his invitation to Portland's gun owners to at least attend police-sponsored safety classes for their use.

Even as he faced such varied challenges as coordinating a city-wide drug sweep that netted 18 street dealers, trying to save a suicidal barricaded man who had lost his job, promoting a new jail to be placed next to the troubled youth center, supporting a gay-rights bill in the Maine legislature, and dealing with the brutal murder of a teenaged girl on Portland's waterfront, Chitwood still found time to be a "celebrity waiter" at a dinner to raise money for the American Heart Association and serve as grand marshal of the annual Memorial Day parade. Following that sort of unpredictable, concentrated schedule, perhaps he might welcome some personal use of that counseling program he had set up to deal with the stress of police work.

With the ongoing gun controversy, the letters kept coming to both Chitwood and the media, now more than ever. A local resident wrote to the *Express:* "Maine vs. Pennsylvania. Portland vs. Philadelphia. I've had enough of this. Why can we not support our police chief Michael Chitwood to restore Portland to what it once was—a clean, safe city?" Her sentiments were echoed by a woman from South Thomason: "It is refreshing to see someone in the public eye champion a cause because it is what he believes, not because it will win him a popularity contest." On the other hand, a local activist challenging Chitwood's renewed use of that old Portland sunrise-to-sunset law in Cumberland County Superior Court insisted that the chief "is circumventing state law and he has no more right to do that than I do. Legal precedents will show the police have gone too far."

On to year two.

*   *   *

Despite such setbacks as the passage of a lobbyist-supported state gun law in the Maine legislature that superseded Mike Chitwood's stronger stand in Portland, throughout 1989, he restated his affection for his new home. The *Express* reported that after returning to Philadelphia for his daughter's college graduation, he couldn't wait to get back. "Highly visible and eager to face issues, he's a popular speaker and fully involved with city life." Chitwood still spoke two or three times a week, noting to the newspaper, "The problem is I'm starting to go back to groups. So my jokes are the same jokes."

Of course, there was nothing funny about the increasing relationship of drugs and crime. In mid-1989, under the heading "Operation Ice," the Portland police broke up a drug ring by arresting 18 suspects. It was also an extensive fencing operation involving over five million dollars in stolen goods. Old issues recurred as the tenacious chief tried again to increase security at the Maine Youth Center. Renewing his campaign for at least a compromise on Maine's gun laws, Chitwood started meeting with House Speaker John Martin at the state capitol in Augusta. They agreed to work together. Peter Binzen of *The Philadelphia Inquirer* knew Chitwood wasn't about to give up. "Can a big city cop find peaceful retirement in a rural state?" Binzen asked in the fall of 1989, "Not if he takes on the pro-gun crowd."

Portland's refurbished and handsome Old Port area, by day its major tourist attraction, had become on weekend nights, with its many bars and concentrated night life, a scene of excessive congestion and rowdiness, drawing unruly, largely youthful crowds of after-midnight revelers. One city councilor called it "a complete zoo" from 12:00 to 2:00 a.m. The prevalence of fistfights, vandalism, and public urination was scaring away tourists as well as the bulk of the local citizenry. Chitwood would have to stretch his modest resources to better patrol its streets, especially on Friday and Saturday nights. Always looking beyond the immediate challenge, he also sought to limit new liquor licenses in the area. To Chitwood, it was all of a piece—public safety was his charge, whether in terms of drugs, theft, guns, or alcohol. He wasn't out to stop anyone's fun, just to keep order. He also had to deal with such issues as senseless vandalism at a major cemetery and to balance civil liberties with license in cracking down on local panhandlers and loiterers.

There remained the customary diversions, always of interest to local media, such as the chief's long-running confrontation with an eccentric named David Koplow, the self-proclaimed "Dogman," who insisted on letting his six unleashed canines run free all over town, including to the federal courthouse. Along more serious lines, a second long-term sting operation led to the arrest of 11 individuals and the recovery of $43,000 in stolen property.

Chitwood had high praise for the quality of his officers, while consistently expressing his concern that they were underpaid and perhaps under-appreciated. So much so that some members of the public volunteered to pay for their body armor after it was revealed that some officers had paid out of their own pockets to secure more advanced weapons. An editorial in the *Evening Express* on October 13, 1989 lauded Chitwood as "a cop's cop," pointing out that he had become Maine's "most controversial law enforcement official. But that shouldn't obscure the more important fact that he's also arguably the best." The article praised his "style and verve that have reinvigorated and boosted morale," his infectious enthusiasm and limitless determination. "We're better off because he's here." Other than the gun controversy, the most public criticism of Chitwood was just that—for example, the objection of a local district attorney, Paul Aranson, to the police chief's proclivity for giving local reporters advance notice of such stories as major arrests to dominate the headlines. It was Aranson who dubbed him "Media Mike."

*   *   *

In a remarkable recognition of just how recognized Chitwood had become nationally, later in 1989, *Esquire* magazine named him one of 36 men and women to be honored in the sixth annual "Esquire Register." This was a lot bigger than coverage in *Philadelphia* magazine. The letter from *Esquire*'s editor, inviting the Chitwoods to a black-tie dinner at New York's famed "21 Club," noted that "a citation outlining your accomplishments, as well as your photograph, will appear in our upcoming December issue." Honorees, "whose vision and determination are reshaping . . . the future of American life," were in six general categories. They included celebrities as disparate as Michael Jordan, Billy Crystal, Michelle Pfeiffer, Oprah Winfrey, and Spike Lee. Chitwood was the only policeman and was listed under the "Education and Social Service" category. Tom Wolfe was the emcee, but Liz and Mike Chitwood were most impressed by the amiable Walter Cronkite, one of the guests they met. In responding to the honor, Chitwood expressed appreciation that the award reflected his entire career.

Throughout Maine, it was a source of pride, even among those in rural areas who had vehemently criticized this outsider from "the flatlands" for tampering with the state's most cherished traditions. Next to J. Edgar Hoover, who was now better known in American law enforcement? Characteristically, near the end of 1989 in a guest editorial in *USA Today*, Chitwood returned to the theme of drugs, even more basic a concern than the prudent control of firearms. Under the heading "The Police Aren't the Villains," he concluded: "The people have always supported the police in efforts to keep our streets and communities safe. I doubt that they will agree with those who suggest that, in fighting drugs, the police have become a threat to the constitutional rights of all."

*   *   *

By 1990, journalists were already writing about Mike Chitwood as a kind of legend. Martha Englert's front-page saga in the *Maine Sunday Telegram* featured a photo of Chitwood from 1980, emoting as he negotiated for the release of hostages in a Philadelphia standoff. "'Dirty Harry' is Gone," it proclaimed. "The courage that made Michael Chitwood Philadelphia's most decorated policeman gets him into confrontations in Maine." In an exhaustive biographical article pieced together from extensive interviews, media accounts, and records, Englert went all the way back, covering all the old ground familiar to Philadelphians. "In 26 years of police work," she summarized, "Michael Jude Chitwood has been revered as a hero, vilified as a brute and reviled as a meddler. . . . The story of Chitwood's career is that of a man constantly in the midst of controversy. . . . It is also the story of metamorphosis, the transformation of a cold yet compassionate street cop into a progressive law enforcement manager." There was nothing, however, about his projected elevation out of Maine in about five years. "I have an excellent department of hard-working people," she quoted the chief as affirming. "I'm happy here. For now, the future is on hold."

Although increasingly concerned about drugs, Chitwood persisted in his attempt to find common ground in revising firearms regulations. Pointing out that Maine had some of the loosest gun laws in the nation, he pushed a step-by-step approach. At the very least, applicants for a gun permit ought to have some basic knowledge of how to handle the weapon. Isn't it simply common sense to prohibit carrying concealed weapons into bars, churches, athletic events, hospitals, and public buildings? These dual concerns presented parallel perils. Just as Chitwood had predicted, drug crimes increased significantly. In the first 10 months of 1989, Portland police had seized illegal drugs with a street value of over $650,000 and arrested 223 people in connection with them.

There would be no letup in either area. Five separate incidents of accidental shooting of children by others who were also underage impelled Chitwood to urge enactment of a state law making it a crime to leave a loaded gun within the reach of children. Chitwood's tentative agreement to work with House Speaker John Martin foundered on the familiar ground of the police chief getting publicity for his proposals prematurely. Martin was now "convinced" that Chitwood's real interest was to get into politics himself, heaven forbid. Chitwood offered to quit the firearms panel reviewing the state's laws if it would help. "He's guilty of making sense," Bill Williamson commented in the *Press Herald*. Maybe it was because Chitwood "isn't a politician that he's been able to take on the uncomfortable task of championing sane gun control measures in Maine." The chief was finally getting frustrated. Recommending a statewide referendum on a seven-day waiting period for handgun permit applications and reiterating his other proposals, Chitwood said, in his talk to the Portland Club, "I can't do this alone. It's time someone else took up the banner. I must run my six-million-dollar operation, the Portland Police Department. I can't dedicate my whole life to the issue of a waiting period for gun permits."

Nor did he. Expanding on his emphasis on psychological aid for police after a troubled officer barricaded himself in his apartment, Chitwood went on to offer the Portland-based Rape Crisis Center space in the city's police headquarters building. His concern was the whole realm of social issues.

Letters from legislators poured in as Mike Chitwood celebrated his 25 years of dedication to law enforcement. He observed the milestone by sharing it with his customary certificates of commendation to his officers and supportive civilians. Keeping visible, he doubled as both starter and participant in the 61st annual Boys' and Girls' Club race on Patriot's Day. His efforts to better secure the Maine Youth Center and protect children from access to guns only grew more insistent. Foot patrols were heightened in neighborhoods facing increased crime, and they proved productive.

When Chitwood endorsed a candidate in the Democratic primary for Cumberland County district attorney, it is not surprising that the incumbent, Paul

Aranson, already his antagonist, accused the police chief of breaking the law. Characteristically, Chitwood responded by challenging Aranson to arrest him. The dispute simply simmered with no resolution, and Chitwood moved on to other areas. To reduce traffic accidents, he insisted that his officers obey traffic signals, even when responding to burglar alarms, and began using roadblocks to deter drunk driving.

Meanwhile, official support seemed gradually to be shifting in favor of a statewide referendum on gun control. A full-page cartoon in the *Maine Sunday Telegram* of December 30, 1990 featured, among other prominent state personages, Chitwood "on gun control and canine containment" exchanging water pistol discharges with his opponents as a dog nipped at his jacket. Another cartoon showed the chief saying ruefully, "I'd rather be in Philly." Asked in January 1991 about how the car he drove reflected his personality, Chitwood replied, "It's getting old, has high mileage, but takes a licking and keeps on ticking." After the state supreme court upheld Portland's concealed weapons statute, granting Chitwood at least one legal victory, he even participated in an ad for the *Casco Bay Weekly*, pushing for his proposed statewide waiting period to take home a handgun. Its caption, next to a photo of the smiling chief, read: "If you can wait seven days for the next *Casco Bay Weekly* . . . then you can wait seven days for a handgun." Anything to press home his point.

Celebrating his third anniversary in Portland on April 11, 1991, Chitwood was surprisingly negative about his hometown. He told Frank Sleeper of the *Press Herald* that Portland, with drugs the biggest challenge, now had the same crime problems as Philadelphia, except that *its* problems were still controllable. He also predicted that he would soon bust a major heroin ring. Other concerns included the spread of graffiti and downtown blight and the negative portrayals of police, particularly in terms of using excessive force. Chitwood decried threatened cuts in the Portland police and fire departments, while admitting that "these are tough times, and this is economic reality." The cuts were to cost him 17 employees.

Still, Mike kept moving, running the five miles in the 1991 Boys' and Girls' Club race in a respectable time of 39:05. In May, he was profiled nationally on the CBS-TV program *Top Cops*, reliving that incident 20 years before when a drug dealer had used a small child as a shield and Chitwood risked his own life to subdue the man without firing another shot. Those career-shaping Philadelphia memories would never recede. Another vivid reminder came that July when his 70-year-old mentor, brash-cop-turned-mayor Frank Rizzo, suddenly collapsed and died while campaigning to recapture his old job in City Hall. "A stand-up guy," Chitwood recalled, all the memories returning. He may have come to love Portland, but South Philly would always be in his DNA.

*   *   *

There was more repetition than dramatic new developments through the fall of 1992. Chitwood's public appearances went well beyond Portland. To the Rotary Club of Oxford Hills, he warned again that spin-off crimes from drug smuggling, sales, and widespread use, including the prevalence of firearms, were one of Maine's primary threats. Property crimes, which accounted for some 92 percent of the state's reported criminal activity, were frequently related to illegal drug use, which had been working its way into the state "like a cancer." A typical letter from the Council on Alcoholism in Lewiston glowed, "Your ability as a police officer is exceeded only by your keen oratorical skills." Having to do more with less resulted in warning the public against potentially hazardous activity, such as cautioning young women not to jog alone along popular public paths. Chitwood's constant call was for education; the best way to inhibit crime was to combat it as early as possible.

Occasionally there was an incident so horrific that it recalled the violence of Chitwood's earlier career, such as the rape of a baby by a teenager in the home of a convicted heroin dealer. But most of the time Chitwood's concerns were ongoing ones, which advanced so slowly because of ingrained bureaucracy. This was surely the case with the Department of Human Services in dealing with child welfare and juvenile crime. Plans to privatize the youth center stalled. The customary excuse for inaction was an inadequate budget, the same challenge Chitwood was confronting. On a lighter note, Portland finally closed the book on over 450 citations against Chitwood's perennial nemesis, "Dogman" David Koplow. No one knew where he had gone after his unleashed canines had been impounded.

There was a major credit-card theft scam; confiscated drug money was keeping the police department's two remaining horses on patrol; cuts in human services were putting more of Portland's poor in peril; and balanced gun control remained an issue. One of Chitwood's allies, Maine representative Thomas H. Andrews, cosponsored the "Brady Bill" in Congress, insisting that sensible restrictions on the sale and use of guns didn't conflict with Second Amendment rights. Security was beefed up around Senate Majority Leader George J. Mitchell when a Boston fugitive known to be armed and dangerous had reportedly fled to his home state of Maine and threatened Mitchell for unclear reasons.

There did indeed seem to be a more pervasive sense of potential violence, as Chitwood had predicted. Biker gangs had taken up residence in Portland, and there were more reports of prostitution and attacks on gays. Old Port rowdiness had, if anything, escalated as hundreds of partygoers hurled bottles and epithets at police around closing time for city bars. Despite having to reduce services elsewhere, Chitwood doubled weekend patrols to curb rowdy, obnoxious behavior in an area that by day still represented the keystone of Portland's physical renaissance. Perhaps even the chief had slowed down a few seconds. His time in the 1992 Boys' and Girls' Club five-mile run had risen moderately to 39:46.

In his commencement address to the 70 graduates of Cheverus High School, Chitwood hit a new note. He said that persistent racism—not crime, poverty, or disease—was responsible for many of the problems facing America, and that the nation's economy should be more equitable "before it separates us as a society of the very rich and the very poor." This in 1992.

*   *   *

A new scandal involved, of all things, the trash-hauling business in Portland. After a thorough investigation, police had gathered evidence to support criminal charges of forgery, theft, deception, and misappropriation of funds against 12 people who owned or worked for trash-hauling companies. In addition, criminal cases were being developed for at least 265 violations of a city ordinance requiring all of Portland's trash to go to regional waste systems. It was estimated that taxpayers might have lost over $1.2 million through the illegal diversion of trash to other, cheaper, unreported destinations, with haulers pocketing the profit. It gets complicated, but essentially involved haulers making more, offering less, hiding the information, and avoiding their legal requirements.

Somehow Chief Chitwood came in for his share of the blame by prematurely disclosing his trash-hauling investigation, which had taken months to develop, in a talk to the local grange. A weekly newspaper publisher was in the audience. Following rumors, local editors had decided to delay publication of what they already knew so as not to jeopardize Chitwood's investigation. However, when the story broke on local radio and TV after the weekly *Portland Journal* published the news, the daily newspapers felt undercut. It was hardly the first time that, even if unplanned, a spontaneous Chitwood had jumped the gun. Response was swift, with cartoons showing the chief with his foot in his mouth and telling a smirking trash collector in his office to just "shut up!"

It did turn out to be a major scandal as many haulers, who kept scanty records in any case, were charged with violating the Portland solid-waste ordinance, avoiding payments of fees, and making immense profits, but only for themselves, by disposing of trash in the cheapest way possible. The *Press Herald*, finally in on the story, quoted Chitwood as announcing that these civil complaints were only "'the tip of an iceberg' in a wide-ranging probe that may result in criminal charges against some haulers."

Throughout, the chief was happy to receive positive feedback about his valued key associates. Sergeant Russell Gauvin's job as head of the department's internal affairs unit made him responsible for policing his fellow officers. He was the author of a new booklet detailing how citizens should complain to or commend the Portland police, and his duties had him reporting directly to Chitwood. With national complaints against excessive police behavior on the rise, Gauvin's job resulted in some ambivalence—welcomed by many in the community, but inevitably a figure of potential suspicion within the ranks. A major article in the *Press Herald* detailed how he worked. Although only about 50 of the 80,000 incidents involving the Portland police in a given year resulted in complaints, the article stressed the department's sensitivity to the public's sentiments and promoted the distribution of Gauvin's booklet.

Another welcome bit of news was the naming of Lieutenant Mark Dion, one of "Portland's finest," by *Parade* magazine as one of the top 10 police officers in America. Four years before, taking his concerns about gay-bashing directly to his new boss, Dion earned his confidence, leading to a new anti-bias unit. "He's one of the most committed professionals I've ever dealt with," said Chitwood, whose own sentiments against any form of prejudice were already well established.

*   *   *

Almost as if by design and just on time, prior to his fifth anniversary in Portland, the call came. This time Mike Chitwood didn't have to respond to an ad. Now something of a celebrity himself, he was contacted by a recruiter representing St. Petersburg, Florida. Talk about a contrast in locales. Would he be interested in submitting his name for consideration as their next chief of police?

Would he? There was no hesitation, although as soon as the news inevitably got out, for once Chitwood may have protested a bit too much. Portland, for all the genuine good the chief had found in the place, was projected in his grand career plan to constitute about a five-year tour. Chitwood was now 48, just the age to move on and up. To the *Press Herald* he insisted, "I wasn't looking. I've got a good job here and a good department. But in the long-range picture [St. Petersburg] is a career challenge I want to explore."

Reportedly, one problem in the southern city had been a lack of sensitivity by the current police administration to "hate crimes" involving racial or lifestyle bias. Their previous chief had been pressured to resign. Although Portland totaled roughly three percent black, Asian, and Hispanic residents, Janet P. Johnson of the local branch of the NAACP gave Chitwood a glowing letter of recommendation. She also cited Mark Dion and their united stand against any form of bias. Expressing her gratitude to the chief "for his commitment to civil rights" and his vigorous opposition to all forms of bigotry, although she would "hate to see him leave," Johnson "overwhelmingly" supported his candidacy. Chitwood was also put in good stead by his positive relationship with Portland's gay community.

In all, 79 people accepted the invitation to apply for the position. St. Petersburg, with an average of 360 days of sunshine a year and once known mostly as a haven for retirees, had developed into a far more diverse city. With a population of some 250,000 within the greater Tampa Bay metropolitan region of almost three million, St. Petersburg had 505 sworn police officers, over 300 more than in Port-land, and a police budget seven times that of his current base in Maine. The new salary would be only $10,000 to $20,000 more than he was making—but money was never Mike's primary consideration.

Most of the intensive controversy about gun rights and the like vanished with Portland's outpouring of appreciation for their chief, exceeding even what he had received in Middletown. "I've got 100 calls saying 'Don't go,'" Chitwood told the *Casco Bay Weekly*. "It has an impact." The *Weekly* printed a drawing of "Media Mike" pondering a container of sun-block. He was to fly south for an interview on November 5th. Already interviewed over the phone by St. Petersburg's director of employee relations, Chitwood had been described by him as "an impressive candi-date." The city had reduced its list down to eight, each of whom would be inter-viewed over two days by a 10-member panel of citizens. Those making the final cut would be asked by the city manager to return for another extensive interview later in November.

A *Press Herald* editorial, featuring a photo of Chitwood in his shirtsleeves, allowed that "St. Petersburg . . . is bigger and richer, but it can't value him more. . . . Chitwood's high-profile advocacy here and at the State House hasn't always won him friends, but it's made him rich in admiration. There's no better currency in Maine." The gleeful response of a few gun enthusiasts from surround-ing communities was countered by a deluge of support in the Portland Press:

"As far as I'm concerned, Chitwood is one of the finest, most competent police chiefs."

"I applaud Chitwood for his efforts to make Portland a better place to live."

"What's this guy from Falmouth's concern with our city government here in Portland? We've been lucky to have a police chief of Chitwood's character."

"I suggest the writer . . . move to St. Petersburg, or at least out of state. . . . In that way he can avoid observing laws that . . . do not require enforcement."

Not surprisingly, Chitwood was called back to St. Petersburg for a third and final interview, having been named one of four finalists for the job. The last of the four asked to take the full tour, he met with everyone from members of the police department and its unions to the city's budget department. It surely seemed a good sign. As in Portland, two of his three remaining competitors were police chiefs from other, smaller communities within the state.

Mark Journey of the *St. Petersburg Times* wrote an exhaustive account of "Media Mike," his first article describing the four finalists. Journey went back to Chitwood's colorful, productive years in Philadelphia, including the pivotal Caser-ta and "scumbag" cases that had shaped his future. It was so extensive an account, however, that it also dealt with Chitwood's old "Dirty Harry" image, including those unproven but lingering accusations of brutality. It had been some years since they had surfaced. The article also contained the now-familiar recent photo of Chitwood strenuously working out. The December 5, 1992, St. Petersburg edition of the *Tampa Tribune*, headlined "Candidate's Past a Mix of Hero, Tough Guy," featured an almost-as-thorough article by David Sommer, also bringing up the full scope of Chitwood's prior reputation. When questioned about the supposed brutality incident involving a black murder suspect, Chitwood gave the same explanation he had in 1975. It was good enough for Lendel S. Bright, president of Minority Law Enforcement Personnel of Pinellas County, Florida. He was among those who interviewed Chitwood and pronounced any allegations of past misconduct irrelevant. "That was Philadelphia, and this is St. Pete," Sommer quoted Bright as saying, "You don't need to bring up that stuff from years and years ago."

His chances looked good, but Chitwood came in second. Perceptive Martha Englert of the *Portland Press Herald* may have put her finger on precisely the reason. Chitwood didn't lose out because of his "Dirty Harry" past but because of his "Outspoken Mike" present. The St. Petersburg officials had not chosen either of their local police chief candidates, but rather soft-spoken Darrell Stephens, executive director of the Police Executive Research Forum. Praised by the city manager for his "low-key administrative style," Stephens wasn't going to scare or unsettle anyone. Chitwood's very prominence may have worked against him, although he was known to have had the support of St. Petersburg's police unions. Even without a gun, a straight-talking tough cop was undoubtedly what *they* were looking for.

At least on the surface, Chitwood took his disappointment well. "I'm glad to be staying," he insisted, ostensibly relieved. He expressed his continuing regard for Portland's city manager, Bob Ganley, and his appreciation for the more than 175 phone calls and 40 letters asking him to stay in Maine. He even ruefully referred to the small number of messages from gun owners offering to help him pack. Chitwood stretched it a bit, saying he might not have taken the job even if it had been offered. He smilingly admitted, however, that his one regret was the weather. He had seen those strolling St. Petersburg residents in their shirtsleeves and short skirts in the midst of a typical Portland bundle-up December. "I did think about the weather there," Mike commented, "when I was out running the last couple of days here."

Yes, it had certainly constituted a significant challenge, and more—the projected career advancement. That Chitwood would admit. With his schedule unexpectedly sidetracked, the real question was this: How soon would such an opportunity come again?

9

Coming to Terms

D espite the sense of satisfaction in Portland that Mike Chitwood would not be departing for the west coast of Florida after all, there was bound to be a certain ambivalence—or perhaps, more accurately, a sense of surprise that he was actually staying. How could any city turn down someone with his credentials? It was almost an insult to *them*. As for Chitwood himself, after his whimsical reflections, however he may have actually felt, he kept going without skipping a beat. As before, many of his heightened challenges resulted from reduced funding for what he viewed as vital city services. As activist as ever, he initiated a lawsuit, in concert with other Portland officials, to prevent the state of Maine from releasing mentally disabled people into communities without the proper supervision.

One typical case publicized in the press represented the relevance of this issue to police. A 30-year-old retarded man named Steven Wayne Gagnon, released from a facility called Pineland Center in 1991, had set fires in his apartment, shoplifted, abused drugs, and worked as a prostitute. With the state's new policy of closing such institutions and limiting supervision to a former patient's own preferences, in Chitwood's view the whole community was put at risk. The budget crisis affected everyone.

In January 1993, the "tip of the iceberg" in Chitwood's year-long investigation of the region's waste-disposal industry yielded its first results with the arrest for theft of the owner and manager of a Yarmouth trash-hauling company. The gun controversy continued unabated as a judge upheld Portland's ban on firearms in housing projects, a victory for the chief in this extended struggle.

With increasing concern about packs of "hoods" terrorizing citizens, both gay and straight, still largely in the Old Port and "cultural corridor" areas, Chitwood sought cooperation with officials of the Justice Department in Washington. For the first time, a local arrest was made on federal civil rights charges of a young man who had harassed, threatened, and poured a drink on a black businesswoman.

Chitwood also investigated the crude painting of a swastika on a Jewish-owned business. As always, in his public pronouncements, he denounced such "cowardly acts" and urged victims to "stand up" and promptly report them to police. Chitwood's attempts to contain violence anywhere in Old Port extended to excesses at an after-hours dance club. Naturally, it resulted in yet another lawsuit against him on the grounds that he was exceeding his authority. "If I had to worry about getting sued all the time," he responded at a press conference, "I'd be mute." Of course, he'd been known to initiate legal action of his own to promote official response to situations he decried. He would uphold the law by any means necessary—including making use of the law itself.

*   *   *

Chitwood's own notoriety hardly receded. A local librarian, conducting a survey covered by national media, asked such varied celebrities as Robert Redford, Chuck Yeager, Lena Horne, Frank Sinatra (answered by his son), Mike Wallace, Ed Bradley, Gerald Ford, Linda Ronstadt, and, of course, America's police chief, Mike Chitwood what books they were reading. The librarian, Glenna Nowell, stressed to the *Press Herald*, "People didn't want just any celebrity. What they want are suggestions from their heroes." Chitwood's choice was *The Firm*, by John Grisham. He described its content, fiction based on experience, as "very thought-provoking and enjoyable," dealing with "corruption and a lack of ethics." Did anyone anticipate a romance novel?

Meanwhile, the commendations kept coming, several to Chitwood personally, from such groups as the Portland Chamber of Commerce and the Maine Public Health Association, but also to the overall Portland Police Department. The National Commission for Law Enforcement Agencies named it one of 250 out of some 18,000 departments nationally to win accreditation for excellence. Nor did Chitwood's light touch diminish. To help promote the nine-day Portland Dance Festival, he participated in it personally, demonstrating some graceful dexterity and insisting, "I can do a split." After all, such moves should come as no surprise. He was likely the best-conditioned public official in Maine.

*   *   *

In March 1993, an ominous incident in New York City alarmed citizens throughout the nation, none more than those entrusted with law enforcement. Although the Cold War had ended, a new kind of conflict had replaced it—terrorism by widespread Muslim fundamentalists unified by their resentments against the West, particularly the perceived policies of the United States. In organized groups and as individual fanatics they sought ways to strike at the very symbols of American strength.

An amateurish terrorist named Mohammed A. Salameh managed to penetrate one of the twin towers of New York's World Trade Center and explode a bomb. It killed five people and for a time shut down that vital center of commerce. When Salameh actually returned the truck in which he had carried the bomb to the rental agency so that he could regain his deposit, it enabled the New York police to quickly place him under arrest. The bombing, however, emphasized how easy it would be under current security procedures to mount a far more lethal attack.

To Mike Chitwood this presented a dilemma he had considered. How do we preserve the most open society in the world while protecting Americans against unprecedented threats of terrorism? He suggested in a *Press Herald* interview: "America can make it tougher for known terrorists to enter this country. It can pass sensible legislation regulating the use of weapons and explosives. And it can take these actions without treading on our fundamental rights." He also stressed the importance of every level of law enforcement working more closely together in this ongoing effort. Prophetic words.

*   *   *

Moving into his fifties, Chitwood must have pondered how that decade was still generally viewed as the most productive of most peoples' lives. Where he might yet be headed could still be influenced by where he had been, the milestones of his career thus far, and the visibility and vigor of his current policies and pronouncements. To Clark DeLeon of *The Philadelphia Inquirer*, Chitwood stressed again: "I'm not anti-gun. I'm anti-violence. I'm pro-public safety. I'm pro commonsensical gun laws. I'm for a ban on assault rifles." DeLeon referred to Mike Jr., a chip off the old Chitwood, whose career was following his father's with striking similarity. Now a five-year veteran of the Philadelphia police force, young Mike had wounded a suspect in a shootout with three men outside the Richard Allen Homes in North Philadelphia. No wonder his father was so gratified when that Portland judge had turned down the NRA's suit to reverse the ban on guns in Portland's housing projects. "Yes, I'm partial because my son was in a gun battle in which 45 shots were fired," Chitwood told DeLeon. "Thank God he wasn't hit." The pride was as palpable as his relief.

*   *   *

Chitwood's father died of cancer at 74 in January 1994. For some time, Mike had traveled down from Maine on weekends to help him keep going. Mike's parents had moved from South Philly to suburban Delaware County, where his mother died in 1990. There were major obituaries of Walter Franklin Chitwood in both Portland and Philadelphia, but a particularly poignant one titled "A major dad," by Jim Nicholson in the *Philadelphia Daily News*, included the reactions of his policeman son and grandson. Walter Chitwood's other two sons, as noted, college-educated Walter Jr. and Mark, had both achieved success, one a highly regarded psychologist and the other an esteemed school administrator.

As Nicholson wrote, everyone respected this "retired navy petty officer who cut no slack for himself or for those he loved. . . . They all learned lessons they didn't quite understand as kids." To his sons, home could sometimes seem sort of like a boot camp, with firm rules and standards stemming from their father's inner toughness. There was that memorable tattoo incident when he threw Mike out of the house. Yet Walter Chitwood could be warm and friendly, even humorous, to just about everyone he met, irrespective of their background or status. Respect was a two-way street, a sentiment Mike would impart to his own son and daughter. Mike Jr., who had become very close to his grandfather, told Nicholson, "He was a man of high ideals and high principles who lived his life by a certain code of ethics and morality." When Mike Sr. leaned down over his father's bedside for the last time, finally there were shared tears. "I love you," Mike whispered. "Every success I've had in my entire life is attributable to you"—the same sentiments his own son had in a prior year imparted to him.

Another reminder of the passage of years was the death in Philadelphia of Mike's first partner, Anthony M. Kane, at only 55. Described by Diana Marder in the *Inquirer* as a "star police officer," Kane "was a man so successful in crime fighting that he and his protégé Michael Chitwood were dubbed 'Batman and Robin.'" Chitwood commented to her, "I probably learned more from Tony Kane about the street and about police work than from any other officer in my 30-year career." For Michael Chitwood, all his early mentors—Kane, Rizzo, and Ferguson—were now gone.

*   *   *

Passages in life. Those extensive feature stories about Chitwood's past and present, such as "On patrol with Media Mike" in the *Press Herald*, were reading more like valedictories now. Who could imagine he would choose to remain in Maine, despite periodic inquiries about other locales, for all of 17 years. The average tenure of a police chief, Chitwood's original projection, is only five years. The lure of Casco Bay dispelled even the attraction of a potential job in Pompano Beach on that other Florida coast. Whatever the duration, capture him while you can. There won't be many more like him. The new photos accompanying such stories mirror the old—an earnest Chitwood punching the heavy bag; a still very dapper Chitwood exhorting his audience; a smiling Chitwood, like a gaunt pied piper, only in shorts and T-shirt, leading a covey of kids on some new fundraising adventure. The mustache is gone now, the hair gray, the six-foot-one frame even more spare. How can anyone look so seemingly slender yet so strong? The taut muscles stand out on his lean arms and legs like a distance runner's. Which, of course, is what he is.

"There never was a day I lost my passion for what I do." That is Mike Chitwood today, still looking much the same, and that is also the essence of it all, deriving from that first day as a school safety patrolman when he was inspired by the cop on his beat. "We protect people" was that enduring message.

The new century, a new millennium in its import, would too soon try anyone's resources and resolve. For Chitwood, it combined incomprehensible events with a degree of controversy he hadn't endured since his days as a Philly homicide detective. Yet he would weather it all and wind up, by common consensus, back on top. His bedrock, then as now: "There never was a day I lost my passion for what I do." It would encompass admitted mistakes and missteps, shock and surprise, without blurring that basic perspective.

The first decade of 2000 started out almost deceptively placid for Chitwood, if any period in such a profession can be deemed quietly calm and pleasant. His career was still being summed up, somewhat prematurely. "Lockstep conformity," wrote Paul Mills in his April 1, 2001, essay, "Inside Maine," for the *Lewiston Sun Journal*, "is certainly not what democracy is all about. . . . If there is one person in Maine who had demonstrated that you can stand apart from the crowd yet at the same time win popular support it's Mike Chitwood . . . a figure who somehow is able to balance the surfboard atop the maelstrom of controversy yet at the same time ride the crest of a popular tide." Another image for the cartoonists: Midwave Mike hanging five.

He wrote his own piece, as he would from time to time, in the *Press Herald*, on a familiar subject—government's neglect of "at risk" children. Now that there was actually a budget surplus in Washington, what better place for investment than in "the best way to reduce crime . . . to help kids get the right start in life, so they never become criminals." Noting that "the hours immediately after school closes are the peak hours for juvenile crime," Chitwood had joined with a thousand others nationwide in preparing an "Invest in Kids—School and Youth Violence Prevention Plan" to assure that school districts and parents have access to after-school programs. It also outlined a variety of steps to make certain resources for everything from fully funded sports activities to child care would be available on every income level. Practicality merged with idealism.

In presenting a new form for Portland's citizens to make complaints (and compliments) about police easier and less intimidating to fill out and submit, Chitwood restated his intention to read them all personally. He also vowed that he or a deputy would meet with anyone reporting a civil-rights violation or the use of excessive force. Despite this, another lawsuit was aimed at the chief, this one by a convicted sex offender who charged that his constitutional rights were being violated when police distributed his photograph to warn new neighbors of his presence. His lawyer pointed out that his actual offenses that resulted in incarceration had occurred 20 years ago in California. To Chitwood, more recent local incidents still made John D. Corbin a "high-risk" offender, and he stayed with the policy.

With the unending drug wars, Chitwood came out conditionally in favor of a new Portland clinic providing methadone, drug counseling, and rehabilitation to addicts. That might be helpful, so long as it wasn't simply the "drive-through" sort of meth facility he well remembered from his Philadelphia days, doing more harm than good. Along another familiar front—to help finance enhanced police patrols throughout the Old Port—Chitwood proposed a controversial bar tax of $4.25 per seat. It cost $100,000 a year to pay for patrolling some 28 bars in the district.

Other incidents similar to the Corbin case highlighted Chitwood's perennial intent to balance individual rights and protection of the public. Norman Dickinson, a convicted kidnapper who had spent more than a third of his life in jail on a variety of charges, bolted from house arrest after his release on probation, warning that he was still a "ticking time bomb" and couldn't handle any form of incarceration. After Dickinson was recaptured, Chitwood sympathized with his emotional state but concluded that a police chief's first "concern is for the community."

Hate crimes escalated, at least in number, during May 2001, with anti-black and anti-Semitic graffiti in some 17 locations. So did Chitwood's response, joining others in "a sense of outrage" and putting two detectives in charge of finding the culprits. "They" turned out to be one emotionally challenged 16-year-old boy, on probation from Chitwood's original nemesis, the Maine Youth Center, who claimed not to be a racist.

The main crime story in June was that of an angry, unemployed loner, with a criminal record trailing back to Florida, who had tried to shoot a convenience-store manager at point-blank range. He had been asked to leave the store because of a power outage. Fortunately, his handgun jammed and he was quickly apprehended, averting a horrific homicide.

Chitwood's activities in July ran the customary gamut of celebratory to controversial. He spoke with fondness and humor at the memorial service for Frances Charlotte Wilson Peabody, a legendary 98-year-old Portland socialite turned civic and AIDS activist. The same week, he courted controversy by setting up an elaborate seven-day videotaped police "sting" operation, advertising a bogus brothel that offered "forbidden pleasures." It pulled in 26 men, aged 25 to 63, each of whom was cited for seeking to engage a prostitute—a misdemeanor. The women were police officers. Another 130 people called with inquiries. Chitwood claimed one motivation for the sting was the complaints of legitimate massage parlors. After some consideration and media objections, however, he decided not to post publicly the names of those who showed up. A few days later, he was out leading the "Bikin', Bladin', Rollin', Strollin' Saturday Trail Blast" to raise funds for a network of regional trails and agreeing, to the extent possible, to have his hair styled in July for another charity event.

*   *   *

By mid-2001, a heightened pattern of contention was beginning to rise with the daily temperatures. Early in July, Chitwood—in cooperation with the major local grocery-store chain—announced a "Campaign for Civility" to counteract an increasing sense of tension throughout the area. As he said at the news conference announcing the campaign, "This program is a response to the stress and antagonism that seems to have become so much a part of our daily lives." He noted to David Hench of the *Press Herald* that there had been 1,200 incidents of violence in Portland during the preceding year, and many more incidents involving intimidation, harassment, and threats of one kind or another. Among other measures, inserts would be stuffed in grocery bags urging shoppers to "keep cool." As Chitwood put it to Hench, "People are in a hurry, and if you're in their way, it becomes an altercation that leads to violence." A plaintive electronic message flashed in the room at Chitwood's news conference: "PLEASE DO NOT GET ANGRY."

That wasn't quite good enough for Lewiston attorney Charles Williams. Because of increased immigration, the Portland area, widely publicized as a welcoming place to settle, was inevitably becoming more diverse. Often the English language comprehension of newcomers was less than perfect. Called in to subdue a suicidal Sudanese youth, Portland police were attacked by members of his family, who feared that they were doing him harm. A melee followed, and three women of the Okut family were arrested for obstruction and assault. At a city hall news conference, attorney Williams, representing the family, announced the filing of a lawsuit against the police department, seeking $1.5 million in damages. Scott Miller of Peace Action Maine, a group working closely with refugee relief and relocation, added a demand for "an internal and external review so the community can find some way to believe police officers are not abusing members of the immigrant community." Indeed, there had been incidents, inspiring increased police patrols, of white youths assaulting African immigrants in multi-ethnic neighborhoods. Later, Williams threatened to file a $100 million federal lawsuit unless Chitwood apologized and dropped all charges against the Okut family.

Of course, the chief had seen it all before. "What am I going to apologize for?" he replied. "They can sue me for $500 million. I couldn't care less." His officers were merely doing their jobs, and it was not a particularly easy assignment. Given his own record, he was especially incensed at any charges of racism leveled at his department, an insult to their—and his—integrity.

Another intended lawsuit, this one for three million dollars by colorful criminal defense lawyer Daniel C. Lilley, was over the arrest and imprisonment of a teenage girl. She had been charged with murdering another teenager but was eventually released by the state when her guilt was contested. This suit was put on hold at least temporarily when Lilley had a more immediate priority to deal with. He had been arrested for driving while intoxicated. But Lilley soon returned with yet another lawsuit in U.S. District Court, charging civil-rights violations when a Portland man named Vincent Dorazio was chased "without provocation" and severely beaten by Portland police. Dorazio may have been wanted on a warrant for a prior offense and ran away from an arresting officer. "These are acts of malice," Lilley charged. "There's certainly a gang mentality." It appeared to be open season on the Portland Police Department.

In September, Chitwood responded in his customary fashion, both calm and confrontational, defending his own. It simply wasn't enough to urge citizens to be restrained and rational, particularly when targeted by litigation-happy lawyers. For those really concerned, he launched a citizens' police academy, an 11-week course explaining how police officers do their jobs, from routine traffic violations to the most heinous crimes. It would cover everything—from ethical considerations to how patrols operate, from drug surveillance and computer crime to when and how force should be exercised. As Chitwood told the *Press Herald*, this glimpse into the realities of police work should help demolish stereotypes and improve mutual trust and cooperation. "It's just another way of opening up the department to community members." True enough. Similar efforts had been helpful in other, smaller communities. But unless it reached into a cross section of Portland's far more diverse population, how much effect could it have in stemming the rising tide of complaints against the Portland police force?

Meanwhile, Chitwood was also supplementing extra patrols with mediation and community intervention to quell the escalation of violence between gangs of white youths and African immigrants in Maine's most racially diverse neighborhood. "My greatest fear," he told local media, "is that when people start using bats and knives, there's the potential for death or serious injury." Gun control wasn't enough.

Even when the charges of drunk driving were eventually dropped against Daniel Lilley, the lawyer continued to insist that his arrest had been entirely inspired by a personal vendetta against him by Chitwood, in retaliation for his activities highlighting the use of excessive force.

Another familiar complaint reminding Chitwood of his days in Philadelphia emerged with the consideration of the city's new budget. It turned out police and fire personnel in Portland had made over $1.6 million in overtime during the 2001 fiscal year, just ended, almost $800,000 more than had been budgeted. At least some progress had been made along gender equity lines. Leading in police overtime was Detective Cheryl Holmes, whose gross pay of $70,573 had been supplemented by $27,395 in overtime, plus another $6,659 in the new fiscal year thus far.

Of course, Chitwood joined with the fire chief in defending the necessity of overtime. He particularly decried vacancies in the vital police dispatch center. "That's such a tough place to work, and it's such a thankless job." Like an air traffic controller's, but without the salary.

Back to the future. Still in 2001, but already in fiscal 2002, and still concerned with issues of overtime, police brutality, control of drugs and guns, community and media relations, juvenile crime, gang violence, racial unrest—everything Chitwood had faced from the streets to the police Roundhouse all the way back in Philly seemingly so long ago.

*   *   *

On September 10, 2001, two engineers named Mohamed Atta and Abdulaziz al-Omari drove up from Boston in a rented blue Nissan and checked into a Comfort Inn across from the Portland International Jetport. They made several stops in the vicinity that evening between 8:00 and 9:22—a Pizza Hut, a Key Bank ATM, a Fast Green ATM, a nearby gas station, and a Walmart. The following morning they checked out of the motel at 5:33 and minutes later pulled into the parking lot of the jetport. Checking in at the US Airways counter, they passed through airport security without incident. By 6:00 a.m., they were on board a Colgan Air Flight from Portland to Boston's Logan Airport, rather peculiar in that they had driven from Boston to Portland only the previous day. Once at Logan, they quickly boarded American Airlines Flight 11 for Los Angeles, which took off at 7:45 a.m. It never arrived. At 8:45 a.m., it struck the North Tower of the World Trade Center in New York City, killing all aboard and so many others, and changing everyone's world. After all the subsequent carnage horrifying the nation, no Americans were more stunned than those charged with our security, from the FBI to the police chief of Portland, Maine.

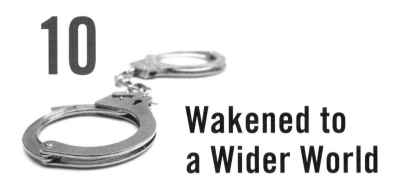

10

Wakened to a Wider World

Although only two of the 19 terrorists who coordinated the hijacking of four passenger jets on September 11, 2001, went through Portland, their overall domestic ringleader was one of the two. Mohamed Atta hardly conformed to the typical Middle Eastern suicide bomber profile. At 33, a German-educated engineer and a licensed pilot, he had used a credit card to pay for his motel room and rent his car, and he bought his airline ticket over the Internet, recording the miles with his frequent-flyer number. Nothing beyond an ethnic stereotype would have led anyone to view Atta with special suspicion prior to the unimaginable horrors of 9/11. Yet he and Abdulaziz al-Omari had been caught on a security videotape as they quickly boarded their initial flight at the Portland Jetport, and Atta probably flew the American Airlines Flight 11 jet they commandeered with their confederates from Boston, turning it back east to its final deadly destination.

Of course, the ultimate mastermind of the four-jet operation and its resulting destruction, claiming more than 3,000 lives, was Osama bin Laden, from his hideout, probably along the border between Afghanistan and Pakistan. Although not admitting responsibility until 2004, he had long been planning such a devastating assault aimed directly at the United States, viewed as the archenemy of militant Islam. Bin Laden, the estranged son of a Saudi Arabian billionaire, had founded al-Qaeda (Arabic for "The Base") in the late 1970s. In our convoluted Middle Eastern policy over the years, we had once viewed the young bin Laden as a "freedom fighter" when he took up arms to oppose the Soviet invasion of Afghanistan. Similarly, we had supported Iraq's Saddam Hussein when he invaded the Iran of the Ayatollah Khomeini, and we were pragmatically friendly with such despots as Egypt's Hosni Mubarak, who obligingly sustained Anwar Sadat's peace with Israel.

It was not the history of our foreign policy, however, that preoccupied horrified and bewildered Americans in the wake of 9/11. Amidst overall confusion, emotions ranged from fury to fear, the sense of alarm shared by those charged with our security. Rumors of imminent new attacks were rampant. How could this have happened? Only one of the four jets had failed to reach its target, presumably in Washington, DC, due to the remarkable heroism of its passengers in the skies over Pennsylvania. How could something similar to this tragedy be prevented in the future? To Mike Chitwood, his twofold focus came down to how to guard against renewed, locally based terrorism and why he was still being told so little by federal authorities. As Portland police were tracing hundreds of leads from people who insisted they'd seen both Atta and al-Omari in the area previously or had observed others who looked similarly suspicious, Chitwood voiced his frustration about how little the FBI was reciprocating the flood of reports he was sending them. "My concern is for the safety of our community," he reiterated in the *Press Herald*, "and I think [we] have a right to know who is here and who is not here."

As to the possibility that Portland's airport might have offered less stringent security than larger facilities, why had the other 17 suicide bombers come through Boston, Newark, Dulles, and Reagan International? Of course, having several locations of entry increased their chances for greater success. Moreover, Portland's director of transportation, Jeffrey Monroe, pointed out that if there were a problem in airport security, it was nationwide. "We follow the same security procedures everyone does," he told the *Press Herald*. The hijackers went aboard with nothing illegal under existing FAA regulations. There were no bombs or automatic weapons, only such items as knives and box cutters in their shaving kits.

Federal security remained Chitwood's preoccupation. "I have 160 cops and the FBI has two agents in Portland," he kept stressing through every available media outlet. On the one-month anniversary of 9/11, the *Press Herald* repeated Chitwood's conclusions that the FBI was putting lives at risk by refusing to share information about their ongoing investigations. "I don't have to know what's going on in Boston, and I don't have to know what's happening in L.A.," he stated, "but if it impacts on Portland, Maine, I need to know about it. . . . It's a new day and new collaborations are needed." For example, Chitwood was particularly rankled when he learned that an Afghan native living in the city had bragged about his links to terrorist organizations and his intention to take flying lessons, which the FBI had known about for five months. For what conceivable reason had they kept him in the dark? Federal agents told the chief to back off in his own investigation, warning him that he could be charged with obstruction of justice. Infuriated, Chitwood challenged them to just go ahead and "Arrest me!" He was also angered that the FBI had earlier information on Atta and al-Omari being in Portland, which they failed to share with him for 12 to 18 hours after the attacks.

With the FBI focusing on their "most wanted" list of major terrorist leaders, Chitwood's concerns about potential neglect of lesser localized figures were shared by others. In New York City, Mayor Rudolph Giuliani, a former prosecutor, said the FBI should be required to share "real-time information about what is happening," even proposing that Congress pass a law mandating it. But he added that the FBI should do it carefully, giving top-security clearance only on a need-to-know basis. The FBI did ultimately respond in a more positive fashion. Director Robert Mueller, addressing a meeting in Canada of the International Association of Police Chiefs, drew sustained applause when he pledged improved cooperation between FBI personnel and local police. After all, they were allied in the common cause of combating future terrorism. *Newsweek* took note of the controversy in its October 15, 2001, issue, quoting Chitwood's comment that "They're not sharing anything with anybody." However, the magazine also updated Mueller's vow of a new "spirit of teamwork and cooperation" and Attorney General John Ashcroft's recognition of local police as "our partners."

In subsequent weeks and months, things did improve, particularly as fears of major new attacks receded. Chitwood sent a detective to work with the local FBI task force. Both were obliged to follow up such periodic concerns as local reports of the pervasive anthrax scare, which turned out to be bogus. Another rumor that the next terrorist attack might be launched by a truckload of explosives led to an investigation of truckers. The rhetorical war of words diminished, as well; there was no arrest of Portland's outspoken police chief. But the possibility of terrorist assaults has remained an additional priority of hard-pressed police departments of all sizes throughout the nation, surprise being as great a fear as the possible size of such attacks. From time to time there are still complaints from one quarter or another that now we simply have too many separate, virtually competing agencies devoted to fighting terrorism on every level, and too little cooperation between them.

*   *   *

Even as potential terrorism, the inevitable aftermath of 9/11, continued to dominate public consciousness, Chitwood's perennial concerns had hardly simmered down. The Dorazio lawsuit alleging police brutality was only the most visible, but one well-regarded officer had already resigned from the force after being placed on leave for undisclosed offenses. Attempts were made to revoke the liquor license of a particularly rowdy Old Port bar, and Chitwood proposed that habitual offenders who drove with suspended licenses should have their vehicles impounded. He ascribed the increase in sex-assault reports to more victims being willing to report them, and decried the use of a drug popularly called "Ecstasy," coming from out of state, by "younger and younger kids." He kept running, at least in the literal if not political sense, in one notable race to promote "peace through sports." Occasionally, bizarre incidents made their way to the docket, from a cockfight arranged by Vietnamese immigrants (but against the law in Maine) to home invasions by a 14-year-old boy (more to go through women's underwear than to steal it). What next?

*   *   *

The most lurid crime, however, was the disappearance of an attractive, popular young woman on Saturday night, October 21, 2001. Amy St. Laurent, a striking blue-eyed blonde, was a very responsible, perennially upbeat 25-year-old with a wide acquaintance of friends. She had been raised in Portland but was now living in South Berwick, and had gone out on the town to show Old Port's attractions to a friend from Florida. But she had not returned to her job the following Monday morning, nor had she returned home to feed her cat in the interim. She was last seen around 1:45 a.m. on Sunday at the Pavilion, the Old Port club that Chitwood had most recently complained about. He was particularly concerned because most missing-persons cases in Portland involved unstable young people running away from home, and those were quickly resolved. Only a few over the years had led to tragedy or had never been solved. With the encouragement of Amy's parents, police quickly distributed hundreds of flyers throughout the area. Chitwood repeated to the *Press Herald*, "Certainly we're concerned. These things don't happen in Portland," even in the Old Port area. Her family offered a $35,000 reward to anyone who might be of help in finding her. A candlelight vigil was held in the city's Monument Square by Amy's family and a hundred friends. As one young coed at the University of Southern Maine put it, "This could have happened to any of us."

Chitwood was candid in admitting that, while "we're following every lead, the longer this goes on, the more difficult it's going to be to find her." By late November, the circuitous trail had indicated the possibility of evidence of some kind in Casco Bay. In the process, the search for this missing young woman led to the fortuitous rescue of another. Portland police and the coast guard turned back a depressed, possibly mentally disturbed woman bent on committing suicide in the frigid water and had her taken to Maine Medical Center.

On December 8th, after revealing he had settled on an unnamed suspect in the apparent crime—the last person to have been seen with Amy St. Laurent those seven weeks ago—Chitwood announced the discovery of a body. Found in a shallow grave in Scarborough, it was almost certainly Amy's. An extensive search, engaging the efforts of many groups including the state police and canine units, had finally centered on a wooded area. "We follow up on all credible leads," Chitwood had said, from seeking evidence in Casco Bay to a murder weapon in ponds near where the body was actually discovered. Maine warden service volunteers had trod upon an uncommonly soft patch of ground in the woods and then had seen spade marks under its pine needles. Digging carefully, they hit the remains of a body two feet deeper. Part of it was covered with a sweatshirt from Pratt and Whitney, Amy's employer. She had worn such a shirt and jeans on the night she disappeared. A state medical examination followed. There was no doubt about the body's identity. "First and foremost," a grim Chitwood affirmed, "this means closure for the family." Chitwood praised their resolve, in the midst of such a haunting tragedy, to help in trying to prevent others in the future.

On February 8, 2002, 22-year-old Jeffrey "Russ" Gorman was indicted for the murder of Amy St. Laurent. The wooded area in which her body had been found was only half a mile from the current home of Gorman's mother. Although he was now living in Maine, Gorman had spent most of his troubled youth in Florida and Alabama.

Revealing the extraordinary extensiveness of the search, which involved many agencies and some jurisdictional disputes between them, the *South Florida Sun Sentinel* reported on February 9th, "A former Delray Beach resident was indicted Friday in Maine on murder charges in a case that brought detectives to Palm Beach County in search of evidence." Although the Maine medical examiner didn't reveal until the following month that the exact cause of death was a bullet to the head, Chitwood was quoted on February 9th in media reports from Maine to Florida that he was convinced, given the unstable, violent nature of Gorman's past, that Amy St. Laurent must have suffered terribly before she was murdered.

For once, Chitwood was praised locally for his quiet approach to so deadly serious a case. Back in December, prior to the arrest, a *Press Herald* editorial observed that "Chitwood's silence has served him well." It went on to point out that although "he's taken a lot of heat over the years for his obvious taste for the limelight . . . as Chitwood's leadership in the Amy St. Laurent murder case has proven, when information is critical to a criminal investigation the chief seems to know exactly how to balance the public's appetite for news with the department's need for secrecy."

When in Maine, Gorman, who had been in trouble of one kind or another most of his life, had been known to hide stolen merchandise in the same wooded area near his mother's current home where Amy St. Laurent's body had been found. He had come forward soon after seeing the posters of her disappearance, indicating that he was one of many people to have been with her that night and vowing his desire to help. It must have seemed sensible. He was bound to have been contacted eventually. Gorman claimed to have met Amy at the Pavilion, where she had come after playing pool elsewhere, for a night of dancing and partying. Later he had taken her to a private party at an apartment with a friend. When the party had failed to materialize, he said he'd returned Amy to the club and gone back to the apartment on Brighton Avenue to see what might still develop. They had all been doing a lot of drinking, and later, when Amy's parents had learned more about Gorman's past, they feared he may have drugged their daughter's glass before abducting her. For one thing, it was out of character for Amy, even surrounded by others, to leave a party with someone other than the person she had come with.

Chitwood suspected Jeffrey Gorman's involvement only two or three days after he was met and interviewed by Portland detectives. For one thing, no one else could corroborate his story. No one remembered him dropping Amy off back at the club. No one had seen her after she left with Gorman around 1:45 a.m. If he had later left the after-hours party with Amy, it wasn't to return her anywhere. Evident contradictions included the fact that he had been stopped by police for using his high beams on Main Street in the nearby town of Westbrook around 3:00 a.m. when he claimed to have been in Portland. When police confronted him with questions about his story, Gorman was so upset that they had to obtain a search warrant to look through his car for possible forensic evidence. Chitwood had his suspect, likely a lone one, but no trace of evidence or a body.

It can be prejudicial, as attorneys tend to attest, to hold a person's past against him, particularly in so potentially serious a case. However, Gorman didn't help his circumstances when he left Maine about a month later for Alabama and was promptly arrested on violation of probation charges stemming from a four-hour standoff with police in the town of Troy. Years before, in Alabama, after his parents had divorced, he lived for a time with an uncle who had served time in prison. When Gorman was 14 years old, in Florida, his mother, who personally feared his violent, brutal outbursts, had him committed to a mental health institution. Shunted between the two states, he was frequently suspended from school and convicted of burglary, theft, assault, and later failure to pay child support. His most recent incident involved robbing two college students in Troy and then holding off police with two handguns. At one point, he had threatened to shoot himself. Eventually surrendering, Gorman had violated probation so many times that he was held without bail, and with evident relief on the part of local law authorities, extradited to his current place of residence in Maine.

However brief their acquaintance, what could possibly have attracted an intelligent young woman like Amy St. Laurent to such an apparent misfit as Jeffrey Gorman, or to go anywhere with him? Even with no knowledge of his homicidal proclivities, she must have been, if not drugged, at least a bit high.

After a protracted, painstaking investigation and trial that riveted widespread attention well beyond Maine, complicated by Gorman's mother recanting her earlier grand jury testimony that her troubled son had actually admitted the murder to her, Jeffrey Gorman, now 23, was finally convicted in January 2003 and sentenced to 60 years. He escaped a life sentence because there was no proof of premeditation and in view of his possible mental state. There is no death penalty in Maine, to the profound regret of many within and outside the courtroom. The shocking murder inspired a TV drama and a 2006 book by then-captain but at the time Portland police lieutenant Joseph K. Loughlin and former assistant attorney general Kate Clark Flora, titled *Finding Amy—A True Story of Murder in Maine*. It might have been subtitled instead, "So Rare a Story of Murder in Maine."

*   *   *

This uncommonly high-profile homicide overshadowed the fact that for the second year in a row no police officers were killed in the state—this in the face of the deadliest year for police fatalities nationwide since 1974. In 2001, 231 officers were killed throughout the United States, including 70 at the World Trade Center on 9/11, the largest number to die at one time in the nation's history. Chitwood's explanation, beyond luck, since police officers in Portland alone were assaulted some 50 to 70 times in an average year, derived from the state's overall low crime rate and the "tremendous amount of training in how to deal with violent situations" his officers received. Left unsaid was how his own aversion to using firearms had influenced the nature of such training, at least in the most populous part of Maine charged to his care.

At the same time, local sentiment was turning against such Chitwood proposals as impounding the cars of people who continued to drive with suspended licenses. The *Press Herald* suggested that serving time in prison would be a greater deterrent to the 700 or so such habitual cases in Portland. A far more serious setback for Chitwood, a harbinger of conflict to come, was the stunning settlement by the city of Portland of $600,000, the largest sum ever paid in the city's history, to end a lawsuit asking for over a million dollars. It had been brought by tenacious attorney and Chitwood critic Daniel Lilley in behalf of Vincent Dorazio, the man beaten and pistol-whipped by two Portland police officers. Lilley insisted that a neurologist would have testified that his client had suffered permanent brain damage. Later investigation placed that assertion, and others, very much in doubt. Chitwood was infuriated about the resolution of this case and also by some subsequent, less sizeable settlements. He would always insist that the more aggressive city attorney to come would have taken the lawsuit to trial and won, a view soon shared by others. Although hardly given to reticence himself, Chitwood was never one to submit meekly to the accusations of publicity-seeking lawyers.

Still, the chief had acted promptly when the original incident had taken place in 2001. In a *Press* Herald article of January 9, 2002, Gregory Kesich thoroughly explored the ramifications of both the disputed circumstances and the settlement, as announced by city manager Joe Gray. Directly after the beating of Dorazio, Chitwood had opened a criminal investigation into the conduct of the two police officers involved—Stephen Taylor and Kevin Haley. He also initiated an internal affairs investigation. Either officer, or both, might conceivably have been dismissed or charged with assault. Instead, they remained on the force but were taken off patrol duties.

Nevertheless, the case—and now this immense settlement—had opened the floodgates to already existing rivulets of resentment. Kesich quoted Portland mayor Karen Geraghty: "We are incredibly disappointed and saddened by the action of two employees in the police department. This is not what the citizens expect and we will not tolerate this behavior." Kesich added Geraghty's intention to take steps "to change the way we do business" and win back public confidence. The prior week, Portland's legal team had decided not to appeal a $50,000 judgment against another officer, in that instance found guilty by a federal jury of using excessive force. Adding legal fees to the plaintiff's attorney, that total would likely rise to over $100,000. In addition, the city had paid to settle a third such case in October, and two others were pending. It all came to about $720,000. Because Portland carried no liability insurance for its police force, all settlements would have to come from an already tight city budget, ultimately paid for by the taxpayers.

Daniel Lilley was having a field day, depicting Chitwood as heading a sort of down east equivalent of the Gestapo. The problem comes from the top, he insisted. "This city has got to hold Chitwood more accountable," he told Kesich. "He has to start disciplining people who use violence as a means of law enforcement. . . . There's an 'us versus them' mentality. . . . They are convinced that they are a law unto themselves." Lilley further portrayed Portland's peculiar problems as stemming from the "big city" attitude of its longtime police chief, echoing the earlier complaints of such Chitwood critics as all those gun owners that he could never shed the aggressive mentality of his Philadelphia roots.

As for 40-year-old Vincent Dorazio, the largely overlooked victim of this case, the incident leading to Lilley's original lawsuit had stemmed from a case of mistaken identity. Seeing him strolling Portland's India Street, Officer Haley thought he recognized a man named Frank Fournier, a violent criminal wanted on a warrant for his arrest. When Haley tried to talk to Dorazio, he ran away. Dorazio later claimed that he was fearful because he had been beaten by policemen before, but he had never filed a complaint. By the time Haley caught up with him, Officer Taylor and two others had joined in surrounding their suspect. After he struggled to get away, Dorazio was hit with a baton and then reportedly with the butt of a pistol, suffering head wounds. The lawsuit alleged that he was also punched in the face and kicked repeatedly by Haley and Taylor as he lay on the ground, while the other two officers yelled anti-Italian epithets and may also have laughed. How all that must have elicited in Chitwood still vivid memories of prior accusations, exacerbated by the press. There is little doubt that Dorazio, treated in Mercy Hospital's emergency room, was seriously injured. However, the extent of his injuries, their ultimate and potential results, and the actual time the entire episode entailed might well have been questioned at a trial. Dorazio was charged with "criminal threatening" and resisting arrest, but both charges were later dismissed. Even though Dorazio was in fact not the man Haley had thought he was, Officer Taylor did claim to have felt threatened by his resistance.

The city had already approved creation of a Citizen Review Board to provide at least some oversight of police activities, including a review of Chitwood's own internal affairs process. Daniel Lilley was among the first to volunteer for the new board. Chitwood had always opposed such a review process, insisting in a prior *Press Herald* guest editorial that the police force could and should objectively discipline its own personnel and asking for patience. Now, however, he admitted that perhaps such an oversight board might be necessary to win back the public's confidence.

Characteristically, Chitwood took the offensive to expand the process. He didn't exactly relish having Daniel Lilley and his ilk perpetually just over his shoulder, prejudging his every action or utterance. Asserting that he was "as outraged as everyone else" about these cases and vowing to "do the right thing" in reviewing every aspect of police work and shining the light on every single patrolman's actions, Chitwood went directly to the Civil Rights Division of the United States Department of Justice. Launching an unprecedented request for their oversight, Chitwood joined with Portland's mayor and city manager in a major press conference to request a thorough federal audit and review of all the activities of its police department as the most effective way to restore public trust. It would likely take over a year, the first such investigation of its kind in New England, and was instituted with the cooperation of Maine's congressional delegation. Including the appraisal of other police chiefs, it should objectively determine whether unlawful practices of excessive force were prevalent in Portland and suggest ways to end them.

Among those in support of the review was Robert Dougherty, president of the union representing police officers, who expressed in a statement his conviction that such a federal probe would dispel erroneous perceptions of the department, which had culminated in so many "frivolous lawsuits." Dougherty insisted: "They certainly have given incorrect impressions of the department and police officers. We are tremendously confident that the Department of Justice will see us as a fine organization."

He was hardly alone in that view, although the actual review of police practices didn't start until June 2002, with the arrival in Portland of a three-person investigative team. Letters to the editor of local and regional newspapers, recently critical of Chitwood, turned in favor of this new development that they identified with him. Public opinion, of course, can be as fickle as the Maine weather that Chitwood had originally decried. He had long since learned how to help shape it, as adroitly as he'd mastered the hard lessons of dealing with unpredictable, sensation-seeking media, wherever their locale. Always take the initiative; the response rarely catches up to the accusation.

By March 2002, the *Casco Bay Weekly*, by the vote of its readers, had named Chitwood, for the fourth time, the area's "best local person." As the periodical put it, "Despite a troubling year . . . he reclaimed the honor. . . . It must be especially welcome this time, because the chief's force is under federal investigation for being overzealous." That isn't quite the way Chitwood would have characterized a probe he had himself requested. However, he responded, when informed that he was once again "beloved by the masses" (in the proletarian phrasing of the editor), "I am honored to think people in this town think that much of me and what we are doing. It shows people in this community are paying attention."

In an even more telling example of the turnaround, in April, Officer Kevin Haley, a central figure in the $600,000 settlement, was named the Portland Police Department's "Officer of the Month." Unlike most such selections, made each month by a committee of lieutenants and sergeants, this ceremony was well attended, with some 25 colleagues of Haley's on hand at City Hall to lend him their support. Councilor Philip Dawson, breaking tradition as had some other councilors by commenting publicly after the ceremony, wondered aloud, as had Chitwood, whether the city would have had to pay Vincent Dorazio anything "had we fought the good fight," adding that "Haley is a fine example of what our police officers are all about."

A Cumberland County grand jury had declined to indict either Haley or Taylor for excessive violence, despite the settlement granted to Dorazio. His original lawsuit, filed by Lilley, insisted he had been chased without provocation and badly beaten. As reported by David Hench in the *Press Herald*, "Cumberland County District Attorney Stephanie Anderson said the investigation of Officers Stephen Taylor and Kevin Haley showed that initial reports about the degree of force used against Vincent Dorazio, and his injuries, were exaggerated." Anderson concluded: "The police took a horrible rap in this case. It seems to me everyone jumped the gun. . . . I think the city settled on insufficient evidence." With so few witnesses there can be many versions of reality. There was spirited applause when the jury's decision was announced. After the ceremony honoring Haley, Chitwood reiterated Councilor Dawson's opinion that "Kevin Haley is an excellent officer." Attorney Daniel Lilley was unusually unavailable for comment following both events.

* * *

Even a modest incident, however, can turn media attention back around again, rarely more quickly than in the volatile environment of the year following the trauma of 9/11. This particular tempest-in-a-terminal dispute involved a police chief under uncommon stress. If Mike Chitwood's emotional breakdown at the trial of the scumbag who had killed Nicky Caserta demonstrated his humanity, his outburst at a Global Security guard in charge of parking at the Portland

International Jetport demonstrated it in a different dimension. Security at airports throughout the nation had become incomparably more stringent, nowhere more than in Portland, where those two terrorists had simply sauntered through. When Chitwood's unmarked police car rolled into the jetport and he was told by the guard that he could no longer park by the entrance to its fire station because of new FAA security regulations, the chief went surprisingly ballistic, reportedly including an impressive string of expletives. Chitwood then sped away in his Ford Crown Victoria. There were about 50 spectators, so the news quickly made the rounds. Although Global Security's Portland office was headed by two of Chitwood's former subordinates, the fact is that this poor security guard really didn't know who his verbal assailant was. At least not at first.

Both City Manager Gray and Mayor Geraghty expressed their concern, and an editorial in the *Press Herald* joined in, suggesting that Chitwood, whatever the challenges to his customary public demeanor, "might have provided better leadership by biting his tongue for once." Chitwood agreed to a mea culpa, admitting that "I screwed up" and later added: "I feel like I let the organization down. I'm supposed to set a tone." He apologized to the guard—and, in effect, to the city—agreeing to carry an identifying placard on his car in the future. However, despite this singular lapse amidst all the pressure he faced, Chitwood returned as always to his upbeat mantra: "The bottom line is I love this job. I love this city. And this is a great department."

Apparently, that was good enough for most of the local citizenry, at least as evidenced by "Voice of the People" letters to the editor of the *Press Herald*. One woman wrote: "The city of Portland is lucky to have Chief Chitwood protecting our citizens. . . . This is a man who is on call 24 hours a day, seven days a week. . . . He is a dedicated professional and—gasp—a human being." Another noted: "How admirable and refreshing for a public figure to take responsibility for his behavior. . . . Thank you to Chief Chitwood for setting an example!" Other letters stressed the balance of his underappreciated good works—including aid to immigrants, the homeless, the mentally ill, and the gay population—and the "sensitivity and understanding" he has brought to his department. Another, from a Scarborough writer, took the *Press Herald* itself to task: "Please do not be so anxious about finding a flaw in the city of Portland's police chief! Your paper is amazing as to what you print about Chitwood. . . . The man is a frank, no-holds-barred person, but Michael Chitwood is the face of your city! Try cutting Chitwood some slack. The man gives you and your city a lot more than you give him." And from a Portland resident: "So, police chief Michael Chitwood has shown . . . that he is a human being." All he has done is "made our city one of the safest places" to live in.

A letter from Portland resident Patrick Eisenhart, arriving at the *Press Herald* in the midst of this latest brouhaha, posed a few pertinent questions transcending the immediate story: "Can anyone tell me why Portland Police Chief Michael

Chitwood, a 'top cop' by national standards . . . has never been formally decorated by the Portland City Council? Can anyone tell me why the council appears to 'fold' rather than 'fight' the alleged claims of police brutality? [Chitwood's] performance here has certainly demonstrated that he is truly a 'top cop' worthy of formal recognition by the city, along with strong support for his department and his recommendations—politically popular or not!"

Still the people's choice, if not always that of the politicians or the press. Admittedly, police have one of the toughest jobs in our society, and while their responsibility is not to abuse the public's trust, most of those in Maine seemed willing to balance so much difficulty and danger with an occasional lapse in judgment, even by the outspoken cop at the top.

* * *

As anticipated, after Portland attained its "bigger-city" status, the homicides, if not more frequent, seemed more dramatic, and sometimes as horrific as those in the most urban of environments. Portland police shot and killed a man as he threatened a city cabdriver with a stolen 9-mm. handgun. John S. Dawson, a 21-year-old resident of Gardiner, Maine, was wanted in connection with an armed robbery there and had told family members he would not be taken alive. Hiding out in a Portland apartment, he emerged to catch a cab to take him to buy some cigarettes. Tipped off to Dawson's location, three Portland police cruisers surrounded the cab. Dawson pulled out his gun. Asked to drop it, Dawson aimed it at the cabbie's head. A melee ensued, the cabdriver escaped, and several shots were fired. One killed Dawson. "Any time someone dies, that's a tragedy," Chitwood remarked, while defending his officers' actions in protecting an innocent cabdriver and themselves.

A stabbing death following a fight between Somali immigrants over a woman in front of the Whit's End bar in Old Town, the scene of frequent disturbances, reinforced Chitwood's call for the nonrenewal of the club's liquor license, slated to be considered the following month. Using one of his favorite expressions, the chief called this latest tragedy "only the tip of the iceberg." The body of Anne Marie Caouette was discovered in a pool of blood by a maintenance worker at her apartment building. She had been scheduled to testify against a former boyfriend jailed on an abuse charge. The most heinous example of the city's underside was the rescue from near death of a 34-day-old child. Her youthful parents had allegedly killed their two prior children, unable or unwilling to learn how to cope with infants. It had been estimated that child abuse cases in Maine had risen from 10 to 14 percent of the total workload of the state Department of Human Services in the previous four years. To Chitwood, hardly overstating this heartbreaking case, "It's absolutely pure evil."

While awaiting the results of the federal investigation of his department and preparing for the possibility of more terrorist activity, Chitwood continued to pursue his ongoing areas of concern. A woman named Sharon Forbis filed a notice of complaint against the city, alleging that police beat her up after they were called to her house to break up a fistfight between her two sons. In this instance, her lawyer—yes, it was Daniel Lilley—was only planning to sue the city for $500,000. Chitwood had instituted training of his Crisis Intervention Team in more tactful techniques to defuse conflict in cases dealing with those afflicted with mental illness. A new ordinance permitted Portland police to impound for 30 days any car driven by chronic offenders of Maine's drunk driving and traffic laws. However, it included the right to appeal, to either the police or city hall. The new emphasis seemed already to be on restraint. As he had suspected, Chitwood found that the use of methadone might be doing more harm than good, and he urged rethinking the city's drug take-home policy. Addicts needed aid, but not every clinic was preventing the increase in drug overdoses.

A particularly violent daylight attack on a gay man during the annual Southern Maine "pride" weekend shocked both Portland's mayor and its police chief, united in this instance to denounce hate crimes in the most outspoken terms. To Chitwood, it represented a "despicable, cowardly act," familiar words for a still-too-frequent event.

Just as an earlier decade had been defined as the "Age of Anxiety," the year following 9/11 launched an age of uncertainty—its stress shared by almost everyone.

Hail to the Chief!

Well, Chitwood had asked for it. Characteristically, instead of waiting, as had been the case in other cities, for a mandated investigation of the policies and practices of their police departments, Mike had requested such a probe. And the United States Department of Justice had complied. Such a proactive "we have nothing to hide" approach engendered a positive environment of cooperation, almost of partnership, from the start. Everything was open to the Justice Department's Civil Rights Division. Nothing was off limits. They exhaustively interviewed everyone from Portland's city officials and individual police officers to those who had complained of being victimized by them. They reviewed tens of thousands of documents detailing every aspect of police work over a considerable span of time.

It took three years to complete the Justice Department's final report. However, their ongoing conclusions were issued in three roughly annual installments, enabling Chitwood to combine their recommendations with his own reforms, many of which he had already begun to initiate. The first interim report, made public in March 2003, emphasized improving the department's review system and developing alternative training methods. Chitwood put in place tighter internal controls and assigned more personnel to his internal affairs department, including a lieutenant and a second sergeant. He strengthened officer oversight and better integrated patrol teams with community involvement. The joint review also led to a new, less overtly aggressive technique called "verbal judo" in handling challenging situations that might lead to an arrest. Hopefully, this de-escalation approach, reminiscent of what Chitwood had developed on his own back in Philadelphia, would reduce complaints of excessive force that had led to this investigation in the first place.

It drew a response from Shanetta Y. Cutlar, chief of the special litigations section of the Department of Justice. In an open letter, she commended the Portland Police Department, from its chief on down, for its wholehearted participation in her work. "Our ability to conduct and conclude this investigation is a testament to [their] cooperation," she wrote.

However, the second interim report, in June 2004, drew an equivocal headline from David Hench's article in the *Press Herald*: "Report Gives City Police Mixed Reviews." Hench summarized its conclusions as finding no pattern of civil rights violations that might require enforcement action, but still raising concerns about how quickly police resorted to force when making arrests and the biased way they might be permitted to report such incidents. However, as then Portland mayor Nathan Smith pointed out, the report was "somewhat retrospective." Relevant reforms were already well under way to address these concerns.

The final report, issued at the end of June 2005, highlighted additional improvements that Chitwood had implemented: a specific Use of Force Committee to look quickly into any such reports or complaints, and an early-warning system to monitor the behavior of officers. As Kate Bucklin added in the *Falmouth Forecaster* of July 6, 2005, "Other changes include the addition of video cameras in all marked police cruisers, establishing a permanent Old Port beat team, an increase in peer support available to officers and rewriting of several department policies."

City manager Joe Gray had held a joint press conference with Chitwood on June 30th to announce the findings. Lauding the chief for his initiative in originally requesting such an outside investigation, Gray remarked, "Before this began I said [to Chitwood], 'Once we go down this road, we don't know quite where we'll end up.'" But three years later there was more commendation of Mike Chitwood's stewardship than criticism. In its 2004 use-of-force report, the Portland police's Internal Affairs Department noted a 25 percent drop in citizens' complaints against officers since the prior year. Chitwood pledged continued improvements, while cautioning: "Obviously, mistakes were made in the past, and will be in the future. We'll continue to monitor how we do things. . . . We want to maintain a high standard of credibility and integrity." Transparency pays.

*　　*　　*

Of course, as all this reviewing and ramping up was proceeding, the old issues had an annoying habit of recurring. By the start of June 2004, there had been 263 car break-ins in the city, an increase of 10 percent over the prior year. Chitwood joined with the police chiefs of surrounding communities in distributing bright yellow bulletins to motorists, listing commonsense precautions against auto theft. Leaving items in view simply invited such attempts. He also noted the increasing problem of more aggressive "smash-and-grab" robberies in public places, ascribing it to "feeding their expensive drug habits." Identity theft was another increasing concern, with 424 cases filed in Maine in 2004.

Then there were the individual cases of bizarre behavior. An 11-year-old girl was stabbed by her agitated mother in an apparently "ritualistic" attack, the knife wrestled away by an older child. Another baffling stabbing incident involved a deranged young woman attacking the 15-month-old son of her purported best friend, and then setting a fire to destroy the evidence. Stopped by police for evidence in a drug case, a Portland man turned his gun on himself. He had been despondent since the death of his two-year-old son. The child had ingested his father's pain medication. A bomb scare, written on the wall of an Old Port bar, was, in those tense times, taken seriously enough to be investigated, but turned out to be a hoax.

Beyond crimes based on the insidious influence of drugs, Mike Chitwood's concerns continued to focus on gun control and attempts to reduce government funding, even for vital law enforcement activities. Accounts of teenagers accused of aggravated assault and posting photos of themselves on the Internet holding guns were troubling, particularly in terms of the recent Columbine tragedy. Chitwood was frequently photographed holding aloft an ominous-looking assault weapon, stressing again that his aim was at violent crime, not Maine's legion of sportsmen. "Do you hunt with an AK-47?" he repeatedly questioned in public. In July 2004, Chitwood took part in a "Halt the Assault" rally, one of many held throughout the nation, to raise awareness of the imminent expiration of the federal assault weapons ban. Although often viewed as insufficiently enforced, at least it was on the statute books. Ever outspoken, never more than on this issue, he exhorted the crowd: "The clock is running out. President Bush says he supports the ban. It's time for him to start acting like it."

With the 2004 presidential elections looming, the first since 9/11, Chitwood was particularly engaged in the security of campaign events and polling places. Gun control was on the national agenda. The Democratic aspirant, Senator John Kerry, himself a hunter, accused Bush, running for reelection, of bowing to the powerful National Rifle Association lobby. "They're spending tens of millions of dollars to support his campaign," Kerry insisted. "Is George Bush going to stand with special interests or with the safety of the American people?" Kerry lost. The assault weapons ban expired.

A new tax cap referendum under consideration by the state legislature in August, brought by a group called the Maine Taxpayers Action Network, threatened to limit arbitrarily the ability of every municipality in the state to raise revenues by taxation, setting a specific percentage. In Chitwood's view, if passed, it could potentially decimate his department, its resources already severely strained. Allied with officeholders from throughout the state, he vigorously opposed the measure, and it failed. Win some, lose some.

Protecting a more vulnerable Portland required, if anything, increased resources. Chitwood had warned early on of more violent crimes invading its precincts.

Scumbags come from everywhere, and even if local homicides remained relatively few, their threat had escalated. As the *Press Herald* pointed out on September 30, 2004: "Portland's broad social services attract many homeless and transient people from outside of Maine . . . like the population generally, most are harmless and obey the law. Some are not, and police say they are seeing more criminals from outside the state."

In November 2004, a young woman suffered a particularly brutal attack by a transient from Florida, reminiscent of prior crimes against women by outsiders in previous years. She had been raped and beaten so repeatedly "she is lucky to be alive," a grim Chitwood commented. Not all the brutality came from out of state. Noting that Portland police respond to some 700 reports of domestic violence each year, after one particularly horrific case in which a Rockport woman was beaten to death, Chitwood resolved to toughen Maine's sex-offender laws. He took this, his latest crusade, to *The Montel Williams Show* in New York, insisting it had national implications. Accompanying him was activist Michelle Tardif, who had been beaten, raped, and left for dead back in 1989 when she was only 10. When her attacker was released from prison the previous fall, Tardif conducted her own neighborhood notification. Chitwood wanted such criminals, sentenced for crimes before 1992, to have to register as sex offenders wherever they move, to have their neighbors warned, and be barred from living near children's facilities. None of that was currently the case.

As November neared, both the FBI and the Department of Homeland Security were taking precautions to assure a safe, secure election nationwide, protecting all 200,000 polling places. There had been terrorist attacks in Europe, one on commuter trains in Madrid in March, killing 191 people. With memories of 9/11 still fresh, Chitwood joined with officials throughout the state to set up Maine's Joint Terrorism Task Force. The irony wasn't lost on him that this was at the request of the federal government, a recommendation made to every state. He wryly observed that only three years before "The feedback I got from the FBI is that I was obstructing justice because I was doing an independent investigation. Today . . . they want us to be part of the terrorist task force, and it's a great idea."

In another longtime concern, Chitwood continued to urge more funding for extensive pre-kindergarten programs in schools throughout the state—indeed, the nation. It was an investment not only in education but in public safety. "To keep Maine safe," he stressed to every audience, "we need to be as willing to guarantee our kids a space in pre-kindergarten as we are to guarantee a jail cell to a criminal." When the budget crunch threatened to close Portland's Help Center, offering psychiatric services to hundreds, Chitwood weighed in, warning, "We're going to see an increased need for people in mental health crises." His department received some 1,000 calls related to this issue each year.

* * *

Perhaps even more than in the past, Mike Chitwood's public utterances dwelled on areas well beyond the limitations of a police chief's customary concerns. But, after all, doesn't public safety have an impact on every aspect of community life? And when Chitwood was criticized from Middletown to Maine for not being averse to publicity, he responded that it represented a positive more for the people he represented and the policies he espoused than for himself alone. Yet more than once "Media Mike" had been accused of using his office in harboring political ambitions. Certainly, he had sometimes seemed to others a logical candidate for public office. In a reflective mood years ago in Philadelphia, he had pondered such a career change, perhaps even to public relations or as a consultant. Moreover, he had been approached to run for both sheriff and city council. But such contemplations always returned to the reality that, whatever its frustrations, Mike loved what he did, and police work involved public service more directly than getting involved in speculative local politics. Still, since the next logical step in his chosen career, progressing from Maine to a bigger job in Florida, hadn't panned out, and his tenure in Portland had extended far beyond its intended expiration date, there was still time to consider other options. What do they say? Sixty is the new 50, or some such.

In terms of career enhancement, under the heading "All in the Family," Trevor Maxwell of the *Press Herald* wrote about another Mike Chitwood who had policed the mean streets of Philadelphia for nearly 20 years. He, too, had been "chasing down killers and dealers," while collecting both commendations and critics. But now this tough, often-quoted cop surprised his superiors. He, too, was leaving to serve as police chief in a small city, with only a fraction of Philly's crime. Mike Chitwood Jr. continued to follow a career path like his father's. Only his first transition to administration, after finally receiving his bachelor's degree, wouldn't be the few miles away to a suburb like Middletown, but all the way to the prairie town of Shawnee, Oklahoma. Go where the opportunity is, his parents had counseled. "This must be in my genes," the younger Chitwood commented. His relationship with his father had gone full circle—from idolizing him as a youngster, to rebelling as a teenager, and now to becoming closer than ever. From whatever locations, the two talked every day, sometimes as much as four or five times.

The result of a brief visit to his daughter, Beth Ann, in North Carolina, Mike Chitwood Sr. produced a somewhat more embarrassing piece of news. Returning to Portland, his face decorated with an ugly pattern of bruises, scrapes, and scratches, he announced to the media, "I just want people to see stupidity." Borrowing Beth Ann's bike to take a spin in the mild weather, he failed to take a precaution he'd always followed, whether riding bikes or motorcycles. He neglected to wear a helmet. Cutting through a parking lot to get to a bike trail, he approached a speed bump. Unfortunately, the bike he was riding lacked the extensions on its handlebars he was used to. He hit the bump and was catapulted over it, landing on his face and winding up on his stomach. Fortunately, a passing motorist took the copiously bleeding Chitwood to a nearby hospital for treatment. It could have been worse, but it could hardly look much worse. At least he would now even more vigorously preach, to adults as well as children, the absolute necessity of never riding without a helmet, a fairly obvious aspect of public safety, even in the long bike lanes surrounding Portland.

*　　*　　*

Biking featured in much of the local crime throughout 2005, but it was motorcycles, along with the customary cases involving drugs and alcohol. Chitwood supported an act introduced in the Maine legislature to penalize adults distributing alcohol to underage users by, among other things, suspending their driving privileges. He led an investigation of a high school dance where a dozen students showed up intoxicated and three were treated for alcohol poisoning. Who had provided the alcohol? The investigation led to charges against a 25-year-old man from nearby Cape Elizabeth, abetted by three juveniles, and to a more intensive crackdown on underage drinking.

An argument in a Portland tattoo parlor between members of rival motorcycle gangs left one man with serious gunshot wounds. Just as with mob clashes back in Philly, members of both gangs weren't about to cooperate with police in nabbing the assailant. "They are going to handle it themselves," Chitwood commented. "It's the code of stupidity." Fearing potential violence among rival motorcycle gangs, the city of Portland called off a country music concert. Despite the lack of violence from the heavy gang presence at a motorcycle show at the local exposition center, Chitwood increased police presence to counter a potential turf war. A motorcycle gang called the Outlaws was trying to expand its local dominance. Every gang had to be monitored.

From the start, Chitwood had warned of the inevitable intrusion of outsiders in both new and established forms of violent crime. In June 2005, sometimes it worked both ways. A Portland man was extradited to Texas, where he faced a murder charge in the slaying of another man with ties to Maine. A 38-year-old Portland man named Victoriano Dubon had fled to Boston after fatally stabbing his roommate following an argument in their second-floor apartment. Although only Portland's second homicide of 2005, somehow the environment seemed more threatening. However, Chitwood retained his confidence that the police force under his command remained up to any challenge. "Going in, we were a very, very good department," he had said, flanked by city manager Joe Gray, in that press conference announcing the receipt of the Justice Department's final report. "Coming out," he continued, "we are better than that."

*　　*　　*

But a surprise was coming. In July, Chitwood announced that he was thinking about moving back to Pennsylvania. At age 61, 17 of his 41 years in law enforcement had been in Maine. After St. Petersburg, he had not followed up other possibilities. This time it just seemed right. He had responded to an invitation to apply to replace retiring Vincent Ficchi as police superintendent of Upper Darby, a diverse, urban-suburban community adjacent to West Philadelphia. He had submitted his application in June and was interviewed by a five-man committee, met with officials, and toured the township earlier in July. As Chitwood told Linda Reilly of the *Delaware County Daily Times* in mid-July: "I told the committee . . . it was an opportunity I'd like to pursue. . . . I've been notified I'm a finalist. They said they would make their decision by Monday." But it sounded like the decision had already been made, as Chitwood added, "Obviously, we are negotiating a package."

Even though the package would include a $40,000 pay raise (although Upper Darby's police force was smaller than Portland's), Chitwood had still been a bit conflicted during the negotiations. He retained many friends in Philadelphia, many within the Drexel Hill neighborhood of Upper Darby, but his own family was now scattered. Going home was more a matter of roots than relatives. Although Ficchi was leaving under a cloud—a grand jury investigation of whether he had quashed the fourth drunken-driving conviction of a well-connected friend of the department—Chitwood insisted, "It has nothing to do with my ability to lead."

Yet Mike had come to love Maine. He felt that he should at least talk things over with Joe Gray. They had been through so much together. Before the job possibility had even been publicly announced, he went in to see Portland's longtime city director. Gray's calm response to hearing about the Upper Darby job possibility was simply, "Congratulations—good luck." With that, Chitwood decided he would definitely take the job.

"WE LIKE MIKE" trumpeted the July 16th *Daily Times*. At his public announcement in Portland that he was leaving, Chitwood, flanked by Gray, talked with genuine emotion about leaving this city he loved, and a position he once described as "the best job in the country." As he had when departing from Middletown Township, he pointed out what a "difficult, gut-wrenching decision" it had been. "I will always consider Portland, Maine, my department . . . my people." Indeed, he had made every promotion of officers then on the force. Chitwood also stressed that as a professional, this was the first time he had made a career move more for personal than purely professional reasons. Philly still held that pull. "I love what I do," he concluded. "I've . . . learned a lot here in Portland and I think I can take it to the next level."

Consistent to the end, the *Press Herald*, while praising Chitwood's energy, passion, drive, and dedication, concluded that he departed with "mixed reviews." His style—"blunt and frequently in the public eye—has earned him high praise in some quarters and sharp criticism in others. It also has earned him a celebrity status almost unrivaled in the state." David Hench wrote, "Crime in Portland declined significantly . . . but his high-profile style brought critics." However, Bill Nemitz's column on July 20th put it more personally. Headlined "Ultimately he's a chief who cared," it concluded: "Without question, Chitwood used his bully pulpit as no chief before him ever did. . . . But as he clears out his desk and says goodbye, he leaves Maine with far more friends and foes." As always, Mike Chitwood had the last word. Summarizing more than just the Maine years, he responded to an extensive interview in the *Maine Sunday Telegram* of July 24, 2005: "Maybe my passion shows I'm a tough guy. I've been involved in a lot in my career. I've been shot at. I've been beaten up. . . . I've done it all in this job, but I like to think I'm a decent human being who has a lot of compassion." His last official act was to swear in six new police officers, wishing them a career in Portland as fulfilling as his had been.

It was not quite the last word. In the next morning's *Press Herald*, ordinary Maine citizens had their say, and it wasn't quite as "mixed" a review as the newspaper's coverage. Typical excerpts from "Voice of the People" letters to the editor:

"He is a true champion of the people . . . holding no fear of reprisal for doing the right thing: addressing crime, the homeless, issues within his own department and Portland's vulnerable children and elderly. What a fine man you are losing. Best to him, from a friend in North Yarmouth."

"Every intelligent, aware, thinking person I know is devastated by Portland's loss of Police Chief Mike Chitwood to Pennsylvania . . . fearless and fabulous! . . . Farewell to a dear friend. We shall miss him."

"We all felt safer with him and his staff watching over us daily. And he's a super nice guy. . . . We wish him the best of everything. He'll be missed by so many!"

"Mike Chitwood—*awesome*! Chief Michael Chitwood of Portland, Maine, for 17 years—*essential*."

"He stayed with Portland and kept hitting grand slams for 17 years. He has set the tone, so we will probably continue to be in good shape. We certainly will miss him! Thank you to our chief a million times over."

"About a decade ago [we] sponsored a fashion show fund-raiser. . . . Chief Chitwood, the only male model, performed with great panache, style, and humor for a surprised but receptive audience that responded with prolonged applause. . . . Thanks for the memories."

On August 17th, more than 200 guests gathered at the Holiday Inn By the Bay to bid their chief farewell, with everything from a band, an honor guard, a video presentation, speeches, a cake featuring his portrait, and commendations from both of Maine's senators, to guests ranging from David Turner, the prominent protestor who had been Chitwood's very first reluctant arrest, to the chief's family, including his son, who had flown up from Oklahoma. Chitwood stepped to the podium last. "I work with the best men and women in police work anywhere," he repeated. "I just want to say thank you, I love you, and I'll miss you."

*   *   *

To Gil Spencer of the *Delaware County Daily Times*, Mike Chitwood was returning home because he "couldn't resist the challenge." It was an Upper Darby political leader who had urged Chitwood to apply for the job. "This is a great department," said councilman Tom Micozzie, and now "we're bringing in a leader who can take it to the next level . . . a 'cop's cop' who can lift the township and its police force out of scandal. We need a fresh start." Chitwood concurred, "I'm looking for a new challenge," he said from Portland. He echoed the same reflections as when he'd started at his two prior postings: "I don't know anybody. I don't owe anybody. I have no agenda, no allegiances, other than to the community. . . . My goal is to have Upper Darby be proud of its police department, and to make it a safer place."

And so, as Spencer put it, Chitwood was willing to trade in the scenic, spectacular view from his Portland office of Casco Bay, its ferries, even its rolling fog, for a "far less scenic view of cement, blacktop, and a bunch of police cars. After 17 years in Ferry Land, Mike Chitwood is coming home."

At 10:00 a.m. on Monday, August 29, 2005, Chitwood was sworn in as the new police superintendent of Upper Darby Township, Delaware County, Pennsylvania. The previous day he had already visited evening and afternoon roll calls to personally meet the rank and file, introduced himself to everyone of relevance in and out of the department he hadn't already met, and vowed to the local news media to take an activist approach, including regularly riding in police cruisers and on bike patrol. He invited community leaders to do the same, gaining a personal appreciation of what their law enforcement officers actually do every day. Chitwood would do some looking, listening, and learning himself, expressing his intent to address the issues and always be accessible to the public. He'd had one very hectic day even before officially taking charge the following morning.

In a well-attended but "brief and breezy" swearing-in ceremony, as the *Philadelphia Daily News* characterized it, "the lean, graying" Chitwood echoed themes he had stressed when taking over in Portland, only with more urgency in this less stable environment: "My goal is to create and maintain a quality of life," he said, "making Upper Darby a great place to live and raise a family. . . . [Battling] the increase in crime—in burglaries, robberies, and domestic violence" is the first priority. To something approaching a returning hero's welcome, Chitwood reminisced about how he had once shopped on 69th Street, dined at the old Hot Shoppe on

Market Street, and cooperated with Upper Darby police in the past. "I will open up my heart as I live, work, and embrace Upper Darby as my own. . . . I will be a visible leader. I truly believe that crime is a community problem and needs a community solution."

There was a light touch at the end. Michael Chitwood Jr., still following his father's route, arrived at the ceremony late. "Because you gave me the wrong address!" he blurted out at its conclusion, drawing laughter from the standing-room-only assemblage and a smile from his dad. He had been introduced to a standing ovation, but left to a laugh. Only a month later, the laughter merged with surprise as the irrepressible Chitwood, in full clown costume, including a bulbous nose, visited a delighted class of preschoolers at St. Alice School.

The remainder of his first month wasn't quite so light-hearted, ranging from arresting scam artists and dealing with child abuse to homicide and the death in a police station's holding cell of a Drexel Hill man arrested for public drunkenness. A thief who stole a badge and honor-guard hat from a slain officer's memorial display case was predictably labeled a disrespectful "dirtball" and "scumbag" by Chitwood. He had already initiated administrative changes and plans to set up sobriety checkpoints, hire more minority officers, and increase overall visibility, including a refurbished headquarters building open to all.

All of this was par for the course. There are unpredictable, unexpected events in the daily docket of any police superintendent. But only two months later the good citizens of Upper Darby were stunned by a bombshell. Their highly esteemed new law enforcement chief had been asked to run for governor of . . . Maine, the state from which he had so recently and emotionally departed. Worse, he was considering it. The fact is, he had been tentatively contacted before his departure by unnamed business and political leaders to declare as either a Republican or an Independent contender to take on the incumbent Maine governor, Democrat John Baldacci, someone Chitwood had worked with and liked personally. All Chitwood would volunteer was, "People have called me and asked . . . if I would be interested. . . . I'm flattered by it. That's all I can say. It's just too early to say one way or another." Too early? The election would be in 2006. Later, Chitwood added that a "very prominent politician" had called. Apparently, he wasn't the first. "I never thought of getting into politics," Chitwood added, but they were looking for two things: high visibility and proven leadership. He would surely be a high-energy candidate, with the proven ability to ignite almost any audience.

Imagine, turning to an outsider, even one who had served so long as Portland's police chief, as a serious contender for governor. But Maine isn't like other states. Chitwood, although a registered Democrat at the time, wasn't that committed to any party line. He had always spoken out more in terms of issues. Yet Maine's Republican Party remained a big tent, accommodating many opinions. Its two senators, both moderate Republicans and both women, were well disposed to

Chitwood. Polls had already shown, not surprisingly, that he would do very well in populous Portland and southern Maine and not at all well in less-populous, gun-friendly northern Maine. But he was still a reasonably viable statewide candidate.

Back in Maine, Chitwood's early success in Upper Darby was duly noted. David Hench, still writing for the *Portland Press Herald*, observed on November 28th that "Chief is big hit in new job," quoting an Upper Darby police lieutenant: "This guy is a breath of fresh air. He's out there with you. He's one of the guys. I've never seen somebody come in and be respected by everybody." Meanwhile, Upper Darby's police superintendent admitted to receiving hundreds of phone calls and emails from Maine residents, urging him to return and run. "I was honored," he concluded in mid-January 2006, and obviously tempted, but finally decided not to make the race. "I'm very happy doing what I'm doing here," he had insisted throughout the process. The letters to the local press, praising his performance, were already as glowing as had been the case so recently in Portland. The natural desire not to be uprooted again so soon certainly played a part in Chitwood's decision. But there was also that little matter of having to raise nearly two million dollars to wage a statewide campaign, with little certainty of success.

Chitwood, however, was hardly finished with politics. In 2007, only two years into the Upper Darby job, he was contacted by Delaware County Republican powerbroker John McNichol to take on first-term Democrat Joe Sestak as the GOP's standard-bearer in the 2008 Seventh Congressional District election. Sestak, a former admiral and another office-holder Chitwood rather admired, had won this normally Republican seat in an impressive 2006 upset victory. However, running against him certainly represented a more viable race for Chitwood than had the prior Maine possibility. For one thing, he could retain his Upper Darby police post should he lose, a position not covered by civil service. Should he win, his annual congressional salary of $168,000 was a good deal higher than the $124,000 he made currently in Upper Darby, but that was never a major consideration for Chitwood. Fundraising still was, especially running against an incumbent with a war chest already at well over a million dollars. Liz and the children left the decision entirely up to Mike. As he had pointed out to McNichol and other Republican leaders, as quoted by Timothy Logue in delcotimes.com: "I've been a Democrat, an Independent, and a Republican. I've always voted for the person.... I wouldn't be telling people what the political party says. I would be telling them what I think is right for the community."

But could Chitwood have as much influence writing laws as only one of many members of Congress in Washington as he would enforcing them as a vigorous superintendent of police? And even though Delaware County had traditionally elected Republicans, it had increasingly supported Democrats for state and national offices. Even so independent a Republican candidate as Mike Chitwood might have difficulty in the potential voter backlash against the continuing Iraq war and other policies of the departing Bush administration in 2008.

Moreover, although an experienced expert in law enforcement, how knowledgeable would Chitwood be in such areas as foreign policy? Still, any opponent would view him as a quick, conscientious learner. And, as the *Daily Times* put it in a September 28th editorial titled "Is Media Mike Ready for Prime Time?"—"Chitwood is an interesting choice. Few police chiefs or superintendents in the country have ever been the lightning rods for comment Chitwood is. There are those who compare him to a rock star. Upper Darby residents have been known to applaud when the colorful crimefighter enters a local restaurant."

On Tuesday, November 20, 2007, Mike Chitwood announced his decision not to run, encouraging Alex Rose of the *Daily Times* to declare, "Scumbags Won't Get Break in Upper Darby."

Chitwood, now 63, told Rose, "Congressman Sestak and the Democrats don't have to worry about me. I'm with an organization that I've been with [for] two years and we've done a lot of good in the community. I want to stay." He went on to relate his discussions with elected officials to gauge what the job might entail, but concluded: "I've been doing what I do for 43 years and I guess I'm fortunate [that I love it] today as much as I did in 1964. Why give up something you're happy doing for something you don't know whether you'd enjoy?"

He added that the scales really tipped several weeks earlier when a four-year-old girl had gone missing. In Newtown Square at the time, Chitwood raced back to Upper Darby while contacting various commanders who were conducting the search. Shortly after he arrived, the girl was found safe and sound. "But the pumping adrenalin," Rose wrote, "the passion of the moment, and of course the relief of the happy ending, was all too much for Chitwood to simply walk away from." As Chitwood himself put it, "If I do this political thing and I win, I would lose all this. I didn't see that passion in the political world."

* * *

The two most vivid accounts of Mike Chitwood's police career, now nearing a half-century, were both in *Philadelphia* magazine, but some 26 years apart. In 1981, Mike Mallowe wrote: "DON'T MESS WITH MIKE CHITWOOD—Philly's toughest, most decorated cop hates criminals almost as much as he hates guns." With the customary grim, trim photo of the newly mustachioed Philly homicide detective, his arms folded, staring straight at us, the article starts with Chitwood "alone in the house of the dead," the city morgue. He had seen thousands of corpses there and had become an expert in this sad specialty. As Mallowe noted: "Chitwood has taken college courses in forensic pathology He does this sort of thing because he is a professional . . . convinced that with enough time and enough patience . . . any crime, any homicide, can be solved." He had achieved so high a rate of success "by working ungodly hours, interviewing hundreds of people in the course of an investigation, risking life and limb daily and relinquishing any semblance of a personal life. . . . Chitwood has been lionized, damned, deified, accused of brutality, held up as an example."

Mallowe probed back beyond Chitwood's South Philly roots to those of his maritime father in the land-locked hills of Tennessee. His grandfather was a small-town sheriff. "I've got quite a family tree," Chitwood remarked. Mallowe filled it in: "He's part Irish, part English, and more than a little Cherokee Indian, with the high cheekboned, almost gaunt look to prove it," a brawny bull of a street cop favored by Frank Rizzo transformed now to a stylish but sinewy 175-pound homicide detective, adaptable to any situation, using his wits instead of fists and firearms. Yet Chitwood still remembered summers when he and his brothers had traveled down to the mountains to visit their grandfather's one-cell office. He'd let them run wild, hardly the case with Chitwood's strict but devoted parents.

Mallowe concluded in the present, 1981, with Chitwood stalking the streets of South Philadelphia, "still trailing a killer who has eluded the police for weeks, but whom he is determined to bring in." Chitwood should be exhausted, but even as morning comes, he isn't. Sometimes he must question the very point of it all. "No matter what Chitwood does, the killing and the crime will only get worse."

But Chitwood conceded nothing. "I do this because I love it," he insisted to Mallowe. "Can you understand that?" he said with some intensity, his eyes ablaze. "I love what I do. It challenges me. I've been good to this job and it's been good to me. This is me. This *is* Mike Chitwood." He might have added that no job could be more important.

Mallowe concluded, "That may be enough."

*   *   *

It's March 2007, and a grayer but no less grim police superintendent Mike Chitwood is still staring straight at us, only seated in a chair, surrounded by four tough-looking members of his Upper Darby drug-busting team, two with hoods over their heads. The title of Richard Rys' article is "Not in My Town, Scumbag." Chitwood is being proposed for a promotion again. This time it's only indirectly political. The article's lengthy subtitle: "Upper Darby police chief Mike Chitwood was known as 'Dirty Harry' in his 19 years as a cop in this city. Today his tough talk is tempered with compassion. Could he be the solution to Philly's crime problem?"

Rys gets to the point quickly, describing how Chitwood's "show" deals directly with crime in Upper Darby, how involved he is with his personnel, as proud as with his own family. "Chitwood backs up his proactive policies by spending more time on the street than behind his desk . . . taking action—and letting everyone know about it . . . is the essence of Chitwood's philosophy of policing, and it's exactly what's missing in Philadelphia." Rys quoted an 11-year veteran of the Upper Darby force, Lieutenant Dave Madonna, as stressing that Chitwood could simply sit behind his desk instead of going on patrol with them, joining in the dangerous job of hunting down criminals. "He doesn't have to go anywhere, but he's a doer. . . . You get caught up in Mike Chitwood—his personality is contagious."

Trying to keep his feelings in check, Chitwood wasn't demonstrative about how much the top Philly job would mean to him, how invested he had been for so long in the city's life, from whatever vantage point. Instead he handed over a detailed, two-page, typed outline of what would be his priorities—starting with the optimistic figure of 2,000 new cops and a reenergized narcotics unit like the one he'd established in Upper Darby. He'd talked it over with his son, now police chief in Daytona Beach, Florida, described by Rys as "perhaps the only ex-Philly cop as headline-grabbing and controversial as his father." Mike Chitwood Jr. had pointed out to Rys how Mike Chitwood Sr. had evolved over the years. "I don't want to use the word 'sensitive,' but he is. He's more sensitive to the police, more sensitive to the victims of crime." He still harbored his attachment to the Philadelphia Police Department, akin to a "surrogate parent" in his youth. As to his own family, necessarily neglected during his Philly years, he'd tried at whatever distance to connect even more closely with each of his kids and their kids, and now a great-grandchild. As Rys concluded, with a reference to how Chitwood was making a difference in Upper Darby: "He knows he can do the same" for that larger family, the entire Philadelphia police force. "As with his own. . . . He's ready to make up for lost time, if they'll let him."

As if this were not explicit enough, Larry Platt, then editor of *Philadelphia* magazine, added a candid commentary: "After reading Rys' terrific piece, I want Michael Chitwood to be the city's new police commissioner. . . . Few believe the next mayor will appoint a white commissioner, but I think black people want bad people put away—period. . . . Bring down the murder rate and you'll get political credit. All it will take is a sense of urgency and leadership, like they have in Upper Darby." If it's so, reverse racism is just as odious as the opposite.

Of course, for whatever reasons, it didn't happen. Seven years later, energized Mike Chitwood is still in Upper Darby, coping with the influx of crime from West Philadelphia and tighter budgets in tougher times than he'd ever experienced in Maine. The real losers are the rest of us.

12

Are the "Scumbags" Winning?

S
ometimes it almost seems so. To much of our pervasive media, "If it bleeds, it leads." Of course, whatever the transitory trends and seeming triumphs, there can be no final victory in the ceaseless struggle between law enforcement and violent crime. For those defending us, however, especially in these troubling times when virtually every police department is obliged to do more with less, some battle fatigue is inevitable. The pressure never recedes. One always wants to get at the root causes of crime, but with lives at stake, taking the long view can be an unaffordable luxury. A drawn gun demands immediate response.

Nothing can be more misleading than raw statistics. By any measure, overall crime in the United States has declined in the past quarter-century. But why, where, and from what levels? Most significantly, how have violent crime statistics changed? For one thing, improvements in medical care have greatly reduced fatalities. Yet how successfully have we dealt with the underlying causes of violent crime, especially in densely populated urban areas like Philadelphia's? Difficult times have only made the challenges more acute. For example, a typical letter to the *Philadelphia Inquirer* cites the heightened local incarceration rates, with their attendant costs, while schools, recreation, and community development programs are cut. Sean Damon, the letter-writer notes that over the past 30 years in Greater Philadelphia, the number of people convicted of crimes leading to imprisonment has increased by more than 500 percent, with African Americans incarcerated at a rate nine times greater than whites. A disproportionate percentage of murders throughout the area continues to be of young African Americans killing other young African Americans.

Still, of our nation's 10 largest cities (Detroit no longer qualifies), Philadelphia has not only the highest rate of poverty but—with 331 homicides in 2012—the highest rate per capita of gun-related crimes. Historically, it has been one of the nation's most crime-ridden cities. Add to this a low rate of "closure"—that is, of finding and convicting the guilty. Yet our jails are overflowing. Certainly, some statistics can be misleading, but there's a stark reality about murder.

No one knows this better than Philadelphia's mayor, Michael Nutter. For all the vibrancy it projects, from the gleaming towers of Center City to the expanding enclave of productive young professionals in Old City, the underside of Nutter's vast metropolis is a population some 25 percent of which is in "deep poverty," with a higher rate among children. Starting his second term as mayor in 2012, Nutter outlined improving education and crime prevention as his two highest priorities, although combating crime already consumes an excessive part of his severely straitened budget. And even with an energetic, ambitious new superintendent of schools and potentially increased sources for revenue, the long-escalating crisis in public education defies solution.

* * *

Memories of Maine. When he heard the news, Mike Chitwood must have nodded in wry recollection. At the end of May 2013, Philadelphia Police Commissioner Charles H. Ramsey called for an independent investigation by the U.S. Justice Department not into the extent of violent crime in Philadelphia but of the degree of "deadly force" used by his department's officers in dealing with it. Was it excessive? "We've been looking into this issue since December," Ramsey told the *Inquirer*, stressing that an internal investigation wouldn't carry the same credibility, particularly in the crime-centered communities.

As quoted by Sandy Bauers of the *Inquirer*, John McNesby, president of Lodge 5 of the Fraternal Order of Police, put a slightly different emphasis on things. Hopefully, the justice department would "find we're outgunned, under-manned, and under-equipped." Look at the weaponry criminals have access to today. How about more federal funds, McNesby concluded, "so we can put another couple hundred cops on the street?" As the saying goes, don't hold your breath.

By the next day, Ramsey had backtracked a bit. His request wasn't so much for a full justice department investigation but more a sort of joint cooperative study of the issue to spur positive change. After all, even an audit would indicate that, whatever the justification, Philadelphia police officers shot 52 people in 2012, compared with 35 in 2011. The number has been reduced this far in 2013, but Ramsey's call followed a traumatic week during which the police shot four people, three fatally. Statistics paled before the perception of a "trigger happy" police force. However, as Ramsey countered to the *Inquirer*'s Mark Fazlollah, everyone must recognize that his officers on the street are "facing an enormous level of violence." Then Mayor Nutter weighed in, holding his own press conference at police headquarters. Look, the mayor pointed out, if someone aims a gun at a policeman, there is a high probability that individual will be shot. "I expect our officers to protect themselves and the public." Back to square one.

* * *

In the midst of all this, *The Philadelphia Inquirer* of June 30, 2013 featured a startling headline in bold type: PHILADELPHIA KILLINGS HIT 45-YEAR LOW. Just-announced statistics for all but two days of the first six months of 2013 indicated a 38 percent drop in homicides from the same period last year. Indeed, violent crime was down in every category—by seven percent in robberies, nine percent in assaults, and so on. This reduction paralleled that in other major cities. For example, as featured in the cover story of *Time* magazine of June 10, 2013, murders were down in Chicago by an almost identical 37 percent of the same period in the prior year. They had reached a high of 506 for all of 2012, giving the Windy City the dubious distinction of the highest homicide rate per capita of America's three largest cities: New York, Los Angeles, and Chicago. Clearly, something was happening.

Of course, such promising statistics must be encouraging to everyone, none more than a longtime law enforcement professional like Mike Chitwood. However, he prudently cautioned not to put too much premature emphasis on such "snapshots" of cities that had so long held the dubious distinction of being the nation's most violent. It's much too soon to celebrate, a conclusion surely shared by Philadelphia Police Commissioner Charles Ramsey. In Philadelphia and Chicago, initiatives are in place that mirror Chitwood's suggestions:

Targeting by police and prosecutors of "hot spots" where violent crime has long been a constant, such as North Philadelphia's 22nd Ward. Resources should be focused at the heart of the problem.

A crackdown on specifically criminal activity using guns—with more apprehended and incarcerated than ever before, a program locally called "gunstat." A majority of offenders and victims of gun violence are between ages 15 and 24.

An overhaul and reform of the city's criminal justice system, with closer cooperation between police, prosecutors, and judicial authorities, resulting in courts increasing conviction rates for the most violent criminals.

Intensive community involvement to portray police as protectors rather than adversaries, particularly targeting crime's "hot spots" and its juvenile potential perpetrators. Gangs can be turned to productive activities.

Data-driven policing. In the world of modern technology, data can not only be collected, it can be analyzed to predict patterns of crime—allowing the police department to be proactive rather than reactive.

Most of all, the constant accountability of command and supervisory personnel to take personal responsibility for implementing crime-fighting plans. And, of course, the issue of dealing with the root causes of crime.

Although Philadelphia appears to be taking such a conscious program of crime-fighting to heart, only time will tell. With fingers crossed, the city hopefully will continue these initiatives, tweaking the strategy as more information becomes available, and violent crime will continue to decline. But it would be well to await a full year's statistics.

*   *   *

No one can appreciate what Philadelphia is trying to do more than Mike Chitwood, observing it all from his vantage point just a few miles away. Not only had he championed so many of these potential reforms, but he could also appreciate such sentiments as those that had earlier induced Commissioner Ramsey to call for an investigation of his own department. How long had Chitwood tried to balance concerns with the immediacy of crime and the complexity of its underlying causes? When he had called for a justice department investigation of the use of "excessive force" by his own department up in Portland, Maine, so many years before, at least it had led to some positive procedural reforms. But Portland still wasn't quite the same as Philadelphia. As Chitwood often remarks today, "It is easier to buy a gun in Philadelphia than a cheesesteak." He has viewed the overall rise of crime in Upper Darby—positioned as it is on the porous border with West Philly—as having a lot to do with location. Any reduction in metropolitan crime should be reflected across county lines.

From its higher elevation, you can see Center City Philadelphia's skyline from Upper Darby's police headquarters, close to the 69th Street hub. You don't need a passport to cross. To Police Superintendent Police Michael J. Chitwood, he really leads what amounts to Philadelphia's 13th Police District. Technically, only a township, Upper Darby is in reality the sixth largest city in Pennsylvania, a mix of densely populated streets of row homes and neighborhoods with more spacious individual homes, but overall, beyond the 69th Street corridor, more suburban than urban in layout. Even with its own mayor, council, school system, and police force, it is hardly a self-contained suburb. Change is a constant. The prominent department stores that once dominated still-bustling 69th Street may be gone, but major redevelopment projects are well under way. The signs on larger buildings in this extensive retail corridor today are often in Korean. The iconic Tower Theater still draws top musical talent from across the country. Although the municipal budget is under severe stress, the local high school's summer music festival, which once featured alumna Tina Fey, is still renowned. Talk about an urban complex.

Upper Darby has always attracted immigrants and encouraged hopes of upward mobility. As the *Inquirer*'s Alan J. Heavens wrote on April 7, 2013, under the heading "Vibrant Mix of Cultures," bustle still characterizes Upper Darby's 69th Street Transportation Center, "where 100,000 travelers a week . . . pass through to connect to high-speed lines, trolleys, or buses," many staying to shop or simply saunter into the residential neighborhoods beyond the ever-evolving business district.

With a diverse population encompassing over a hundred ethnicities and nearly as many languages and dialects, Upper Darby's neighborhoods are said to house some 83,000 inhabitants. The fact is, nobody really knows. In some of the lower-income and immigrant neighborhoods, there may be 11 or 12 people living in houses where the census bureau counted only three. Income levels vary from those in the near-slums to authentic affluence in the mansions of Drexel Park, but there is far less unemployment than in neighboring Philadelphia proper. Only some seven percent of the residents of Upper Darby are considered to be below the poverty line.

Upper Darby also differs from Philadelphia in the breakdown of its population, characterized by Mayor Tom Micozzie as "American Pie." A great many recent immigrants never had reason to trust police or other authority figures in their homelands, one reason Chitwood always wears a suit instead of a uniform. Over 46 percent of residents are white, over a quarter black, less than five percent Hispanic, and a significant 11 percent Asian. Geographically so near and statistically so much better off than most of Philadelphia, this suburban "township" city is an obvious lure to lawbreakers, especially those bent on burglary.

Crime in Upper Darby has not yet been excessively violent, although, as in Maine, it is the potential that keeps Chitwood up at night—not that he sleeps all that much anyway. The five homicides committed within the township's borders in 2010 were reduced to three in 2011. There were four homicides in 2012, three solved and one still open. An imaginative local headline writer, however, might discern a trend: "Murder rate up 25 percent in Upper Darby!" There have been only two homicides in the first half of 2013, one the celebrated shootout at the Summit Inn Hotel. A former veteran and police officer named Michael Galla had broken into his former girlfriend's home in Mount Carmel, Northumberland County, and fired seven shots, one of which injured her current boyfriend. The heavily armed Galla then fled and was finally cornered by U.S. marshals in the Upper Darby motel. In the subsequent shootout, Galla was killed. As Chitwood put it, Galla was intent on taking himself out "in a blaze of glory," a dramatic form of "last stand" suicide. Thankfully, no bystanders were injured, but the incident illustrates the perils of homicide in any locality.

By far, the most calls to police within Upper Darby still involve domestic disputes. There were about a hundred more burglaries than robberies last year. Both may seem of equal concern, but a robbery is when actual force or the threat of force is involved. Particularly in Upper Darby's more affluent neighborhoods, burglary—the nonviolent theft variation—poses a far more immediate threat and elicits more fear. Apparently, breaking-and-entering is still more likely than street muggings or even the "smash-and-grab" variety of robbery.

However, in Mayor Micozzie's American Pie, there are some pretty strange slices. Some individuals have a proclivity for burglaries that border on the bizarre.

Take, for example, those two teenage lesbian lovers described by the media as Upper Darby's "Thelma and Louise." They seemed to steal for the sheer joy of it, and they would take almost anything. For two months in 2011, they burglarized, often in broad daylight, some 29 homes throughout the area, accumulating an estimated $30,000 in cash and valuables, largely electronics.

"They used people's homes as their own private shopping center," an incredulous Chitwood told the *Inquirer*, taking everything from a Nintendo Wii, a Sony Play Station, iPods, and assorted jewelry to toiletries, purses, baseballs, knives, medicines, a .22-caliber revolver, and even a statue of the Virgin Mary. One imagines drugs must have entered this mix somewhere, because each one claimed that running into a fierce "live lion" was the only thing that dissuaded them from ransacking house number 30. Or so they insisted after they fled and were finally arrested by Upper Darby's police in the modest flat they shared. In reality, it appears that they were greeted by a somewhat less ferocious, rather large dog of uncertain breed. Chitwood concluded, almost with reluctance, "If we find a lion, it will be a bigger story than this." However, in Upper Darby, what wouldn't be possible?

* * *

Although his daily docket may today be dominated by burglary and domestic disputes, the larger issues facing law enforcement throughout the nation have never departed from Superintendent Chitwood's consciousness. His fervent advocacy of sane gun-control laws goes back decades, and personal reflections of 9/11 always remain vivid. To much of the nation's population, the terrible shock of such unthinkable terrorist attacks on our soil had receded into a kind of generational Pearl Harbor or Kennedy assassination memory, the "where were you?" syndrome. To Chitwood, his involvement remained painfully personal.

The February 2013 issue of *Police Chief* magazine notes, "In a recent Gallup poll, less than one-half of one percent of respondents ranked terrorism as the most important issue facing the United States. Contrast that with a similar poll taken months after 9/11, when terrorism was ranked one of the top issues facing the country. . . . While we want citizens to be vigilant and to report suspicious activity to law enforcement, we do not want them to be preoccupied with concerns about terrorism. . . . We do not want citizens in a free and democratic society to be fearful." Two months later, on April 15th at 2:45 p.m., came the horrific bombings by two terrorist brothers at the Boston Marathon.

* * *

While generally viewing the immediate, intensive response favorably, including apparently close cooperation between the FBI and local police on every level,

Chitwood observed that later revelations indicated some of the same difficulties he'd had with the FBI back in Portland directly after 9/11. Perhaps had earlier information about potential terrorists been shared in time, now as then, they might even have been apprehended before being allowed to strike. In Portland it had involved only two of those who participated in the 9/11 attack, but one was the pilot of one of the planes. In Boston, the FBI had obtained information forewarning of the potential for violence of both of the brothers responsible for the bombing. Certainly there are a considerable number of potential terrorists residing throughout this country, but our technology and covert activity in targeting them have surely improved during the past decade.

However relevant, this apparent lapse in communication between the FBI and Boston police only came to light after the general euphoria following the killing of one of the brothers and the capture of the other. With justifiable relief at such prompt resolution and praise for both police and first responders, the entire nation joined in Boston's pride. This Boston Massacre had been dealt with in a remarkably timely fashion, but at what a cost.

To Michael Chitwood, the Boston bombings and their aftermath elicited acute professional interest. So much about them seemed almost to defy credulity. Two young brothers originally from the embattled former Soviet republic of Chechnya, Dzhokar Anzorovich Tsarnaev and Tamerlan Anzorovich Tsarnaev, both raised as traditional Muslims, planted two delayed-remote-reaction pressure-cooker bombs within the densely populated area adjacent to the finish line of the Boston Marathon on Boylston Street. The race was only half completed when the bombs detonated, killing only three people, one a child, which seems almost miraculous. However, by the insidious nature of these explosives, with metal fragments widely dispersed, of the 264 people injured, at least 36 underwent amputations and are maimed for life. In the immediate carnage and confusion, medical personnel on all levels were among the most heroic and immediate to respond.

Why and how did these two brothers come to such a decision, to plan and carry out so horrific a crime? The younger, in particular, Dzhokhar, not yet 20 when the bombings took place, if it matters, doesn't look anything like our customary conception of a fanatical terrorist—with his clean-shaven, handsome, boyish face and curly hair. Did his older brother, 26-year-old Tamerlan talk him into it? Dzhokhar had come to this country with his family when only eight, became a naturalized citizen in 2011, settled in Cambridge, was attending college, and seemed well adjusted to American life. His older brother had already married an American, who converted to the Muslim faith.

The radicalization of the Tsarnaev brothers must have evolved fairly gradually. It is known that they began attending a mosque espousing greater militancy and expressing grievances against the west. However, even before Tamerlan's mysterious visit to areas of Russia in 2012, where apparently he was in contact with extremist groups, there were concerns within his own family about his emerging anti-Americanism. An uncle expressed them as early as 2009.

Indeed, Russian security itself warned the FBI about Tamerlan, and the CIA also had him under surveillance, but nothing came of it. Extremism took a terrorist turn on September 11, 2011, when three men, all Jewish, were brutally murdered in Waltham, Massachusetts, one reportedly a friend of Tamerlan's, but the homicides were never solved. After the Boston bombing there was some indication that the two brothers had been contemplating a 9/11 anniversary bombing in New York, but it never came to fruition. Whatever the degree of suspicion, Tamerlan's application for U.S. citizenship in 2012 was held up by the Department of Homeland Security, in view of an ongoing FBI review of his implied activities, or perhaps only of his sympathies.

To Michael Chitwood, viewing these facts and the bombings' aftermath were to shape some conclusions of his own. Improved visual resources, including those supplied by individuals, had targeted both brothers with some certainty, at the scene and leaving it prior to the actual detonations, each walking at some distance from the other. There is no discounting improvements in surveillance. According to the FBI, the brothers had learned to construct such lethal explosive devices from an online magazine published by affiliates of al-Qaeda in Yemen, stressing retribution for U.S. involvement in Iraq and Afghanistan.

Unfortunately, the murders were not yet over. Forced to flee as FBI images of the Tsarnaevs were widely distributed and an extensive manhunt was launched, involving a lockdown of the entire Boston area, the brothers took off for Cambridge and then to the suburban community of Watertown. In the process they shot and killed a Massachusetts Institute of Technology police officer, carjacked an SUV (although sparing the owner), and sped to Watertown, where the police closed in. During an extensive exchange of gunfire, a Massachusetts Bay Transit Authority policeman was critically wounded, but Tamerlan was shot multiple times and killed. Somehow, the younger brother, Dzhokhar, although injured, managed to escape in his stolen car. He was finally discovered in a most peculiar fashion by a Watertown resident who thought he'd take a look at the small, tarpaulin-covered boat stored in his back yard. Under that tarp he was astonished to find young Tsarnaev, in weakened condition but unarmed. Dzhokhar was promptly arrested and rushed to the hospital, as local residents, freed from confinement in their homes, took to the streets in celebration and commendation of everyone involved.

That's when Chitwood's conclusions began to form, reminding him of another terrorist incident in 2009. When Dzhokhar Tsarnaev was taken into custody, his injured throat had to be sufficiently restored for him to be able to speak. There were several pressing concerns still unresolved. For one thing, were there any accomplices? Initially, federal law enforcement officials invoked a "public safety exemption" to the customary Miranda warning to anyone who is arrested. After all, Dzhokhar Tsarnaev had been charged with use of a weapon of mass destruction, and malicious destruction resulting in death. In short, terrorism. At first, he wrote out brief answers to questions willingly enough, and after his throat had recovered sufficiently, he responded orally to questioning by investigators for some 16 hours.

However, on the night of April 22, 2013, after federal judge Marianne Bowler read Dzhokhar Tsarnaev his Miranda rights, he simply stopped talking. Apparently, the government had decided to try him in the federal court system rather than as an unlawful enemy combatant. In view of the facts, Mike Chitwood could find no compelling justification for failing to obtain every shred of evidence possessed by a terrorist responsible for such heinous acts. What of the victims' rights to justice?

It all reminded Chitwood with such disturbing similarity of that prior, equally clear case of terrorism at Fort Hood, Texas, on November 5, 2009. On that day, Major Nidal Hasan, a psychiatrist in the U.S. Army, suddenly started firing his semi-automatic weapon in a crowded medical building where unarmed soldiers getting ready to be deployed were receiving vaccines and medical tests. Shouting "God is great" in Arabic, Hasan killed 13 men and women and wounded 52 in the worst mass shooting ever carried out on a United States military installation—before the major was shot by police, paralyzing him from the waist down.

Evidently influenced by Anwar al-Awlaki, a radical, U.S.-born Islamic cleric, Hasan has insisted on defending himself against the death penalty with a "defense of others" argument, claiming that he was only defending Muslims in Afghanistan against an illegal and immoral war. This has been denied by a pretrial judge because he considered it to fail as a "matter of law."

Chitwood's concern, as with the Boston prosecution, is more a case of defending ourselves. Our government has apparently classified the Fort Hood massacre as "workplace violence" rather than an act of sheer terrorism. Quoting the definition in the Code of Federal Regulations as the very essence of terrorism, Chitwood feels it would be a crime to classify it any other way. Unless the Military Code of Justice rules that these deaths and injuries were indeed those of "combat" victims, their families cannot receive the same benefits and compensation as those wounded in combat—or, for example, during the September 11, 2001, attack on the Pentagon. The killer will still get his salary.

To Chitwood, characteristically, what it comes down to is a matter of simple right and rights. He put it to me this way: "As someone who has spent 50 years in law enforcement, I have some very strong opinions about two terrorist acts that have been perpetrated against our country. In both the Fort Hood and the Boston Marathon acts of terrorism, the path of righteousness, accountability, and public safety have been subverted by our government. In both cases, the victims' rights have been compromised. Although the goal of keeping America safe from terrorists is among our highest priorities, the unfortunate reality is that these acts of terrorism will continue. I believe we should call them what they *are*, and prosecute them accordingly." Any questions?

*   *   *

This is a war Chitwood might well want to lead, just as there is a parallel struggle he has championed beyond even the memory of most of us, one that keeps returning with a shattering impact. The worst recent incident was at an elementary school in a quiet Connecticut town.

On the morning of December 14, 2012, in the suburban community of Newtown, where there had been only one homicide in the prior 10 years, a young loner named Adam Lanza killed his mother, a gun enthusiast, in their home. He then took her Bushmaster rifle and magazines containing multiple bullets to the Sandy Hook Elementary School nearby, shot through its locked glass doors, and proceeded randomly to kill 20 children and six adults. In a matter of minutes, he had fired 154 rounds. As alerted police units rushed in, Lanza killed himself.

Shock doesn't begin to describe the universal reaction to this horror. Not that it was remotely the first such gun atrocity committed somewhere in the United States. Now surely, finally, *something* would be done about it on a national scale, starting with control of such lethal, automatic, rapid-fire weapons. Mike Chitwood had been preaching that message since virtually the start of his career in homicide. How many photos have featured him raising an automatic rifle, exclaiming yet again, "No hunter uses this. It's a military and law enforcement weapon only. . . . Controlling its distribution doesn't curtail any sportsman's Second Amendment rights." Now, once more, to anyone who would listen, he laid out a comprehensive program of sane gun control. In many respects, it is similar to the extensive "Common Sense" position paper approved by the 3,000-member International Association of Chiefs of Police. Both detailed proposals clearly reflect the majority opinion of the American people, in poll after poll, despite the vigorous, well-financed propaganda of such vocal opposition groups as the National Rifle Association. As the IACP points out, "In the years since the terrorist attacks of 2001, over 300,000 American lives have been lost to gun violence."

Chitwood puts it plainly: "Columbine, Virginia Tech, Sandy Hook Elementary School [a month later, he would have added Santa Monica]. The list of tragic deaths of innocent people at the hands of violent criminals intent to murder is long and growing day after day, year after year. And this type of violence is not limited to college campuses and schools. It is happening daily in every city throughout America. When we look at these massacres which occur, there are two things that unite them: the number of people killed and wounded and the use of guns to kill so many." The recurring nightmare, of course, is the escalating scale of gun violence, from murder to massacre, using automatic, quick-firing weapons no civilian should ever have or ever need. It's simply a matter of sanity, including keeping guns out of the hands of the mentally ill.

Chitwood goes on to note, in reflections he wrote out for this book, that the United States today has the fourth highest per capita rate of homicides in the world, behind only South Africa, Colombia, and Thailand—an "American tragedy," and an ongoing crisis. With government so unresponsive to these critical issues, Chitwood predicts continuing violence unless we do something now, starting by building a national grassroots constituency for change. Either we finally take action against gun violence or we continue to follow the gun lobby's program to arm as many Americans as profitably as possible. Geographically expanding his "Chitwoodism" that "it is easier to buy a gun in this country than it is to buy a cheesesteak," he recommends the following:

> Ban assault weapons and high-capacity magazines (more than 10 rounds). In 1994, President Clinton and Congress enacted a very specific assault-weapons ban. In 2004, President Bush and his Congress allowed the ban to expire. Buying such weapons remains legal and easy, despite the opposition of law-enforcement groups and a consistent majority of the public. Reinstating a ban—and sustaining it—remains priority number one. There is *no* reason to have time limits on assault-weapons bans, other than in terms of political priorities.
>
> Close gun-show loopholes. They currently allow criminals, the mentally ill, and virtually anyone else to buy guns from unlicensed dealers at these events without undergoing background checks.
>
> Increase use of "microstamping" technology. This approach uses lasers to help engrave a gun in such a way that when it is fired, a code identifying the weapon's serial number would register on the bullet itself, enabling law enforcement to trace it quickly. The challenge today is how to be able to afford such highly sophisticated new technology.
>
> Establish mandatory sentences for committing a crime with an illegal gun.
>
> Enact generally stronger gun ordinances and laws.
>
> Require gun owners to report a stolen or lost firearm within 24 hours or be subject to possible fines or jail time.
>
> Limit the number of handguns that can be bought at one time.

Concurrently, Chitwood would continue and enhance other programs aimed at preventing gun violence and improving coordination and community policing efforts. He favors similarly sensible gun controls on every level—local, state, and federal. Of course, he also has his eyes on what major cities are currently doing.

New York has been a pioneer in targeting "hot spots" for crime and then heavily focusing resources on those areas. In Chicago, where six people were killed over the Memorial Day weekend and at least seven more were injured, even that is a substantial reduction from 2012. As police enter the subsequent months, traditionally the most dangerous of the year, that city's administration is hoping for progress if not victory. Emphasis is on programs, echoing Chitwood's, in community initiatives and partnerships. Los Angeles is targeting such specific goals as reducing gang-related and narcotics-related violence that still dominates entire areas of that sprawling metropolis.

Everywhere, the beat goes on. But strategies to reduce urban crime have no better chance of success in combating such random violence as in Newtown unless progress in sane gun control is finally part of every program. Chitwood summed it up: "During my 29-year tenure as police chief in several cities, I can draw the unmistakable conclusion: We have not done enough in the area of gun control. Gun violence continues to plague our country at an alarming rate. While I respect a gun owner's constitutional right to bear firearms, I believe we need to get serious about this issue and take meaningful action. In short, the 'tough cop' wants a tougher stance on gun control laws." No one seeks to imperil our cherished Second Amendment rights, but there are also some other rights guaranteed us all by our Constitution. Even if still more a goal than a reality, one of Franklin Roosevelt's famed Four Freedoms was "Freedom from Fear."

"The time for action is now!" Chitwood concluded. If anything, it is overdue. To which I add my own conclusion: As with terrorism, would that he had the authority to lead the charge himself.

It is now well over half a year since the senseless murder of those innocents at Sandy Hook. Hopes were high that at least it might finally motivate some action on the federal level, vigorously proposed from the president on down, to start establishing sensible programs such as those outlined by Chitwood and our major law enforcement associations, which polls prove are supported by a majority of the American public. Yet thus far every effort has failed.

Even the relatively mild bill sponsored by two highly respected conservative senators, Republican Pat Toomey of Pennsylvania and Democrat Joe Manchin of West Virginia, to extend background checks to gun shows and gun sales over the Internet, went down to narrow defeat. This at a time when even our emails and personal phone calls aren't always secure. Toomey particularly took heat from both the Heritage Foundation and the NRA. Representative Daryl Metcalfe of upstate Pennsylvania commented, "A lot of people feel Senator Toomey has violated the trust we had extended to him."

Efforts continue, spearheaded by parents of those children whose lives were taken, as well as such prior victims of gun violence as former Arizona congresswoman Gabrielle Giffords. Similar attempts go all the way back to such survivors as James Brady, Ronald Reagan's press secretary, who was crippled by a lunatic assassination attempt on the president. It is beyond discouraging that any pressure groups wield such potent political clout as the relentless NRA, whose "solution" to the gun crisis is to arm all the schools—certainly good for business. To gain remotely similar power in Washington reflecting genuine public opinion will be no simple task, unless there's a wholesale change in legislators.

*   *   *

It was an uncommonly somber Mike Chitwood that I encountered as he paused for a belated breakfast at the historic Llanerch Diner on the edge of the eight-square-mile community he is sworn to protect. That legendary eatery, of course, was prominently featured, along with other Upper Darby locations, in the Academy Award–winning film, *Silver Linings Playbook.* We just missed getting a bit part. For Chitwood, it is already the middle of the day. Up at 3:00 a.m., he had hit the gym for two strenuous hours and had made his ever-flexible rounds for 6:00. His daily schedule is always subject to the immediacy of events, his car a mobile office. It's been almost half a century now, from Philly to Maine and back again, from cop to chief, since Chitwood set out to help anchor that thin blue line holding back the tide of criminality that never entirely recedes.

Pausing only to acknowledge the customary cordiality of everyone entering the place, Chitwood reflects on how little has changed since he took to the streets as a gung-ho patrolman fresh out of the academy.

It was no longer the broad areas of gun control and terrorism that preoccupied him, just those eternal one-on-one confrontations with criminals. The "scumbags" his men are apprehending now seem so similar to those he'd encountered decades ago that they might be the same people. Despite the millions that have been invested to try to get at the core of so much random violence in our society—broken homes, failing schools, shattered neighborhoods, poverty, despair, hopelessness—alienated young people still emerge from the same environment, feeling they have little to lose and less to live for. Two commodities still easily obtained are drugs and guns. And Chitwood worries more about the future: "I look into the faces of those little kids coming out of the same neighborhoods and wonder, what chance do they have in life?"

For just a moment, the enormity of the task seems to overwhelm even so fearless a crime fighter as Mike Chitwood. In his many public utterances, he sounds more like a sociologist: "Although the prevalence of crime and types of crimes has changed over the years, the social issues that underlie crime in America remain the same . . . Poverty, race, and socioeconomic status continue to plague our society despite social programs that have been in place to reverse these trends." Recent years of recession have only made such efforts less extensive, and the capacity of law enforcement more circumscribed.

Two of the highly visible police chiefs Chitwood has most admired—Bill Bratton and John Timoney—have gone on to far more lucrative careers as consultants. Bratton is currently advising the British government on how to deal with escalating riots. Timoney is giving advice to, of all people, the rulers of Bahrain. At 69, Chitwood might well entertain offers to emulate their success. Interviewed in the 1980s, he could foresee such long-term possibilities for himself, considering an eventual career in public relations or even politics, as well as consulting. It's not going to happen, whatever the rewards. Despite or perhaps because of all the challenges, Chitwood will never retire from the you-never-know-what-will-happen excitement of active police work.

The momentary frustrations that even such a tireless chief of police must experience from time to time had already receded. He was back from his reflective mood, smiling and exclaiming, "I love this job!" How often have we heard that, in four locations, over nearly five decades. Perhaps in part because of the enthusiastic support he receives these days, starting with the mayor of Upper Darby, Chitwood added, "Every day's an adventure. They'll have to carry me out." And out he went, from the diner to his movable office in the parking lot, greeted by every new arrival as either a celebrity, an old friend, or both.

Recently, Mike put it this way to a criminal justice class: "Never lose passion for your job. I love the job today as much as I did when I first started. On my first day, I loved that I was a police officer. Today, when I walk into the Upper Darby police station, I still love the fact that I am a police officer. And I still approach each day with the same zest and passion that I did 49 years ago." If you don't feel that, he concluded, find something else to do that does elicit your passion.

It's odd that the most sustained criticism that Mike Chitwood receives these days is still that he is too enamored of personal publicity, too highly and excessively visible, the top cop as celebrity. It may tend to characterize Upper Darby as a supposed hotbed of crime. The fact is, such visible enthusiasm has always represented the essence of his success and remains the most distinctive asset he brings to it today. Philadelphia's current police chief is undoubtedly a most capable, dedicated, and experienced public servant. Recently, he, too, decried the availability of deadly assault weapons. But in the past, he has sometimes seemed about as visible to the public at large as if he were in the witness protection program.

To Chitwood, crime is always a community problem. Had he a "Four C's" of crime prevention, they might well be "coordination, community, cooperation, and communication." As Mike puts it, people want to know what's going on, to have a feeling of security and well-being, and to perceive their police as hands-on professionals. Surely, prevention before a burglary is preferable to sharing information after it happens.

Months ago, however, there were some 24 burglaries in quick succession throughout Upper Darby's most affluent neighborhoods (no, not those of "Thelma and Louise"). Chitwood quickly set up three well-publicized regional meetings with the residents of Drexel Park and Drexel Hill. Over 200 people attended each one. After Chitwood and his team answered questions, detailed how they were going about apprehending the robbers, discussed overall crime issues, and offered tips for future home protection, each meeting ended with a spontaneous standing ovation by the audience. Most if not all of the burglars were caught. And yes, they were all from Philadelphia. It's a simple matter to drive around and find attractive communities so close at hand and then raid these homes when it appears the residents are away or asleep. These particular raids became a short-lived epidemic. But once any category of crime is quelled, it can always break out somewhere else. The best protection is consistent cooperation between cops and community.

Beyond his proclivity for plain talk, not excluding a stream of expletives in appropriate company, Chitwood is still sometimes pictured as a headline hunter who might call a press conference for nabbing someone guilty of parking overtime. In a front-page *Daily News* feature on December 8, 2011, writer Stephanie Farr described what a typical day accompanying Chitwood was like, trying "to keep up with the 67-year-old crazy bastard." The paper's cover photo showing Chitwood lifting weights was headlined—bear with me—"Tough Chit." Well, the *Daily News* is a tabloid. Its inside headline, "The 'Real Deal' or a 'Jackass'?" posed the premise that "salty, brash, U. Darby's top cop tells it like it is." Citing testimony from both sides, Ms. Farr concludes on a positive note, "In the end, the same passion inside Chitwood that makes him scream 'scumbag' at news conferences may be the very same thing that allows him to give a damn about the victims." But then almost everyone admits that the chief has mellowed. Ask his family. If crime is rising again because of hard times, Chitwood stresses that it's an overall community problem and "the community deserves to know what is going on." All the publicity helps, not just for his notoriety, but also to spread the word.

Nor does Chitwood hog the credit. He's set up two police substations, a mentoring program for interaction between police officers and Upper Darby school district fifth graders, and a citizens' police academy to explain to residents of all ages how everything works in and for the community. If Chitwood shows up at the scene of an arrest, it's not to seize the spotlight but to give his people a visible show of support. In the Upper Darby Police Department there is not only an employee of the month, but also frequent commendation and award ceremonies for both officers and local citizens. Even his detractors admit that overall morale in the department is very high. Does this sound familiar?

*　　*　　*

Although he is loath to dwell on it, Chitwood must wonder at times what he might have accomplished on a larger stage, had he been chosen to head law enforcement in a city the size of Philadelphia itself, as reportedly he very nearly was. In the *Philadelphia Inquirer* of January 18, 2012, columnist Karen Heller, agreeing with Mayor Nutter about the interrelationship between crime and failing schools, refers to the approach of a very active academic named David Kennedy. Noting the reality that "crime is driven by a very focused group," Kennedy advises dealing with them directly, accepting that most violent crime comes from a very small percentage of the population. Working within neighborhoods, schools, and the criminal justice system itself is fine, but holding a direct "open conversation" with this relatively small and recognizable group may be more productive. On the one hand, "We want you to live"; on the other, "Keep it up and we'll have to lock you up. . . . A failure for both of us." It may sound like trying to turn the Taliban, but it's a concept many communities are trying out. In Upper Darby, perhaps too many of Chitwood's "scumbags" are invaders from outside, but in a larger setting, an innovative leader like him might have come up with his own variation of Kennedy's "Operation Ceasefire."

Bill Bratton's New York "miracle" and John Timoney's similar success took place in far more salubrious economic times, but so much of what they accomplished, and their similarly high visibility, echoes Mike Chitwood. Bratton, boasting the unique trifecta of being police chief of New York, Boston, and Los Angeles, developed a "predictive policing" model in L.A., stressing an information-based strategy designed to do more with fewer resources. What it largely comes down to is "preventive policing." It's rather like preventive medicine, where doctors emphasize what will sustain good health rather than the more expensive alternative of treating with problems after they occur. As Bratton puts it, police exist to "control behavior, to change it." That was his focus in both New York and Los Angeles, embracing the philosophy of community policing. After the failed philosophy of reactive policing, community policing focused on the prevention of crime, "returning us to our roots."

Named by Mayor Rudy Giuliani to head New York's police force in 1993, Bill Bratton, very much like Chitwood, saw the pervasive crime and fear of crime throughout the city as a community crisis. He promised to reduce crime by some 40 percent in three years. Just as important, he would change the climate of fear by doing what many professionals might avoid. He would stick his neck out and make his own voice a weapon to fight an enemy as insidious as a foreign invader. Eventually, this led to conflict with the ambitious mayor, who wanted to claim more of the glory—and headlines—but it worked.

John Timoney, born in Dublin and still at 65 retaining his Irish brogue, the quintessential New York cop, became Bratton's most trusted assistant and likely successor. Together they instituted a policy of inclusion on the force, giving new precinct commanders more authority and their trust, tremendously increasing morale and weeding out corruption. Using a sophisticated computer system called

"Compstat," encouraging the input of everyone into a kind of command center, the Bratton team reduced crime by 10 percent in his first year as chief. Soon he was on the cover of *Time*: "Finally, we're winning the war against crime." His 1998 book detailing it all is called *Turnaround: How America's Top Cop Reversed the Crime Epidemic.* Talk about visibility.

In his book, *The City That Became Safe*, author Franklin Zimring concludes that a fundamental reduction in the crime rate, as happened in New York, can take place without a similarly fundamental change in the city itself. The root causes of crime, however, have to be promptly dealt with—from open drug deals on every corner to a quarter-million New Yorkers evading fares every day in the subway system. When people see this "broken glass" emphasis of making enough arrests for even seemingly minor offenses, the very quality of life will improve. Perception becomes reality. Of course, it helps to have a lot of cops on the street. The emphasis may be on prevention rather than simply response, but individual and gang behavior, the root of most crime, has to be met in a way visible to every law-abiding citizen. That was the "tipping point" premise of writer Malcolm Gladwell. One of Bratton's obstacles was pervasive cynicism. This is the way it's always been. What can we do about it? But that guy jumping the turnstiles may also be carrying a concealed weapon.

In any case, by 1995, murder was down in New York by 31 percent over the prior year, theft by over 20 percent, overall crime down by over 18 percent. The success Bratton had with over 20,000 police, he repeated in Los Angeles with only about 9,000. It was not done without cost. Whatever their number, police are more visible when a Bratton, Timoney, or Chitwood is commissioner. In 2011, police fatalities in this nation rose 13 percent. There is always a price for peace. And despite so much focus on America's immense prison population, there has been a continuing decrease year by year over the last decade in the number of inmates as compared to overall population growth of the nation.

Today one can walk safely at night through New York's Central Park, once a most precarious proposition. In 1981, there were 731 reported robberies in Central Park alone; in 2011, only 17. And today's New York City police force includes some 6,000 fewer officers. What Bratton accomplished in New York, Timoney attempted to achieve in Philadelphia and then in Miami, using many of the same methods. He particularly focused on avoiding the excessive use of firearms. In Philadelphia, an average of 14 people killed each year as a result of police bullets was reduced to two. With Timoney skillfully and very visibly leading his community-conscious men and women on a bicycle, demonstrations at the 2000 Republican National Convention never disintegrated into violence, the polar opposite of what happened in Chicago at the 1968 Democratic National Convention. When immigrant passions simmered in Miami, Timoney and Mayor Manuel A. Diaz would show up together in their midst. Timoney would tell the crowd, "I'm John

Timoney, chief of police. I'm an immigrant from Dublin, Ireland. And this is our mayor, Manny Diaz. The mayor is an immigrant from Havana, Cuba. What can we do for you?" Talk about visibility. Talk about community. Mike Chitwood must have smiled when he read about it. Yet there will always be controversy. In 2007, a Miami newspaper cited Timoney as "America's worst cop" because of his frequent trips, crude language, and trampling of civil rights.

Investing so much time in one's work can take a toll. Bratton has been married several times, but currently most happily. Timoney's two children had problems with drugs. In Chitwood's case, it only meant missing many family events, but in recent years, he has very successfully made up for it. That his son has risen to become a Florida police chief is no small satisfaction.

* * *

Theodore Roosevelt didn't always follow his own advice, but he once said, "The best executive is the one who has sense enough to pick good men to do what he wants done, and self-restraint enough to keep from meddling with them while they do it." That's right out of Mike Chitwood's playbook. He's a very visible leader and communicator, but his greatest satisfaction is in the achievement of those working for and with him. When he shows up at a narcotics bust or a public disturbance, it isn't to take charge or take over, but rather to demonstrate support for his own.

Much of what Chitwood has learned is reflected in the careers of those contemporaries he most admires. I asked him to put some of it down in his own words. More than bromides, it represents advice helpful to virtually anyone in an executive capacity.

Under "Lessons Learned," he reiterated how critical collaboration with the community is. "Keeping members of the community informed about issues and crime prevention strategies along with a community policing program that focuses on partnership, problem-solving, and prevention goes a long way to helping combat crime."

"Treat others as you would want to be treated yourself"—whether victims, witnesses, or defendants, they deserve to be treated with respect. Lead by example. "Surround yourself with a team of knowledgeable, dedicated individuals who are committed to their profession." Then seek their input and listen to their suggestions. "Connect with your team. There is not a part of my department that I don't know intimately. I go on patrol. I ride with the bike unit. I go on drug raids. . . . I would not ask anyone to do something I have not done or would not do myself." Of course, learn from experiences, good and bad. "Stay physically fit, mentally fit, professionally fit." Make a physical fitness routine a daily necessity. This is one lesson it took Chitwood some time to learn. As our photos show, he is far more lean and fit now, at 69, than he was at, say, 29. It's part of what enables him to maintain such a rigorous schedule, part of who he is, and another example for his colleagues of any age. With so much emphasis on criminal justice majors at today's colleges and universities, simply qualifying to take police academy examinations is far more competitive than it used to be. Physical and mental fitness is a vital component of success.

In terms of "issues facing law enforcement professionals," great strides have been made in recent years, from better compensation and training to the ability to retain the best and brightest. New technologies such as DNA testing and advances in forensic science have greatly enhanced crime-solving ability. Unfortunately, the current economic recession has led to downsizing of departments, "givebacks" of benefits, and diminished resources. Equipment can quickly become obsolete, and cutting-edge research may be postponed. Due to budgetary constraints, there is "a large gap between what is technologically possible and what is realistically affordable." It will be an ongoing challenge for police departments to stay ahead of the emerging increases in Internet crime, including cyber terrorism, online sexual exploitation, and cyber fraud.

The success of a police force may not always be based on its size, but unless it can more readily afford the latest technology and training, it may take another decade, in Mike's words, "for police departments to recoup what has been lost due to the pressure of the economic recession."

Chitwood goes on to outline in some detail how to combat the increase in crimes among adolescents and school-age children, reducing on-site violence and bullying, the proliferation of guns in our society, early release programs in our jails, and the need for an overall strategy based on informative "predictive policing" policies. However, it always comes down to coordination, community, cooperation, and communication. Expect Mike Chitwood, the most decorated cop in Philadelphia history and today the most colorful and outspoken police superintendent in the nation, to be no less visible and vocal in the future. He is still the "real deal," and doesn't mind who knows it. The relentless message from our "Tough Cop" still rings out loud and clear: "Not in my town, 'scumbag'!"